MW01088921

Advance Praise

"Learn from someone I consider to be the best at living life full out! Brad Pedersen is an extraordinary individual who embraces the humility, wisdom, and courage needed to be the great leader and success he has become in business and in life."
—DARREN HARDY, founding publisher of
SUCCESS magazine and international bestselling author

"Brad Pedersen is one of the most mission driven, category creating entrepreneurs I've met. *Startup Santa* is a legendary present founders can give themselves and their friends."
—CHRISTOPHER LOCHHEAD, eleven-time
#1 bestselling co-author of *Play Bigger* and *Niche Down* and
editor of the *Category Pirates* newsletter

"You need to read this book. Brad's advice has made me millions. You won't find these frameworks or approaches anywhere else. It's a book that stands above the rest."
—DAN MARTELL, Founder of SaaS Academy and *Wall
Street Journal* Bestselling Author of *Buy Back Your Time*

"Santa only delivers presents once a year but *Startup Santa* has gifts that will keep on giving to you and your business for many years to come! I recommend you unwrap a copy and start reading today!"
—JOEY COLEMAN, *Wall Street Journal* bestselling author
of *Never Lose a Customer Again*

"If you were looking for a campfire to sit around and hear sage wisdom on life and business, you'd want to pick the one with Brad Pedersen. This book delivers that wisdom from a leader with the battle scars to prove it, but with a thoughtful tone. Grab it, find a campfire, and download the wisdom from a legend."
—TODD HERMAN, entrepreneur and #1 *Wall Street
Journal* bestselling author of *The Alter Ego Effect*

"I have watched Brad use a combination of imagination, discipline, and continuous learning to not only build several successful businesses but also to build up countless people. Now he is opening up his playbook so that entrepreneurs everywhere can learn and understand the building blocks of a successful life and business. Thank you, Brad!"

—MISTY LOWN, Founder & CEO of More Than Just
Great Dancing, #1 bestselling author of *One Small Yes*

"This is a terrific read. Some authors give advice; Brad Pedersen distills wisdom for life with his words."

—DAVE LINIGER, Chairman of the Board and Co-founder
of RE/MAX

"One of the signs of a true entrepreneur is the ability to get off the canvas when you get knocked down, finish the fight and shake hands with your opponent, learn life's lessons, and get ready for the next battle. Brad is that person. I know because I put him on the canvas and watched him get up and shake my hand. He's a friend to this day."

—JAY FOREMAN, Co-founder and CEO of Basic Fun!

"Scaling even a single business into a multimillion-dollar success is a life-defining achievement—and Brad Pedersen has done it several times. In *Startup Santa*, Brad shares lessons from a career of entrepreneurial ingenuity—from bootstrapping in his basement to building a toy empire and ultimately creating a sustainability-driven company. I've known Brad for years and always learn something when I talk to him—his hard-earned, valuable lessons in this book can help you unlock your full potential and achieve fulfillment in your life and career."

—ROBERT GLAZER, *Wall Street Journal* #1 bestselling
author of *Elevate* and Founder and Chairman of Acceleration
Partners

"Many of my greatest business lessons are a result of Brad's mistakes. It's a fresh take in a world where every book on business feels the same. This one is different. Brad has done a masterful job of blending the power and necessity of creativity with the reality of the hard knocks you're bound to experience when you set out to build something meaningful."

—MATTHEW BERTULLI, Co-founder & CEO of Lomi and Pela

"I am a super consumer of counseling, journaling, and reading business books so I can design an exponential future. Yet *Startup Santa* has taken me on a mental journey of insight and epiphanies unlike any other. I loved playing Monopoly as a kid, but I never knew why until now. I never realized the games and toys I loved as a child would be so informative of who I am and who I was meant to be as a consultant, author, and entrepreneur. Do yourself a favor: pick up a copy and go on the journey with Brad Pedersen, the Toymaker from the North."

—EDDIE YOON, founder and bestselling author of
Superconsumers and *Category Pirates*

"Brad Pedersen really knows his stuff. If you have decided to be a lifelong learner, constantly looking to grow and improve, this is your chance to learn directly from a master toymaker!"

—ADAM CONTOS, retired CEO of RE/MAX
and author of *Start With a Win*

"Startup Santa was a joy to read, as it rekindled fond childhood memories while sharing important lessons. I would highly recommend this book to founders seeking to learn from someone who has experienced firsthand the highs and lows of the entrepreneurial journey. Brad is one of the wisest entrepreneurs I know and I love how he uses timeless toys to share business wisdom through the power of play!"

—KRISTI HEROLD, Founder & CEO of JAM,
bestselling author of *It Pays to PLAY -
How Play Improves Business Culture*

"There are a gazillion entrepreneurship books out there, but I've never read one that so closely examines the toy industry—in all its creative joys and unrecyclable faults. Brad has shed light on a niche we all know and love but rarely think hard about. Some of our fondest memories growing up are rooted in the toys we got for Christmas or our birthday. But it was shocking for me to learn how many of those toys end up in a trash pit just a few months later. If you are an entrepreneur, a builder, or an investor, read this book. It will change the way you think about creating things that really, truly matter."

—NICOLAS COLE, author and Co-founder of Ship 30 for 30, Category Pirates, and Digital Press

"Learn from Brad's mistakes so that you do not have to learn them on your own. Brad's vulnerability in this book is revealed in several helpful lessons that, if applied to your life, will help you navigate your entrepreneurial journey."

—HAROLD CHIZICK, Founder and former CEO of ChizComm

"Brad Pedersen's own story is unique and has many of the ups and downs that most entrepreneurs encounter when trying to build their businesses. Brad survived and thrived. His story tells us how, with some imagination, curiosity, and creativity, it's possible to be transformative. Brad Pedersen is the real Startup Santa and will inspire you to live your best life."

—TOM KENNEDY, Chairman of Kensington Capital Partners Ltd

"There is no single incident that made Brad into the incredible leader he is today. In this story we watch the progression of someone from humble beginnings who endures significant adversity and, because of his deep commitment to family and faith, becomes a highly respected business and thought leader. Brad's commitment to excellence, adventure, and mastery shine through the pages of this uniquely written book."

—DON CAMERON, former toy executive at Walmart

A literary masterpiece! Brad Pedersen is a thoughtful and inspiring author who shares with us important principles that are critical to building a successful life and business.

—JODY STEINHAUER, President & Founder of
The Bargains Group, *Wall Street Journal*
bestselling author of *Success Mindsets*

"Brad is one of the most dynamic and insightful entrepreneurs I have ever met. The same courage that caused him to launch new products and businesses is on display here as he honestly shares the good (and often painful) lessons he has learned along the way."

—VIJAY KRISHNAN, former executive at Recipe Brands
Unltd and Lead Pastor at The Well

"This is a story of how everyone can use their imagination, curiosity and creativity to literally transform the world. Brad Pedersen is the real Startup Santa and will inspire you to live your best life."

—ANTHONY DIMARCO, Entrepreneur and
High-Performance CEO Coach

STARTUP
SANTA

STARTUP
SANTA

A Toymaker's Tale *of* 10 Business Lessons
Learned *from* Timeless Toys

BRAD PEDERSEN

M3 ADVENTURES
P   R   E   S   S

STARTUP SANTA
A Toymaker's Tale of 10 Business Lessons Learned from Timeless Toys

FIRST EDITION

ISBN 978-1-7380958-0-3 Hardcover
ISBN 978-1-7380958-3-4 Paperback
ISBN 978-1-7380958-1-0 eBook
ISBN 978-1-7380958-2-7 Audiobook

EXPLORE THE HEART OF STARTUP SANTA

You are invited to join a more intimate deep dive to further unpack and reveal the stories and ideas foundational in the creation of Startup Santa.

Follow along as Brad Pedersen is interviewed by friend and spiritual mentor Vijay Krishnan, who together uncover further wisdom and principles from each chapter.

STARTUPSANTABOOK.COM/VIDEO

Contents

Prologue & Dedication

"The most potent muse of all is our own inner child."
—STEPHEN NACHMANOVITCH

Something unexpected happened while writing the pages of this book; my father passed away. Both of my parents were infected by the COVID-19 virus, were subsequently hospitalized, and ultimately ended up in the ICU on ventilators. My mother, who had underlying health issues, miraculously survived. My father was released on the belief that he had recovered, only later to succumb to the damaging effects the virus had inflicted on his body.

It is one thing to be aware of a pandemic ravaging our planet, and another thing entirely to personally feel the effects of its deathly sting so close to home. My journey over the past number of weeks has been a roller-coaster ride, filled with a myriad of emotions. Disbelief that this virus has landed so close to home; anxious over the possible outcomes; hope when it seemed triumph and recovery were imminent; and ultimately grief when I realized this was the last time I'd kiss my father's forehead.

My dad was my hero. He was a larger-than-life personality, and lived a virtuous life. A man of wisdom, strength, and deep character, who would always strive to do what was honorable and right. My father was an eternal optimist and believed that our lives were God's gift to us—*what we chose to do with our lives was our gift back to God.*

Throughout my youth, he was always there to provide words of wisdom whenever I felt hopeless or despair. He was famous for saying, *"Don't despise the process,"* a reminder that every obstacle in life is an opportunity to "grow through" versus simply "going through." He truly believed that adversities could be turned to your advantage and that challenges were ultimately there to help shape character.

I remember my father telling me that in life I would pay one of two prices: the price of discipline or the price of regret: the price of discipline weighs mere ounces and was certain to cost me something, but the price of regret weighs tons and would ultimately crush me under its weight.

Those words have been formative to how I view the world and make important decisions. To ensure I did not miss the lesson, I wrote these words out and put them in a picture frame next to my bed. Each morning when my alarm beeped in the dark cold air and the warmth and comfort of my cozy bed would suggest I roll over—those words sitting on my bedside table challenged me to roll out—to push my limits and get comfortable being uncomfortable.

My dad would famously say, "You cannot do the wrong thing right," encouraging me to constantly do the right thing even when it hurt or was uncomfortable. He knew that during this life we were going to struggle, no matter how high we jump we're always fighting gravity. He believed that to be our best and to get the most of what life has to offer, we need to go against the grain, to swim upstream, and to have the courage to take the path less traveled.

With all that in mind, this book is dedicated to my dad. To the man who raised me with discipline, encouraged me to dream big, be bold and have courage. My father demonstrated how to live a life of ambition *but tempered with* compassion.

Dad: Since I was a little boy, I have always looked up to and admired you, and I have wanted to make you proud. I have done my best to distill my life lessons, scribed into the pages herein, and I devote this work in honor of you. I miss you!

"In life you may not be able to do all you find out,
but make sure you find out all you can do."
—JIM ROHN

Foreword

You don't know me, but you likely know the leaders I advise.

I'm not a blogger, podcaster, or a personality. I'm a practitioner. All day, every day, I help entrepreneurs get comfortable in their own skin (warts and all) while they clarify their vision, define their goals, and build their leadership muscle so that they can unpack the possibilities in others.

Over decades of this work, I've been fortunate to travel the world—working closely with entrepreneurs and their teams from every edge of the globe and every size of business. I've worked with founders of underwear empires making millions from their kitchen table, and supported the executives of massive multinational conglomerates. I've seen profitable exits and painful journeys that include entrepreneurs who go from rags to riches and back to rags again.

What I know for sure is that entrepreneurship isn't for the faint of heart. Frankly, it's a life choice that is akin to being a professional bull rider.

Bull riding has been called "the most dangerous eight seconds in sports." Maybe it's the fast-paced, adrenaline-filled environment that compels some people to choose bull riding as a career path and knowingly opt into an unpredictable environment fraught with risk with only a small chance for glory.

We may think that bull riders are brave, or crazy—or both—but they are no different than the person who decides to start their own business. Most entrepreneurs are thrown to the ground in the first few years and decide to throw in the towel.

Like bull riders, a select few entrepreneurs find the fine balance between holding on too tightly and becoming "locked onto the bull" or keeping too loose a grip, and flying off, violently. Making a career out of bull riding means spending your life navigating this thin edge.

In more than two decades of working with professional bull riders (a.k.a. career entrepreneurs), few leaders have demonstrated the level of stubborn, relentless, honey-badger-like persistence of Brad Pedersen. If entrepreneurship were a sport, Brad would be one of the unbeatable forces defying boundaries and refusing to give up.

I first met Brad close to twenty-five years ago when I was the president of a local chapter of the young entrepreneur's organization. He attended one of our "lessons from the edge" events featuring a local entrepreneurial legend that went from being millions of dollars in debt, essentially headed for bankruptcy in the real estate business, to founding a scrappy little airline that's worth several billion today.

Even way back then, it was clear that Brad wasn't attending this event to be starstruck or entertained by an exciting story of success. Ever the student, Brad was busy taking notes from a fellow entrepreneur—a peer—about living on the edge of business and winning.

In 2010, he might have been searching for those notes when he found himself teetering off the edge in what appeared to be a potentially unrecoverable fall. As bad as his situation at the time was, his belief in a brighter future ahead was unwavering. He wasn't in denial, or delusional, he just had the kind of faith that we rarely see. In a conversation during that time, I remember him sharing, "You know, Colin, I have a perfect vision for 2020. I know where I'll be, and I'll look back at this difficult time as critical to my success."

Brad persevered, continuing to lead from his principles while innovating and building toward his vision step by step. Brad got to be right about his prediction and he deserves every ounce of the incredible success he's created. Today there are audiences of aspiring and experienced entrepreneurial leaders who are learning from Brad's lessons from the edge and beyond.

In the increasingly uncertain and ambiguous environment we live in, there is no "how-to" guide for entrepreneurship. It doesn't exist because entrepreneurial leadership is both an art and a science. However, if we look carefully enough, we find a book that allows us to take a deep dive into the lived experiences of a successful entrepreneur, learning the principles embedded within the stories to use as guideposts for our own journey.

I believe that this book is Brad's way of paying his success forward by inspiring, informing, and educating the next generation of leaders. Perhaps, to even lend them a bit of faith in what is still possible at a time when they most need it.

Positively,

Colin Collard

Introduction

The Tao of Toys

*"Every child is an artist. The question is how to
remain an artist once he grows up."*
—PICASSO

We can all remember a favorite toy from our childhood.

Like Andy and Sheriff Woody, and later Buzz Lightyear, the relationship is unmistakable and unforgettable.

My favorite toy was a NASA space shuttle kite. Once the kite was flying high, the wind would carry a gyroscope from the handle all the way up the kite line to the top. As the gyroscope reached the end of the line, it would hit a clasp, releasing a space shuttle that came flying back down to Earth.

I was captivated, as the wonder of flight left me breathless. Even now, as I recall watching that space shuttle float back down, I feel it: the rush of excitement that flight always gave me. I remember the excitement I felt as a child when I heard the roaring sounds of my uncle flying over our house as I ran outside to watch him do a low-level flyover with his infamous wing wave.

This magic never lost its grip on me. Wonder moved me from kites to wood gliders to airplanes, and, eventually, to model rockets. I imagined one day becoming a pilot, and I reveled in the idea of being a real-world ace who protected the innocent from tyranny by engaging the enemy in air-to-air combat. Even to this day, images in my office pay homage to Spitfires and Mustangs, my favorite aircraft and some of the most aspirational warbirds of the Second World War.

Likely, you can remember a favorite childhood toy with equal nostalgia. Perhaps you remember unwrapping your toy or the overflowing excitement as you held it for the first time. Instantly, you knew it had limitless opportunities. You carried that joy with you from one playtime to the next, and it likely helped you develop into the person you are today.

Something about toys, and play in general, embed deeply in our emotional landscape. Action figures assisted us in beating the bad guys, dolls helped us host tea parties, and our favorite board game kept us busy on snowy days.

We never forget the moments, but too often we forget the lessons. Perhaps we didn't realize that our action figures were teaching us to stand up for justice. Maybe we didn't realize that our dolls were teaching us compassion and empathy, or that our favorite board game was preparing us for future negotiations in the marketplace.

As adults we've grown up and lost the life-altering lessons those toys were trying to teach. As George Bernard Shaw stated, *"We do not stop playing because we are getting old, we get old because we stop playing."*

Every child, in every corner of the Earth, plays—even if they don't have access to commercially made products. Toys and play are woven into the fabric of the objects all around us as we instinctively reach to make a "magic wand" from a stick, skip a stone across a pond, or blow away dandelion seeds, releasing hundreds of "tiny parachutes."

While the whole world is connected through our ability to play, perhaps none are more united in the need to imagine, explore, and create than kids and entrepreneurs, who by definition are creators. But the child has an advantage: they are given permission to be curious and playful.

Adults, however, must proactively seek out their own inner-child, and we've been implored to do so by philosophers like Marianne Williamson,

Julia Cameron and Jesus–who encouraged his followers to become like little children in order to fully realize the possibilities of God's kingdom.

It's no wonder why. Children, after all, have so many of the necessary attributes that promote growth and innovation: imagination, hope, curiosity, excitement, and faith. Children believe that anything is possible, and they're infinitely curious about the world around them; a leaf, a caterpillar, a raindrop—anything can capture their imagination. Their zest for life is unmatched, and they can inspire us all with their giddiness. Lastly, children have an abounding faith in the world, and they believe in what they cannot yet see.

All these qualities are found in children, needed by entrepreneurs, and best developed and manifested through the art of play.

So, in the following pages, I want to give you, the reader, the opportunity and permission to reclaim your inner child. I invite you to journey back to your early years, to remember the possibilities you once knew so intimately, and to rediscover the lessons you learned so naturally.

Who am I to extend this invitation?

Well, I like to think of myself as Santa Claus's silent partner. I've walked in his footsteps as close as humanly possible. For one, I grew up and reside in Canada, (which is the home of the North Pole). Secondly, we previously shared the same profession—*we were both toymakers.* I too have spent many hours sitting in workshops imagining, tinkering, and creating what I hoped would ultimately one day bring a smile to a child's face.

I started selling my first toy (of course, it was a flying toy) almost thirty years ago in the early 90's. By exploring my own childlike curiosity, and nearly by accident, I became immersed in the wondrous world of playthings. This adventure would send me on a journey through founding a startup focused on promoting children's entertainment that would result in eventually shipping Billions of products around the planet. It started from humble beginnings: including an office and warehouse in my basement, where we facilitated selling products through kiosks in malls. It would evolve to eventually become the largest distribution company of its kind in Canada.

Along the way we made several mistakes, failed multiple times, and experienced significant setbacks. However, by persisting through all the tumult, we eventually pivoted to become a toy *developer* and *manufacturer*. It was a fragile transition, but the business continued to evolve and would eventually become a global contender with multiple offices and mass distribution, generating more than $100 Million in annual revenue. In our pursuit of "delivering joy and creating smiles", we worked with premier inventor groups, entertainment brands, media houses, and toy retailers. I never had a room full of *elves*, but I did have hundreds of amazing employees, several warehouses, and offices across multiple continents. So, while I didn't technically put on the red suit, don the black boots, or carry an overstuffed bag down a chimney, I have been an ally to Santa—helping create play experiences that would inspire hope, spread joy, and leave enduring smiles.

I've experienced firsthand the happiness that results from connecting with our inner child, the Tao behind the toys, and the truth we can learn through the art of play. As kids, we thought we were simply playing with childish objects, but all along we were growing, exploring our humanity, forging a strong character, and helping shape and develop worldviews. There is a reason we refer to musicians as *"playing"* an instrument. It appropriately describes what the power of play is all about: the ability to unleash our inherent creative potential.

In some small way, I believe that the lore of Santa and the childlike faith that kids have about his role in their lives is meant to save us from the malaise that can be found in adulthood. The hope of Santa should help inspire all of us to be endlessly curious, to remain passionately playful, and to revel in the mystery and magic found in our imagination.

I am a toymaker from the North, and in this role I feel privileged to be your guide, to help you reconnect with your past, engage with your inner child, awaken the feelings of joy that came from play, and through my life lessons, help inspire you to see a bright and bold future.

If after reading this book you find yourself inspired and wanting to take action on how to apply these lessons to learn to live your life to the full, then I encourage you to check out FullSpectrumLife.com/Resources.

> *"At the height of laughter, the universe is flung*
> *into a kaleidoscope of new possibilities."*
> —JEAN HOUSTON

CHAPTER 1

G.I. JOE'S HUMBLY MIND THEIR FLANKS

"Resilient people do not bounce back from hard experiences; they find healthy ways to integrate them into their lives. In time people find that great calamity met with great spirit can create great strength."

—ERIC GREITENS, AUTHOR AND FORMER NAVY SEAL

decided to open the first chapter of this book with a quote from a Navy SEAL for two reasons—First, the SEALs are revered in our society for representing modern-day heroes and second, they are directly linked to the men of service who inspired the creation of our first toy of interest: G.I. Joe. The *toy version* was modeled and named after the colloquialism for US soldiers, which historically embodied ultimate heroism. After two world wars and a conflict in Korea, America had put its faith in the virtues of G.I.s as the heroes of courage and justice who protected the free world, eliminating threats of tyranny.

The G.I. Joe figurines are famous around the world as a symbol of freedom and for being the toy world's first action figures.

In the 1960s, Donald Levine was the vice president for the successful toy company Hassenfeld Brothers (now called Hasbro). He was smitten by the "razor-and-razorblade" business model, wherein you sell one, original item (razor) and then enjoy continual revenue off the attachments (blades). Mattel had utilized this model with Barbie, and they were taking the girls' toy market by storm.

The popular thinking was that Barbie, along with other dolls, was exclusively for the domain of girls. This left many toy companies asking the question: Could a similar humanoid figurine be used to capture the imagination of their male counterparts?

In 1945, a movie called *The Story of G.I. Joe* debuted, capitalizing on the heroism of the American G.I.s. By the early 1960s, the Cold War was in full swing, culminating in 1962 with the Cuban Missile Crisis. If ever the Free World needed a hero they could turn to, it was during this dark moment in history.

Then one day, as the radio waves proclaimed the constant threat of nuclear war, and Mattel enjoyed glaring success with Barbie, Levine passed by a store and spotted a soldier mannequin on display. He had an *'aha moment'* and immediately started to draft a plan for a revolutionary idea:

articulated toy soldier with removable clothing and accessories. Shortly thereafter, he presented his concept to his team and was able to convince them to support his vision and launch a unique toy doll specifically made for and marketed to *boys*.

Of course the term *doll* was in the domain of girls, so they instead coined the word "action figures." They launched the G.I. Joe product line with four different soldiers, one for each of the main branches of the US military. The genius behind the toy was that each action figure had nineteen points of articulation, which allowed them to be placed in realistic positions.

The toy launched on February 2 1964, and it was an instant success. Within twenty-four months, G.I. Joes made up two-thirds of the sales of the already-successful Hassenfeld Brothers toy company. While the toy's sales suffered shortly, during the highly unpopular Vietnam War, it enjoyed a resurgence when it was re-released decades later. In recognition of its enduring success, in 2004, it was officially inducted into the (US) National Toy Hall of Fame. The popularity of the brand has even inspired multiple Hollywood action films.

The term *G.I.* itself has a fascinating history. "Words and Their Stories" host Phil Murray explored the etymology of the name. Most believe that *G.I.* originally meant "general issue" or "government issue." Eventually, the term *G.I.* eventually evolved into meaning the soldier himself. But Murray offers another explanation:

Apparently, many believe that the American soldier wasn't just tough, but that his character and physical strength, disciplined and trained for one specific purpose, could only be described as one thing: *galvanized iron.*[1]

I'll leave the true etymology of *G.I.* for you to decide. As for me, when I consider the rigors involved in a military boot camp or in the infamous

---

1 Phil Murray, "Words and Their Stories: Military Expressions," Learning English, October 27, 2012, https://learningenglish.voanews.com/a/words-and-their-stories-military-expressions/1534670.html.

Navy SEALs Hell Week, I see it as a forging process of human potential and as such "galvanized iron" *only* seems fitting.

GETTING FLANKED

In 1994, when I was 21 years old, I read an article in a magazine about the X-Zylo, a simple plastic cylinder about the size of a softball, whose special aerodynamic design enables everyday people to throw it up to 600 feet. I couldn't believe such a simple design could fly more than two football fields, so I ordered a box to test them and discovered that everything I read was actually true.

I enjoyed playing with the X-Zylo for several weeks before calling the US manufacturer and learning that he didn't have a distributor in Canada. I was curious if I could make a business out of selling them. I was fascinated by flight and I had always been a playful spirit; it seemed like a compelling opportunity. I created a business plan and submitted it to the owners and to my surprise, they accepted the proposal. I was suddenly the exclusive X-Zylo distributor in Canada, and I was both excited and terrified. Without realizing it, I'd just joined the ancient profession of play, and little did I know that I was about to embark on a journey that would take me through a very steep learning curve.

At first, I was little more than an old-school traveling salesman, drumming up meager profits by traveling with my hired-hand to carnivals, setting up shop and tossing X-Zylo's back and forth in front of the crowds. I soon realized that I would never be able to build anything great if I was responsible for making every single sale. That is when we made the decision to market the product and to do so by having a celebrity endorsement. Through a series of fortunate events, we managed to sign a promotional deal with Doug Flutie, who was at that time the star quarterback for the Canadian Football League's Toronto Argonauts. We initially tried to launch the product on the Shopping Channel, but soon learned that we were making a cardinal mistake: marketing to the wrong audience. That led to us creating an infomercial and finding the right medium for broadcasting. Suddenly sales started to soar.

Fast-forward a few years. My wife and I, along with a few friends and family members, had formed a real toy company known as Dynatech. With the success of X-Zylo, we had made a name for ourselves in the Canadian marketplace, and a number of other companies started to inquire if we would take on their distribution and marketing. Our portfolio of brands grew, and we added a number of significant brands and products, including: Wham-O's Frisbee, Hula Hoop, Slip 'N Slide; Wild Planet's Night Vision Goggles; and the famous Uncle Milton Ant Farm. Dynatech may have started out as the little engine that could, but it soon became the go-to gold standard for toy distribution in Canada.

We were a scrappy startup with a strong work ethic that had been baked into our ethos from the very start. We viewed every opportunity with a fresh approach that allowed us to customize unique and unconventional marketing campaigns, which in turn generated sales that resulted in rapid company growth. We did not have the big budgets of our competitors, so often our marketing was done through utilizing in-store displays or in-person demonstration events. Our unorthodox approach to marketing also informed the way we would raise money to support the company, resulting in several clever and unique ways to ensure we had the capital to support the extraordinary growth we experienced.

Through determination and hard work, we became one of the largest toy distributors in Canada and for several years in a row, the company was ranked in the top 100 fastest growing companies in the country. Our retail partners loved us because of our innovative marketing and distribution strategies, and we started to garner attention from toymakers, retailers, and distributors from across the globe.

I was also enjoying accolades and recognition, receiving the Fast Growth Award from the CYBF and becoming a finalist for the Ernst and Young Entrepreneur of the Year Award. It felt good for the ego that this "wunderkid" from rural Canada was disrupting an old industry and I enjoyed basking in the applause of crowds, frequently traveling and delivering keynote speeches.

What I did not realize at the time is that fast, undisciplined growth tends to sugarcoat systemic problems that, if left unchecked, can have grave consequences for a company. Unknown to us, our fast growth had lulled us into a "ready, fire, aim" approach. We were growing recklessly—"flying by the seat of our pants," and through grit and the sheer force of will, we somehow managed to always pull off our plans. Every year, we'd start from building out our company's growth plan from scratch, without re-inventing or reassessing the necessary resources required to achieve our goals. It all just happened to work out...*until it didn't.*

In December 2005, I was with my family in Mexico. I was riding high on Dynatech's successes, and my wife and I had just decided to purchase a property in Baja. Our toy company had enjoyed what we thought was unprecedented growth. We were ranked as one of Canada's fastest growing enterprises, we were one of the top toy companies in the country, and with a new joint venture in product development, we were actively gaining market share in the United States. We had just opened up a New York showroom, had hired American staff, and were now working with every major mass-market retailer on both sides of the border.

After soaking up the sun and waves of Mexico, we returned home to Canada and my phone rang. On the other end was my business partner and the company's CFO, who ominously stated, "Brad, I think we have a problem."

"What do you mean?" I asked.

"After extensive review, it turns out we don't have the profits that I have been reporting to you from the system," was his reply. He further elaborated: "It turns out that the data from the new ERP we implemented has been giving us bad information."

Our leadership team met to discuss the extent of our financial problems, and the more we peeled back the layers, the more troubles we found. Over the prior ten years, while we had grown the distribution business aggressively, we had been doing so with lean margins that resulted in meager profits. Now that the truth was being revealed, our balance sheet had been stretched and we were now in breach of a number of covenants with our lenders.

As our situation became clearer, what we had anticipated to be another year of dreamy business growth, instead started to look like it may very well become an emerging financial nightmare.

Within weeks, I found myself having difficult conversations with our debt holders, explaining how a few hiccups in our accounting system had put our entire multimillion-dollar enterprise in the red. After divulging our situation to our bank, they decided to put us into special loans, meaning we had lost their trust. They froze accounts, forced us to cut costs, and micromanaged our financial situation on a daily basis, giving us access to extremely limited amounts of capital to operate. We couldn't move forward with any of our new initiatives; instead, we were paying high interest rates to borrow additional cash just to make payroll and fulfill existing orders.

Within thirty days, we went from one of the most aspirational companies in Canada to being on business life support.

So, what exactly happened? The answer isn't complicated. As we advanced, we forgot to cover our flanks. We let the pride of our so-called success cloud over our vigilance to inspect what we were expecting in our results. As Proverbs teaches, "Pride goes before destruction, a haughty spirit before a fall."

NO ONE FLANKS A G.I. JOE

The modern day SEALs epitomize all that the G.I. Joes represent to young children—a highly revered unit, the elite of the elite, embodying virtues of strength, courage, and honor. To become a SEAL, you need to first overcome the now infamous and grueling *Hell Week*. It has a notoriously high attrition rate, and the lore of this right of passage has inspired films and books.

SEALs, G.I. Joes, and other elite soldiers know that stagnation causes death, while advancement means life. Ergo, they never stop pushing forward. This ever-forward movement creates pressure on their enemies, and helps them overcome their opponents. Yet, as they apply that forward pressure, elite soldiers understand the importance of maintaining a rigorous guard of their flanks. This is crucial because most military defeats happen as the result of a flanking maneuver: one side advances too quickly, and they inadvertently expose their backside. If this happens in battle, the enemy will take advantage of the moment to either attack from behind or to cut off supplies, ammunition, and reinforcements.

The Battle of the Bulge showcased an expert flanking maneuver in which Eisenhower anticipated the "blitzkrieg" German advancement against the Allied troops, even allowing it so he could follow with a pincer maneuver. He believed in the "bend but don't break" philosophy, so he allowed the Nazis to advance. Then Eisenhower directed troops to attack around the sides and cut off the now spread-out enemy from their supply lines. The defeat was legendary as it eliminated one of the last great threats on the western front of World War II.

This same advance-and-defend concept applies directly to the world of enterprise. Growth is certainly the catalyst for most business conversations today, and for good reason—without growth, businesses die. At the same time, we have to anticipate and prepare for the right speed of growth. There is a difference between controlled growth and explosive growth that can precipitate the downfall of a business, if proper measures aren't taken to defend the flanks as a company advances.

It may come as a surprise to learn that more businesses die choking on biting off more than they can chew, versus starving to death due to lack of opportunity. When an organization grows too quickly without the proper anticipation and defenses put into place, the success itself can break the foundational structures that underpin the integrity of the business. The result of an undisciplined pursuit of more can create a lack of focus, a strain on systems, and a quick drain on capital, leaving a company vulnerable and exposed. There are endless examples of growing businesses and intelligent founders who have overstretched their internal capabilities, only to reach their breaking point.

When Steve Jobs returned to Apple in 1997, the organization was hemorrhaging cash and was on the brink of financial disaster. One of his first acts as the CEO was to kill the products that were distracting the company from those they could ultimately be great at. After the great Apple culling, the company went from 350 products down to *ten*. Steve Jobs recognized that too many options in the company's product line had created an inability for them to be truly great in any one product category. The impact of these changes became evident over time, as Apple has gone from the verge of bankruptcy to the most valuable company in the world 20 years later.

As entrepreneurs, we naturally see incredible potential in people, products, and ideas. This optimism is a gift, but it must be disciplined so as to not hinder us. With a deluge of opportunities we begin lacking focus, thinly spreading our resources across a number of projects. Too often founders chase "good ideas" that really are distractions disguised as opportunities. We are better served in applying our energies where we can make our greatest impact.

Consider the effect of a magnifying glass. If you let the sun shine through it while it is out of focus, it may illuminate a piece of paper. If on that same paper you focus the light into one concentrated spot, the energy will be powerful enough to burn a hole through it. Our attention and resources are no different. We must condition ourselves to focus on the few items that help us advance our vision and where we can apply our full agency. As Greg McKeown noted in *Essentialism*, we need to focus on the "vital few" versus being distracted by the "trivial many."[2] Steve Jobs understood the importance of protecting the flank and the vulnerabilities that were created by too many priorities. It is the only way we can become world-class.

> *"I'm as proud of what we don't do as I am of what we do."*
> —STEVE JOBS

SET THE VISION, LIVE THE VALUES, FIND THE TALENT

> *"If you want to go fast, go alone. If you want to go far, go together."*
> —AFRICAN PROVERB

Before going further down the rabbit hole of the potential flanking maneuvers of a business overstressed by growth, I want to take a step back and start with first principles, thinking of what are the CEO's key tasks. Every CEO has three important roles within their company.

First, they need to set the vision and direction for the company and ensure the resources are in place to make it possible. You need to inspire your company and your customers with your bold vision for the future and the roadmap of how you are going to achieve it.

Secondly, the CEO should shape the culture by *living out* the values they espouse to others. According to Gandhi, "Happiness is when what you

---

2 Greg McKeown, *Essentialism: The Disciplined Pursuit of Less* (New York: Crown Business, 2014).

think, what you say, and what you do are in harmony." When we live our values, we find a certain music emanating from our lives, and when a leader projects that music, others listen, and want to come closer. Followers must be able to consider your life and witness you breathing and imitating the values you espouse. When leaders live authentically and when their actions reflect the values, their followers will trust and support the leader's vision. As the wise adage goes, "What you do speaks so loudly that I cannot hear what you say."

That leads us to the third task of a CEO—to find the best talent and empower them to make the vision become reality. The business of business is people; meaning a company is not a product, icon, symbol, or building but rather reflections of the values and creative genius of the people working within. The truth of the matter is that one is too small a number to achieve greatness in any endeavor. Finding, attracting, and retaining the right talent is required for any CEO seeking to achieve a bold vision. This skill set becomes an ongoing process as the business experiences growth. It is up to the CEO to ensure that the company hires the right talent ahead of the breaking points.

THREE CRITICAL BUSINESS FLANKS

It is easy to fall under the allure and intoxicating feeling that comes from witnessing top-line gains without recognizing its inherent dangers. While growth is necessary for a business, uncontrolled growth will ultimately expose the business's limitations. When a business is growing uncontrollably, there are three flanks the leader must defend against:

* The people
* The systems
* The capital

When a growing business gets sidelined, it will almost certainly be because your org chart was not ready, the systems couldn't handle the strain, or the necessary capital structure was not in place. Growing a business means you are stressing it and as a result, you need to be continually increasing its capacity.

Most entrepreneurs operate with naive optimism, thinking, "We can figure this out as we grow!" Many are capable of doubling the size of their company through the sheer force of will. However, if you set a goal to grow ten times, you will quickly realize that it is not possible by exerting more of just yourself. The only logical conclusion to achieve this outcome is by upgrading these three critical areas on a continual basis.

Your ability to upgrade both your cash flow and your operating systems is largely not a "how" question but rather one of "who." As such, your key priority as CEO is finding the right people. You should have a maniacal focus for increasing the talent density within your company.

In the early stages of business, founders are true generalists seemingly wearing every hat. They create systems, answer emails, make sales calls, develop presentations, and even take out the trash. As the organization grows and attracts additional team members, founders must evolve from being generalists to becoming specialists. This includes being highly optimized with respect to time and concentrating on their areas of competency. Focus must also be placed on setting the vision, living the values, and finding the best talent. You need to find people who not only fit the culture and have the desire to perform, but have the capacity to deliver exceptional results under the stress of a scaling enterprise.

A company will never grow bigger than the capabilities of its team. If you are not constantly upgrading and growing your organization's talent pool, you'll inadvertently expose your business to future problems. That includes you, the founder. This should be a stark reminder that we must all constantly be looking to grow our capabilities, capacity, and connections.

In order for a snake to grow, it needs to shed its old skin and put on a new one. You are either green and growing or ripe and rotting; there is no stasis.

Not only is it important for a growing company to constantly reinvent its team, but it's also important to review whether you even have the right people. The team you started with is not necessarily the team that will take you into the future. Business is a team sport, and if your goal is to play in the major leagues and to win a championship, it is crucial to elevate your team with exceptional, world-class talent.

In considering the frequency of when to assess the vulnerability of these 3 possible flanks, if you are growing your business at single digits, you should reassess and upgrade annually. If you are growing by double digits, these three areas should be reviewed and upgraded biannually. If, however, you are amongst the rare few entrepreneurs who are experiencing triple-digit growth, this must be a quarterly or perhaps a monthly process.

Most importantly, as you are monitoring the health of the company, remember to focus on business metrics that matter. Too many entrepreneurs get sucked into focusing on superficial "vanity metrics." Remember the wisdom of this axiom if you want to become an enduring enterprise: top line is vanity, bottom line is sanity, and cash flow is reality!

For additional resources to help you to defend your flanks while advancing your business, visit FullSpectrumLife.com/Resources, where you'll uncover proven strategies for increasing your company's capacity ahead of its growth.

SLOW IS SMOOTH; SMOOTH IS FAST

In the fast-paced frenetic world of startups, most founders start out by doing the majority of work and maintaining a pace that is unsustainable. The business needs this initial input of effort and energy to get the needed momentum to propel it forward and to create inertia. This work ethic turns a creative concept into a business, inspires followers to join the enterprise, and compels the team into action. With high energy, plenty of multitasking, and an immense amount of perspiration, an entrepreneur bootstraps and births a business into being.

This "get it done at all costs" mentality is necessary in the early days, particularly when resources are scarce, and the unknown is so vast. A healthy dose of naivete helps move the business from trial, through error, into creating forward momentum. That said, these extraordinary early efforts often create a frenetic environment that may work amongst a smaller team, but as you add complexity with people and systems, is not sustainable long-term.

When an enterprise is small and nimble, redirection can happen quickly as only a few people are involved in decision-making. As the company scales, the ability to make quick changes becomes more challenging, as there is more friction and drag created by the organizational structure. As such, strategy decisions need to be more calculated and implemented more carefully. This is when entrepreneurs need to set up the guardrails that keep the energy and momentum flowing. Without proper systems, organization, and discipline, a founder will find themselves doing and redoing work, wasting energy, and frustrating the team.

This is common amongst less experienced entrepreneurs. They struggle to slow down long enough, to think about and consider decisions fully before executing. Founders must learn to graduate from impulsive decision making into a more disciplined and calculated approach that drives results. Otherwise, impromptu decision-making can lead to confusing "activity for accomplishment", or what I call the rocking horse syndrome: where you get on the horse and rock back and forth really hard, but lack meaningful direction.

Conversely, more seasoned entrepreneurs may face the opposite issue. They may take too long to make decisions, allowing valuable opportunities to slip by them while they overanalyze and contemplate. I can understand why some entrepreneurs are prone to make such a mistake: you've taken some hits, and are a bit gun-shy to get whacked again since the pain of the last mistake still resonates. In this condition we are susceptible to confirmation bias, where we want to be right and as a result we overanalyze decisions without advancement, otherwise known as paralysis from overanalysis.

In either case—if you make too many frenetic decisions or if you take too long to make any decision—you will frustrate your progress to achieving your vision, mission, and goals. In the former case, the car seems to swerve endlessly, wasting energy, while in the latter case, the car just moves too slowly forward and is easily passed by faster cars who steal away the opportunity.

Regardless of one's tendencies, we should realize that there needs to be a creative tension that pushes us to move both quickly and thoughtfully, considering what exposure our movements create. Like the SEALs, we need to constantly be advancing while simultaneously guarding our flanks.

There isn't an exact measurement of when you should act versus when you should pause, and of course, every business decision requires an acceptance of a certain level of risk. However, Colin Powell offers some insight with his famous 40–70 Rule. Powell argues that you should attempt to gather between 40 and 70 percent of the information needed before executing on a particular decision. He theorizes that if you have less than 40 percent, then you are acting too impulsively, creating unnecessary risk. Conversely, he says that if you tell yourself you're waiting for more information even after you've uncovered 70 percent of the facts, what you're really doing is stalling or hoping for confirmation bias. This sort of procrastination, he says, actually creates *greater* risk of missing the timing for making your move count.

HUMBLE WARRIORS

*"Bad companies are destroyed by crises, good
companies survive them, great companies are
improved by them."*

—ANDY GROVE

Business case studies often point to how large incumbents miss out on great opportunities by overlooking disruptive businesses and technologies. Blockbuster famously turned down Netflix's offer to sell their company for a relatively small amount only for Blockbuster to end up filing for bankruptcy shortly thereafter. Within that mistake, we find the creative tension between the principles of advance and protect the flank, and slow is smooth, smooth is fast.

You could say Blockbuster failed at both pieces of these fundamental SEALs' disciplines: Blockbuster moved too quickly to refute the offer, failing to slow down enough to recognize the changing environment. If Blockbuster had considered the emerging technology and the market paradigm shift it was creating, they would have realized they were going to be left exposed to disruption.

They say that the punch that will knock you out is the one you did not see coming. Hindsight is always 20/20, but by remaining vigilant and on guard, perhaps Blockbuster would have recognized the opportunity afforded by Netflix, and seized it.

Successful companies maintain a level of *active uneasiness*, similar to what Jim Collins calls "productive paranoia." The philosophy of active uneasiness is simple. As a founder you must constantly consider: "Who's trying to take us out? What is changing? How could we be disrupted?"

This is a healthy form of restlessness that helps leaders identify threats from the evolving marketplace and then to make decisions accordingly.

Leaders know that today's success doesn't promise future greatness, and we can never rest on our laurels too long. In baseball, you cannot win today's games with yesterday's home run.

Certainly advance and protect the flank and slow is smooth and smooth is fast are valuable principles that the SEALs use and can easily be applied as a benefit to our businesses. However, these tactics are only effective if implemented with the virtue of humility, and I believe the G.I. Joes symbolically represent this. While we were playing with these soldiers as children, lining them up to defend and attack, we were certainly modeling out their virtues of honor and courage. Our toy soldiers were never acting out of selfish ambition or serving just to please themselves. In our imagination they were elite, well-trained warriors that used their prowess to protect others, to serve humanity, to bring order to chaos, and to repel unjust enemies. They were acting in a way that C. S. Lewis best summarized as "humility isn't thinking less of yourself—it's thinking of yourself less."

G.I. Joes, for all their symbolic bravado and strength, are only celebrated when they use their gifts to serve others. When those with equal gifts use them selfishly, we don't think of them as heroes; we consider them villains.

Of all the characteristics G.I. Joes share—physical strength, mental stamina, resilient fortitude—their humility is the single attribute that makes them aspirational. It's the necessary virtue that we would expect from the heroes who are charged to resist tyranny, subdue chaos, and defend our liberty.

PRIDEFUL WARNINGS

"Choices start with your thoughts. Your thoughts become your words. Your words become your actions. Choose each day life-giving thoughts."
—NICKY GUMBEL

In his book *How the Mighty Fall,* Jim Collins identified how many once-successful juggernauts in business found themselves devolved to utter ruin. Collins studied the 2008 great financial crisis, which resulted in bankrupting many of the world's top financial institutions, extrapolating common patterns. He noted a pattern: a predictable succession of steps that ultimately resulted in capitulation. The first step was hubris or pride borne of success. These were companies who stopped doing the necessary work that had earned their initial success and instead started to believe the success they had experienced was deserved.[3]

Entrepreneurs should heed this warning and learn this principle: nothing fails like success. Blockbuster's arrogance toward Netflix caused them to overlook an obvious threat to their business. An irrational and overly protective belief system blinded Kodak from recognizing the threat created by digital imagery (ironically a technology that Kodak invented). With this strategic misstep, Kodak went from being a top global brand into oblivion. Coincidently the same year that Kodak declared bankruptcy, Instagram was acquired for $1 billion.

In recent history there are several companies who have suffered the same fate by letting pride go unchecked within the leadership of the company. These examples have been popularized by TV dramas recounting the rise and fall of high-profile companies such as WeWork, Theranos, and Uber. The common ailment in all of these stories is that the leaders allowed the pride of their early success to take hold and drive their motivations and resulted in poor decision making.

Pride typically flows from the intoxication of success. At the apex of accomplishment, just when it seems we can rest on our laurels, relish in our achievements, or take delight in what our hands have created, this is when we are most at risk. I know the feeling firsthand as I have swallowed

---

3 Jim Collins, *How the Mighty Fall: And Why Some Companies Never Give In* (New York: Collins Business Essentials, 2009).

a few sips from the alluring drink of self-proclaimed success only to stumble, fall, and then ultimately crash. This has given me firsthand insight into the sobering truth: without humility and discipline as you rise, your enterprise will become vulnerable to ruin. Success often leads to pride, and pride quickly results in excess overhead, apathy, and a lack of vigilance. Left unchecked, it will be the flanking factors that compromise your business and be the beginning of the end of a once promising opportunity.

FULLY FLANKED

Pride and my false belief that we were "too big to fail" made the situation at Dynatech go from bad to worse. When we finally uncovered our financial mistakes, my proposed solution only dug us into a deeper pit. Even though we were strapped for cash, I told myself, "I'll just secure another big distribution brand to pay for our missteps." I set my sights on Playmates, a company well known for brands such as the Teenage Mutant Ninja Turtles, Amazing Dolls, Strawberry Shortcake and Disney Fairies. I falsely believed that if I could juice more sales, that would deliver the profits to solve all of our problems. I was trying to solve the problem using the same level of thinking that had got me into the mess to begin with. More is not better, and working harder is rarely going to fix your problem; however, the one thing I knew how to do was grow the top line.

I courted Playmates, and I won distribution rights for the majority of their brands; however, the financial conditions of the deal were egregious.

In order to secure the capital to fund the distribution deal, our new financier required that we go through 'a restructuring', which I have since learned is a fancy word for bankruptcy. Basically, it means that we would be cleaning up our balance sheet by shedding debt, giving our company's creditors pennies on the dollar and then injecting fresh new capital to support the business plan.

In light of the previous losses and the stranglehold we were in with the bank under special loans, we had little choice. Still, it was not an easy decision to make as in addition to the creditors we had over $1 million of friends-and-family money invested. This weighed heavy on my mind; however, we were out of options and out of time, so with the support of our bank, we filed the Dynatech BIA petition in June 2006. We followed this with a full operational restructuring by shutting down our head office, laying off several dozen staff, selling off a subsidiary, and moving our inventory into a third-party distribution facility. These were the necessary steps we believed we needed to make in order to cut costs while simultaneously recapitalizing, in preparation for the forthcoming Playmates deal.

My pride kept me from questioning the integrity of the business model and zooming out to see the shifting marketplace. As a result, the restructured operation and injection of new capital would instead prove to be the final blow to Dynatech. We struggled to make it work, but the writing was on the wall. I soon discovered that more money doesn't solve your problems, but rather amplifies your inadequacies. Instead of embracing active uneasiness to reassess the changing marketplace and its threats to our business model, we falsely believed more sales would solve the problem. We secured the Playmates distribution deal and our revenues did grow, but we soon discovered that we had saddled the company with massive resource obligations. This only exacerbated the problem of our anemic margins, causing the company to suffer even greater losses than those experienced prior to the original restructuring.

In the spring of 2009, we filed for Dynatech's second and final bankruptcy. We were devastated. It was the end of a chapter, with the company's demise bringing much shame.

The months that followed were dedicated to deep reflection, resulting in valuable business lessons that you will encounter in later chapters of this book.

*   *   *

Jocko Willink, retired Navy SEAL and author of the book *Extreme Ownership*, once wrote that:

> Implementing Extreme Ownership requires checking your ego and operating with a high degree of humility. Admitting mistakes, taking ownership, and developing a plan to overcome challenges are integral to any successful team.[4]

As Jocko points out, extreme ownership is about setting aside your ego and then owning your part in co-creating the conditions that then led to the outcomes. Reflecting back on these experiences in my life, I now recognize how naive I really was. Yes, I had worked hard, but I also had been incredibly lucky, which afforded us the opportunity to grow the business with reckless abandon. I had allowed the pride that came with being labeled a "wunder kid" to go to my head. This resulted in building a business without the needed rigor, resulting in a structure built on a sandy foundation, unable to withstand the marketplace tremors we would later face.

Growth is a double-edged sword. It is a critical component for us and our businesses to continually grow and evolve. Unchecked reckless growth, however, risks the company and can lead to its demise. When choosing to grow your company, take note that you are actually stressing it. The key is to evolve your people, your systems and your capital at a pace that is ahead of its growth.

Through the "school of hard knocks," I've since learned the lesson the G.I. Joes had offered all along. There needs to be a creative tension between moving forward but at a pace that is slow and smooth, without leaving

---

4 Jocko Willink and Leif Babin, *Extreme Ownership: How U.S. Navy SEALs Lead and Win* (New York: St. Martin's Press, 2015), Kindle.

your flank exposed. Protect yourself from yourself by not letting pride from success set in. Ensure you are practicing active uneasiness about the ever-changing marketplace. A leader must be constantly watching the horizon for threats that may come and before they do, be willing to adapt the business to protect its flank. Staying still isn't an option; you do not tread water, you are either moving forward or falling back.

These are some of the valuable lessons learned from the G.I. Joes and the characters who helped inspire them. These important principles would go on to become foundational in both imagining and designing my next entrepreneurial adventures.

> *"You need to know how to control your growth as*
> *things that grow fast tend to die fast also. There are*
> *two types of growth. Growth that makes you fat*
> *and growth that makes you strong. We look at all*
> *our growth in the context of being here 100 years.*
> *Learn to know the difference."*
> —YVON CHOUINARD

CHAPTER 2

WE ONLY PLAY MONOPOLY WITH OTHERS

"When you focus on what you lack,
you lose what you have.
When you focus on what you have,
you get what you lack."

—GREG MCKEOWN

M onopoly's origin story is both fascinating and mysterious. For many years, the story went that Charles Darrow invented the game, and sold the rights to Parker Brothers in the 1930s. Perhaps to bolster sales, Darrow's story reads like a traditional rags-to-riches tale one would hope to hear of any American entrepreneur: Darrow was a nearly destitute salesman who invented Monopoly in his basement. "The tale," suggested a 2015 *New York Times* article, "was that an unemployed man named Charles Darrow dreamed up Monopoly in the 1930s. He sold it and became a millionaire, his inventiveness saving him—and Parker Brothers…from the brink of destruction."[5]

But an accidental discovery in the 1970s shed light on the game's true origins. Darrow had actually commandeered the idea from a woman named Elizabeth, or "Lizzie," Magie. Decades before, she'd come up with a game called The Landlord's Game, which Americans (particularly college students) had begun playing. Darrow took this idea, iterated upon it, and created Monopoly.

Ironically, Magie, a progressive economist and feminist, invented Monopoly's predecessor to spread her notion of the potential evils of monopolistic land grabs by wealthy individuals. With the game, she hoped to evangelize the "single land tax" philosophy: that all land should be owned by the government, and only "rented" by individuals.[6] To Magie, the game would teach Americans (particularly children) to "see clearly the gross injustice of our present land system." In fact, she originally wrote two versions and rules of her game:

An anti-monopolist set in which all were rewarded when wealth was created, and a monopolist set in which the goal was to create monopolies

---

5 Mary Pilon, "Monopoly's Inventor: The Progressive Who Didn't Pass 'Go,'" *New York Times*, February 13, 2015, https://www.nytimes.com/2015/02/15/business/behind-monopoly-an-inventor-who-didnt-pass-go.html.

6 Henry George championed the "single tax" philosophy on land in the late 1800s. His philosophies are monikered Georgism or geoism and have heavily influenced some modern economic philosophies. It was this philosophy that Magie attempted to further.

and crush opponents. Her dualistic approach was a teaching tool meant to demonstrate that the first set of rules [the anti-monopoly version] was morally superior.[7]

To her chagrin the *monopolistic* version is what survived and is ultimately what Darrow sold to Parker Brothers, becoming the global phenomenon we know today.

Magie attempted to use the game to illustrate the market evils, and instead she unintentionally created a fun, free-market experience that has since become a delight to millions of players and has gone on to become the best selling board game of all time.

Today the brand has become prolific with multiple versions of the game introduced, including popular licenses such as Star Wars and an annual marketing collaboration with McDonald's. World champions have emerged from international competitions, and for decades family gatherings have been hilariously (or even heatedly) energized by the game's competitive nature. While Izzie was attempting to use the game to instruct us about the evils of land ownership, I think she may have unintentionally instructed us about something else.

THE PERILS OF THE UNDISCIPLINED PURSUIT OF MORE

Upon deeper reflection behind Dynatech's demise, it has become clear to me that our insatiable desire to grow the company led to reckless business decisions.

The late 1990s were an exciting time for Dynatech. As a small toy distributor, our success was growing based on meaningful relationships we had created with small and mid sized retail shops, the sort of romantic mom-and-pop shops that sell specialty board games and unique toys. We grew

---

7 Pilon, "Monopoly's Inventor."

our business by offering extraordinary products and serving these smaller customers with excellence.

By the early 2000s, mass-market retailers such as Walmart started to notice us, and they wanted our products in their stores. We had a healthy and stable business serving specialty customers; however, there was the juicy temptation to sell into the larger retailers. The illusion we bought into was that if we could get our products in these big-box retailers, we would grow our revenue, increase profits, and become more successful.

However, the mom-and-pop stores with whom we'd spent nearly a decade building relationships with—didn't want to carry products that were also available in the world's largest retailers. Mass retailers often sell products as loss-leaders in order to drive foot traffic, making up profits in other categories of products. Smaller retailers simply can't compete with retailers devaluing prices for loss-leading products. We failed to recognize this issue, as we were enamored by the idea of growing our top line sales. We succumbed to the false belief that more revenue equaled more success.

For a short time, we attempted to serve both the small and large retailers. Unfortunately as our products began to proliferate in mass retailers, our specialty retail customers started losing interest in us. At a deeper level, they even felt betrayed. We offered a few products exclusively to be sold in their stores, but they saw that for what it was—a half-ditch effort to salvage withering relationships. Once the majority of our products were available at mass retailers, the trust and loyalty we'd built over many years quickly evaporated in a matter of months.

At first our revenue increased as expected. Like any well-executed deception, the snake at the tree never told us the full story. We would later learn that the increase in revenue would come at the price of a strain on the business resources and a loss of profit margins. Big-box retailers entice you with large quantities but do so only after tough negotiations on pricing and terms. We placed larger orders with our factories but to finance these orders, we had to borrow an ever-increasing amount of money from banks.[8] Simply put, our sales were growing but our profit margins were shrinking, our capital was evaporating, and we were overleveraging our balance sheet.

To make matters worse, if the product did not sell, the mass retailers would come back to us and ask for either a product return or markdown dollars; issues we'd never experienced with the mom-and-pop market. If we didn't agree, the unspoken truth is that the mass buyers would punish their vendors by reducing future support.

On the flip side, if the product sold too well, the big-box retailers would then penalize suppliers for being out of stock. You as the supplier needed to bear the risk of always having to ensure there was just the right amount of inventory on the shelves. As your listings grew, so did the strain on your people, systems and capital. We had taken the bait and succumbed to the pursuit of undisciplined growth without thinking through the true costs.

I didn't recognize it then, but this was the beginning of the end for Dynatech. We had lost our way; our initial guiding principles had become compromised and we had recklessly started chasing growth without considering the costs. We were selling more, but working harder. We were living on anemic margins, and the happiness we had hoped would come from being bigger was instead a mirage mired with anxiety and stress.

PURE CAPITALISM & PURE SOCIALISM

On one hand, we'd simply done what was seemingly best for any capitalist—grow bigger. Can you blame us?

We made a mistake, and to better understand it, we have to peel back the layers just a bit, on what we all believe about money and marketplaces.

---

8 Typically, in the toy world, the retailer places the order with the distributor—us, in this case—and the distributor pays the factory up front, only to collect the money from the retailer at a later date. So, the larger the orders, the more capital the distributor must front.

Most people believe that there are only two basic forms of economic philosophy:

* **Pure capitalism:** A system in which greedy people race to the top, collecting as much as they can for themselves.
* **Pure socialism:** Supposedly, the antithesis of capitalism is a sharing system with no exorbitant winners.

At Dynatech, we started drifting toward the first notion of pure capitalism; however, we made a mistake in our binary approach. The problem with this "capitalism versus socialism" dichotomy is that they both focus on *greed* as the central component, one suggesting it's the solution, the other, that it's the problem. Throughout history, whenever either philosophy has been exclusively embraced by a nation, it's always digressed into becoming a tyranny. In either scenario greedy people take advantage of another, to devastating results.

It's easy to assume that capitalists are the real greedy ones. The truth is that greed can strike anywhere, in any system at any time. It is a broken condition of the human heart that is prompted by our egos. At its core, the belief is that you will find satisfaction if you chase extrinsic things at the expense of others.

Once, during a visit to our factories in Hong Kong, I ran into a Swedish businessman whom we'll call Sven. He was fabulously wealthy. He'd gained his wealth by distributing Bang and Olufsen's luxury sound systems into the former USSR. These systems are incredibly expensive. I couldn't believe that Sven, or anyone, had amassed such wealth by selling such expensive items in the supposed equalize-the-wealth economy of the Soviet Union. However, Sven informed me that there *was* an incredible amount of wealth inside the USSR, but it was entirely stratified, and only the very elite could access it. Socialism had not equalized everyone's wealth; in fact, it had done the opposite. Nighttime photos of North Korea offer the same evidence. A few bright lights in Pyongyang and a handful of other North Korean cities illuminate in what is otherwise a sea of total darkness. The country is supposedly one that shares wealth; however, greed still reigns, and it seems only an elite few have all the power.

In the Western world we are more familiar with and see the negative results of greed through pure capitalism. Greedy people underpay, fire frivolously, and overwork employees. They bend and break regulations, and accumulate their wealth at the expense of others and then use their wealth as an opportunity to promote their fragile ego.

In any system where ego and greed go unchecked, the false belief that drives the behavior is: "If I had that, I'd be happy." The truth is money will never create lasting happiness, which we will explore in a future chapter.

Money is nothing more than a neutral form of transaction that is a medium of accounting for resources invested. When you have money it allows you to manifest the true nature of your internal character. Money is neutral; it simply makes you more of who you really are. If you want proof, look at the litany of tragedies that accompanies the typical lottery winners. In my experience, more money will temporarily sugarcoat your business problems while magnifying your personal problems. On the other hand, good people can do lots of good things with money, and the world needs more good people with resources who can, in turn, use it to build value and bless others.

Many believe that money is evil, and they cite a verse from the New Testament book of Timothy. The verse is often taken out of context. Money on its own is not evil; it is the *love* of money that is evil. The love of money leads to greed that allows us to justify prioritizing profits over people.

It's the evil of greed that Magie hoped The Landlord's Game would show people. She believed people would play the game, understand how evil the pursuit of "more" is, and revolt against that ideal. She was mistaken.

What she was actually teaching is what I would propose to be a *third* philosophy, one that strikes true in the heart of every person who embraces it: A Truly Free Market.

The Free Market Economy

The idea of a *free market* philosophy starts with the premise that we are free and empowered to imagine and create products and services that in turn build value. When done right, as the phrase suggests, a "free market" promotes *freedom*. Freedom to pursue opportunities, freedom to create, and freedom to propagate optionality for others.

When the game of Monopoly begins, there is a certain amount of chaos—everyone has some money, and there is some order to the arrangement of property, but it hasn't yet been developed or distributed. As a player your goal is to try and create the most value from the potential that is inherent within the game board. Luck will be a factor as you cannot decide the cards you were dealt or the roll of the dice, but you can certainly determine how they're played.

Within our human nature is the innate desire to bring order to chaos. A messy desk inspires anxiety, while an orderly one brings us peace. To plant a garden, a field of weeds must first be tilled in order to create fertile soil for sowing rows of plants. Science, language, agriculture, and mathematics are all based upon orderly, organizational boundaries which create the necessary guidelines for the next phase of human desire: creation.

Creation comes from using our imagination to conjure up ideas of value. By continually exploring our curiosities, expanding our imaginations, and pushing the limits of our possibilities, we increase our chances of creating more value and promote more freedom. Simone Biles and Shaun White do not stop at winning gold. They believe in progression and demonstrate this by developing *new* stunts, *new* tricks, and *new* routines to further expand their respective sports.

Creative desire is at the core of all problem solving that produces enduring value by increasing our human potential and quality of life. Elon Musk was told that space exploration was too expensive to create a viable private company. Using first-principles thinking, he was able to look at each of the limitations, break them down into their basic elements, and then re-create new models from the ground up. That resulted in SpaceX, the modern leader in space exploration that has dramatically reduced costs for advancing our potential in exploring the cosmos. More freedom for humanity has been provided by introducing the possibilities of interplanetary travel and harvesting valuable resources beyond what is available on Earth.

In a free market philosophy, players believe that life is *not* a zero-sum game but rather an infinite one that can benefit all. They use their desires to bring order to chaos and create something that increases everyone's freedom, while growing the overall potential and capacity. Pure capitalism and pure socialism suggest that in order for me to *have*, I must take from others. Free-market thinkers use their abilities to create products or services so *there's more freedom and abundance available for all.*

Consider aluminum: it's one of the most common elements available on Earth, making up 8% of the planet's crust. At one time, aluminum was worth more than gold and you may ask how is that possible? Aluminum is primarily found in nature as a chemical compound. During the 1800s, the process of refining the metal was difficult and as a result it became the most sought-after precious metal in the world. Legend suggests that Napoleon III ate off aluminum plates while his guests had to make due with gold. All of that changed in 1888, when we learned that aluminum oxide could be made very inexpensively from bauxite. As a result, the price of aluminum plummeted by 80 percent overnight and made the metal readily accessible. Think of how different the world would be without this innovation; everything from drinking our favorite soda beverage to our ability to transport ourselves using aircraft and bicycles. Using a free-market approach that encouraged the creative process, we took what was once scarce and made it abundant while in the process enriching the lives of everyone.

That is the true mystery of Monopoly. Behind the veneer of capitalism is the truth of what free enterprise is all about: creating value, freedom, and abundance for all. We use our unique abilities to trade, barter, build, and create, and for it to last, it must be valuable. Perhaps against her knowledge or even will, Magie was illustrating how *fun* competition is, and how it can draw out an individual's best. Within all of us is the desire to imagine, to build and to create. Monopoly doesn't create this desire; it simply highlights it.

You Can *Choose*
To Be a Free-Market Thinker

You get to decide whether to be a capitalist or a free-market thinker. The first mindset is focused on scarcity and the idea that the pie is limited in size. The latter is built on abundance and the belief that as we build *more value*, we create *more freedom* and grow the size of the pie for all.

If you consider the rise and fall of many recent high profile businesses, such as Theranos and We Work; it's easy to see where companies who started out initially pursuing free-enterprise virtues very quickly digressed into becoming selfish capitalists. They first promise disruption and claim empowerment to rally extraordinary people to their causes. Virtue signaling is then carried out via lofty visions, compelling mission statements, and aspirational values, luring the market into believing their intentions are genuine. Finally, empty promises go unrealized, as the company's real intent of pursuing power and status at the expense of others becomes blatantly clear.

To win the game of Monopoly, we must compete by being authentic and in a way that is fair and abiding to the rules. As Magie stated in The *Single Tax Review* in 1902, "There are no fairer-minded beings in the world than our own little American children. Watch them in their play and see how quick they are, should any one of their number attempt to cheat or take undue advantage of another."[9] Magie understood that fairness in competition was a noble goal. As author Theodore Roosevelt Malloch wrote:

> I strongly believe that profit-only companies are, in fact, parasitic, and that they damage the economy at large with their limited and self-focused view of their role in the marketplace. But companies that commit themselves to a more holistic core mission and are steeped in spiritual capital often succeed in righting wrongs and creating genuine personal and social progress, while also succeeding in generating strong profits.[10]

Monopoly teaches us to become the best we can, while also playing according to a set of fair standards.

I believe the free enterprise system is in line with God's intention for our humanity. Christianity teaches us about an abundant Creator, who from nothing, created everything. He created our humanity and then commissioned us to continue the work he started. The very desire to create is innate, essential, and pleasurable. We have been commissioned to carry on the work of a creative God; to paint art, to build buildings, to invent machines, and to build businesses of value.

As we will later learn, human beings have been endowed with unique potential to continue to build upon creation and color in the magnificent canvas that God so generously bestowed upon us. There is a simple underlying rule that must drive our motivations in our creation, and that is love. Love for His creation, and most importantly, love for our fellow humans.

---

9 Lizzie Magie, "An Interesting Invention of a Young Lady in Washington by Which Children at Their Play May be Taught the True Laws of Economics," *The Single Tax Review*, 1902, quoted in The Landlord's Game, accessed October 20, 2022, https://landlordsgame.info/articles/LLG_SingleTaxReview-1902.html.

10 Theodore Roosevelt Malloch, *Doing Virtuous Business: The Remarkable Success of Spiritual Enterprise* (Nashville: Thomas Nelson, 2008), Kindle.

The best way we can demonstrate love is through creating freedom and abundance which is at the heart of the free-market economy.

Conversely, we have one hundred years of experience with what happens when a society tries to wipe out incentives and in the process extinguishes creativity. There have been several attempts to build a "utopian" communist society. Nations have become economically impoverished as a result and millions of people have been left dead. As Winston Churchill so eloquently stated, "Socialism is the philosophy of failure, the creed of ignorance, and the gospel of envy; its inherent virtue is the equal sharing of misery."

We do not see a mass exodus of people trying to escape *into* North Korea, Venezuela, or Cuba. Instead, we see the opposite. People risk everything to leave these oppressive states. Pure socialism dries out human nature, stifling creativity and innovation. By definition, we were born to be creative and free. To repress this is not only unnatural and inhuman, but it leads to a life devoid of meaning and filled with apathy.

THE FOUR CS > THE FOUR PS

"I think everyone should get rich and famous and
do everything they dreamed of so they can see that
it is not the answer."
—JIM CARREY

The differences between a free-market philosophy and pure capitalism may seem subtle, so allow me to clarify. By letting our egos lead our desires, we provoke ourselves into being consumed by greed. Greed leads to the pursuit of the "four Ps:"

★ We chase *possessions* because we believe they'll satisfy us.

* We desire *power* to create an illusion of control over others.
* We want *prestige* to make us famous and to feel important.
* We seek *pleasure* and the desire to feel good in the moment.

Marketers understand these motivators better than most, often targeting them in advertising campaigns. Behind these marketing messages, you're "hearing" that you're not enough, and in order to find meaning and happiness, you are sold that you need to buy this new thing, subscribe to this new service, or travel to this new destination.

We've been duped.

Chasing any of these as a primary motivator ultimately is a worthless pursuit. If we achieve any of them, we may find it exhilarating for a short period of time. Very quickly the feeling wanes however, leaving us feeling empty inside. Like heroin addicts craving their next hit, of which we need bigger and stronger doses, we seek out our next conquest for one of the four Ps. This leads to what becomes an endless pursuit of more.

I remember hearing a story about two men discussing the death of a colleague who had accumulated a sizable fortune. In their conversation, one man said to the other, "Does anyone know how much he left behind?" After a pause, his counterpart bluntly stated, "All of it!" Leo Tolstoy, regarded as one of the greatest writers for his work on War and Peace, questioned how much land a person should accumulate during their lifetime. He concluded that in the end, all that was really needed is about six feet of soil. We are equally leaving it all behind—the endless pursuit of more is folly; as King Solomon would say: "Whoever loves money never has money enough; whoever loves wealth is never satisfied with his income. This too is meaningless."

Pause and reflect for a moment on the most meaningful memories from the last twelve months of your life. You'll notice something significant:

none of those meaningful moments have anything to do with your material purchases, the vehicle you drive, or the title on your business card.

What we ultimately care about and what we *would* include as our most meaningful moments almost always fit into the following "four Cs":

* **Challenges:** moments that mark personal struggles, obstacles, or developments. This category could include running a marathon, becoming a better leader, or fulfilling a lifelong goal.
* **Connections:** moments that deepen our relationships with others. The family vacation you went on, the time your child held your hands, an intimate conversation with your spouse,or the time you supported a friend.
* **Creativity:** moments when you used your life force and agency to create something out of nothing that provides joy and value to others.
* **Charity:** moments when you make meaningful deposits into humanity, using your resources to improve the life of others.

In all of these cases, the benefits extend from yourself onto others and will be marked in how we invest our LIFE (leadership, influence, finance, and expertise) to build a better you, company, marketplace, community, and planet.

While these "Cs" constitute humanity's most treasured moments, we spend little time attempting to curate more of them, opting instead to chase the four Ps. Why? Many of us are driven by our egos, and we are susceptible to needing external validation, falsely believing that in order to "make it," there is some shiny object or title that we need to possess.

When we fully maximize our own potential within the four Cs, we will know what it means to live an enriched life, full of abundance. These in turn become our most fond memories which is ultimately all that matters and truly gives us the soulful satisfaction of living well.

So how do we bridge the gap between our efforts and what matters? Do we sell all of our possessions, live in a commune, become philosophers, hug trees, and chant mantras? Particularly, how do we as entrepreneurs utilize our gifts—of product creation, service enrichment, and problem solving—to find fulfillment?

Here we come to the crux, another mystery of Monopoly.

From a very superficial point of view, Monopoly appears to be a game of greed. The goal seems simple—defeat all opponents by owning all property and cash. That may sound like it's pushing you to pursue the four Ps and descend into becoming a capitalist. Yet, that isn't the ultimate goal of Monopoly. It can't be. If owning everything were the true goal, there would be one surefire way to win Monopoly, every time:

Play alone.

But no one plays Monopoly alone, even though that's a guaranteed way to win. We don't roll dice, pass Go, collect $200, land in jail, and build houses simply because we want to own everything on a square piece of cardboard. We enjoy trading, outmaneuvering, and inspecting the intellectual prowess of our opponents (challenges). We love seeing our own abilities to create new buildings, develop cash, and put together creative deals (creativity.) Finally—and most importantly—our love for playing stems from the opportunity to engage in meaningful time spent with friends and loved ones (connections).

Building a business can be incredibly fun and rewarding. Beyond that it is also *life-giving* to employ others and fill the marketplace with useful products and services. Creating wealth can be noble, if you use that wealth to help promote freedom for yourself and the world around you. Most people see it differently. They value things and use people to acquire them.

True joy in life is found when you value people and use things to build meaningful connections and create more magic memories.

Winning a board game is a great experience, but only when it's won in competition with players beyond yourself. It's a joy to use our talents and skills to shoot a basket, win a football game, earn a title, invent a product, or become a global leader in a category, but would any of these have value if we had no connections to humanity?

That's the mystery of Monopoly. Playing with excellence, with a desire to win, but only while we are living in pursuit of challenges, creativity, charity and meaningful connections.

"We have gone a lot too far in our pursuit of stuff. Nothing is ever enough. We want more and when we get it we want more yet again. We want what we see on TV, we want what our friends have, we want what rich people have, we even want what we already have but in a newer, fancier and bigger model. We want with such emotional intensity that we are able to convince ourselves that they are not wants at all but integral components of our future happiness. Nothing could be further from the truth and in reality our stuff weighs us down and our pursuit of more often distracts us from what is truly important in life. I genuinely believe that our never ending material quest is not only sabotaging our financial tomorrows but also negatively impacting our psychological todays."

—DAVID CHILTON

FROM CANADA TO JAMAICA

*"The best and most beautiful things in the world
cannot be seen or even touched. They must be felt
with the heart."*

—HELEN KELLER

From an early age, my life had one career path. My great-grandfather was the first chiropractor in Denmark, and following in his footsteps, my grandfather, grandmother, father and uncle all became chiropractors. It would seem that I too was destined to devote my life towards this noble career as a health professional.

As others constantly spoke about my chiropractic future, I rarely fought the notion. Yet while I mentally accepted that, my instincts were leading me elsewhere. As a twelve-year-old, I used to kick the ice around the parking meters to find lost coins dropped in the freezing snow. In the summertime, I would sneak into golf courses at night with my snorkeling gear and dive for golf balls that I'd later sell by the dozen. During my teen years, I borrowed my dad's truck and chainsaw and hired some friends. Through sweat equity, we would cut down trees, buck up the logs, split the wood, and then deliver it to customers, charging less than the competition. From an early age, I had shown entrepreneurial tendencies; I was a free-enterpriser, and I loved to use my creativity to fund fun endeavors for myself and my friends.

When I graduated high school, I was prompted to take the next step toward following in my forefathers' footsteps—by attending chiropractic college. However, I decided to take a year off to travel and discover more of who I really was. I joined an organization called Youth With a Mission (YWAM), and for the outreach we booked a trip to Jamaica. I was excited. I'd never traveled outside of North America, and visions of beautiful islands and exotic food filled my mind. All of those visions are realities—in *north* Jamaica, where there are several beautiful destinations including Negril, Montego Bay, and Ocho Rios. Unfortunately, we found out that these locations were not going to be the area of our focus. After my team landed on the island and piled into a van, we found out we would be spending our time *south* between Mandeville and Kingston.

From the airport, we may have only traveled sixty miles, but the journey took nearly six hours, as the narrow, winding roads twisted and turned. As we descended deeper and deeper into the island, away from any tourist attractions, my vision of alluring and exotic beauty gave way to the reality of poverty, graffiti, and boarded-up shops.

Along the way, we were stopped at a police checkpoint. The police boarded the van, carrying automatic weapons. The feeling of intimidation and anxiety amongst our team members was palpable. I started to realize that we were vulnerable and that our personal safety, something we simply took for granted based on living in Canada, was not guaranteed. If the police were corrupt (common in Jamaica at the time), they could take whatever they might want from us. To our relief, after some questioning and reviewing our passports, they let us proceed on our trip.

When we finally arrived at our destination in Mandeville, we learned that the day before, at a nearby village, a local had been caught stealing a goat. As punishment, the villagers had determined he should be executed via necklacing. This is a gruesome practice where others force a rubber tire around the victim's neck, followed by being doused in gasoline, and then lit on fire. A horrific way to die. As a sixteen-year-old kid from the prairies of Canada, to say I was feeling both nervous and intimidated by the strange new world I'd entered would be a gross understatement.

Over time we started to acclimate to the new surroundings, especially as we focused on the tasks at hand and the purpose of the trip. What I initially thought would be an adventurous, fun vacation turned into something much more profound and meaningful. Instead of playing in the waves and surfing, my team spent most of our time working with kids in churches and schools. Instead of eating out at trendy island restaurants, we gave out food and medicine. Instead of hanging on beaches sunbathing, I would spend my days laboring under the hot sun for the benefit of others. It may seem as though my visit left me "short-changed," but in reality, nothing could be further from the truth. The precious memories gained, the valuable lessons learned, and the incredible experiences in service to others left me with a new North Star for my life; a souvenir no tourist could ever purchase.

When I arrived back in Canada, I literally kissed the ground as I reflected back on the unbelievable wealth of life lessons that I had reaped from participating in this trip.

The first realization was how lucky I was to be born in Canada. I'd never considered the incredibly good fortune I enjoyed simply by being born in a country with so much abundance and freedom.

The second was living in faith and recognizing that there was a Higher Power who had an influence on my life. I had watched with amazement as small miracles were literally manifested again and again throughout our trip.

The third was the true value of giving. Like many North Americans, I was caught up in the materialistic worldview that accomplishment and happiness are based on what you could get. What I learned during that trip is that *true joy does not come from what we get but rather from what we give.* That was my initial discovery of charity. I realized that there is nothing in the world that you could acquire that would give you the same soulful satisfaction that comes from the rewards of enriching the lives of other people. The expressions of hope that your actions inspire and the look of gratitude that comes with selfless giving are some of life's greatest moments you can experience.

These three insights were incredibly formative to my worldview at a very important time in my life and have become foundational to how I prioritize and invest my resources.

*   *   *

Eleanor Roosevelt famously stated that comparison is the thief of joy. Have you ever noticed that we are really good at comparing ourselves up? Particularly to those who supposedly have "more" than we do? We are so good at comparing our back of stage with other people's front of stage, and if left unchecked, this can lead to a life of misery. We are the most susceptible to this temptation when using social media, where we find it is so easy to compare ourselves to those we perceive to be the elusive "1 percenters." Ironically, we overlook the fact that by simply having an iPhone and using these platforms, we're actually part of that elite group of individuals. According to a study conducted in 2012 about the distribution of wealth, if you live alone and make $34,000 a year, you are in the top 1 percent *in the world.*

Comparing ourselves to the richest in our rich world is an easy practice that can not only victimize us, but also makes us guilty of the very thing we blame the ultra-rich for: greed. When we allow someone else's status and material possessions to take hold of our imaginations, we've become susceptible to avarice and the pursuit of the four Ps.

> *"These individuals say they have riches just as we*
> *say we have a fever when really the fever has us."*
> —SENECA

PLAY LIKE A CHILD

Taking the time to reflect helps us reveal what is truly valuable and important to us. I firmly believe that in the end, only actions framed within the four Cs will be where we derive meaning in our lives. Everything that falls under the four Ps will fade after a fleeting moment of euphoria.

The thrill of buying a new car (possession) will produce a brief amount of happiness, but not one that will outshine the joy created by a father-daughter dance (connections). Establishing fame (prestige) by growing your social media following may give you a temporary sense of satisfaction, but nothing compared to the soulful satisfaction of training and running a marathon (challenges). Gaining influence over others (power) may feed your ego temporarily; however, ultimately what will matter is the kindness and support you offer to less fortunate individuals (charity).

Earlier in the chapter, I asked you to recall your most cherished memories from the past twelve months. Now, I challenge you to delve deeper and examine your whole life and write out your top three to five memories that hold a special place in your heart. These might include forming a meaningful relationship, witnessing the growth of your family, embarking on a memorable adventure, overcoming personal challenges, building an enduring enterprise, or making a significant impact in someone's life through your kindness and generosity.

As you reflect on these memories, take a moment to acknowledge the emotions that arise. You may experience a profound sense of warmth, joy, and gratitude that resonates deep within your soul. By connecting with these feelings, you not only honor the precious moments that have shaped your life but also allow yourself to appreciate the richness of your experiences and the meaningful connections you've formed along the way. Now look at your calendar for the past month and do an honest audit of where you've invested your time. We invest our time in what we value. I find that most people are sleepwalking through life, unaware of how many of their waking hours are devoted to the fruitless pursuit of the four Ps. Fulfillment and joy in life will only come when we focus on investing our most precious and scarce resource–time–into the four Cs.

> *"Youth is not entirely a time of life; it is a state of mind. Nobody grows old by merely living a number of years. People grow old by deserting their ideals… you are as young as your faith, as old as your doubt; as young as your self-confidence, as old as your fear; as young as your hope, as old as your despair."*
> —GENERAL DOUGLAS MACARTHUR

CHAPTER 3

IN JENGA, SOME BLOCKS YOU CAN'T MOVE

"The paradox of our time in history is that we have taller buildings but shorter tempers, wider freeways, but narrower viewpoints. We spend more, but have less, we buy more, but enjoy less. We have bigger houses and smaller families, more conveniences, but less time. We have more degrees but less sense, more knowledge, but less judgment, more experts, yet more problems, more medicine, but less wellness.

We drink too much, smoke too much, spend too recklessly, laugh too little, drive too fast, get too angry, stay up too late, get up too tired, read too little, watch TV too much, and pray too seldom. We have multiplied our possessions, but reduced our values. We talk too much, love too seldom, and hate too often.

We've learned how to make a living, but not a life. We've added years to life, not life to years."

—DR. BOB MOOREHEAD

Have you ever observed the joy of a child laughing and giggling as they watched a tower of toys come crashing down right in front of them?

Children can watch a mountain of blocks collapse over and over again, stalled only by the time it takes to re-stack them. Why do kids enjoy toppling things over so much? I wonder, just maybe, if it isn't because there's a secret buried in that fallen mountain of blocks.

Leslie Scott brought Jenga to the known world in the 1980s. She and her siblings used to collect wood pieces from the local sawmill, using them for a game where they would take turns trying to stack blocks before the structure toppled.

Jenga seems like a strange name especially considering its inventor is a lady living in England. However, Scott didn't grow up in England; she grew up in Ghana. The moniker *jenga* is based on the Swahili word *kujenga*, which means "to build."

When Scott brought Jenga to market, it was different from traditional games—unlike the two-dimensional classic board games, it literally took the genre to new heights. By adding in a three-dimensional component, this novel game reimagined the game category from the ground up. The game launched and its popularity spread quickly, resulting in spectacular sales results, with Jenga rivaling Monopoly for the top selling spot in the games category.

At first glance, Jenga relies on a relatively simple idea—each competitor must remove one block from somewhere in the middle of the tower, then place it on the top level. We build and build…until one move destabilizes the structure and the blocks come tumbling down. Beyond the obvious fun of removing and stacking blocks, if we dig a little deeper we can find that this extraordinary game offers some profound life lessons.

THE TOWERS OF NYC

It was a beautiful sunny autumn day in New York City. I had traveled to attend the Fall Toy Previews, an annual gathering of toymakers, distributors, and retailers. In our industry, this was an important event which helped provide guidance and feedback on new product launches for the following year.

I was in the middle of a meeting in the Toy Building, when suddenly a receptionist came rushing into the boardroom and said, "A plane has just crashed into a nearby building!" We were all stunned by the news, but we brushed it off as some random incident; perhaps a small plane was on a flight tour over the city and had gotten off course. We went back to work.

A few minutes later, the same woman came rushing back in and now in a panicked tone exclaimed, "A second plane has crashed and both planes have hit the World Trade Center!" Now we knew something was up, so we quickly filed out of the office and descended down the stairs to the streets below.

As we departed the Toy Building, we saw thousands of people standing along the streets to get a view of the situation. Together, we stared at the clouds of dark smoke billowing from the Twin Towers. People were crying, some were yelling; everyone was in a state of shock and confusion. I watched in horror and disbelief, as these towers that had long been proud symbols of financial strength, now had become broken and vulnerable.

While we were watching, emergency and fire crews were racing down the streets towards the scene and we remained hopeful that they would be able to bring the chaos under control. Suddenly, the once mighty towers buckled and fell, creating a massive cloud of dust and smoke, flooding nearby city streets and spreading an eerie sense of despair and hopelessness.

Just an hour before, I was in an office building, in the middle of what I had thought was an incredibly important business meeting. Now on that street, staring at the dark smoke, it felt that time itself had stopped and the importance of our meeting relative to what had happened, seemed very trivial.

The following days were a roller-coaster ride. All travel in and out of the city was suspended as authorities tried to unravel the mystery around the senseless violation. The city was on edge as over the subsequent days there were a number of random bomb threats at prominent locations. We were trapped in the midst of the confusion with no way to get out, and I longed to be home with my wife and kids. Only the relationships with my family stood out as what was truly valuable.

September 11th highlighted the significance of building a sound foundation for the metaphorical tower I was creating in my own life. While the gravity of the loss is clear, I found myself grateful for the experiences and personal growth it inspired within me. The memory of that tragic day continues to serve as a reminder to the importance of carefully positioning the building blocks that form the structure of my life.

WE'RE MADE FOR BIG TOWERS

At first when you start playing, Jenga seems easy. For several moves, the game doesn't seem to progress much. Then suddenly, a player grasps the wrong block and the whole tower wobbles, showing its vulnerability. Gravity, physics, and architecture reveal their importance with a vengeance, reminding players that they are indeed poking holes in a necessary design. As the tower grows taller, moves become more tricky. Without the patient and careful selection by the player whose turn it is, the stability of the tower structure becomes compromised and eventually collapses.

Like Jenga, life follows a similar pattern. Early on, we see a world of possibilities, and every move seems like a good one with few, if any, negative consequences. Most choices seem to have little to no correlated impact on other decisions and as we progress through life, our tower grows taller as we continue stacking on new priorities. These responsibilities include getting an education, choosing a career, finding a spouse, having children, chasing personal passions, meeting new friends, exploring hobbies, and so on. Soon we have built a tower that can suddenly look lopsided and unstable; however, unlike Jenga, if the tower of our life falls, the results are devastating.

Before we discuss how the tower of our life can become unstable, it's key to understand that as humans, we need to grow and we need to build. Think about Jenga—it's only fun because the tower grows larger and takes on a unique shape. Likewise we were made to build grand towers, creating a story of a life well-lived.

Unfortunately, most of us never reach our full potential, which is an interesting attribute exclusive to our humanity. Every other species will reach for its highest potential by default. Trees will grow as high as they can. Grass will push through asphalt to seek out sunlight, and squirrels will gather as many nuts as possible as they prepare for the long winter ahead.

By contrast, humans can choose to forgo achieving their utmost potential. Most people reach a point in life, where through fear or apathy, they stop building their tower and instead try to maintain what they have built. In the process, they let their gifts dry up and the possibility of what could have been withers away. It's a tragic outcome, and quite unlike the spirit of childhood.

As children, we see endless potential for building a future made up of a grand tower that is unique to our own creative design. We let our curiosity and imagination explore the possibilities as we refine our skills to transform ideas into reality. We feel unstoppable…until we choose to stop because of the challenges we face.

We will discuss later in this book the idea of overcoming adversity to turn it to your advantage and thereby grow to your full potential. For now

I'd like to offer a strategy for how to build your tower to its highest potential in a way that is structurally sound.

THE ARCHITECTURE OF LIFE

Perhaps Jenga has been such a universal hit because, somehow, this simple game has tapped into the universal strategy of the architecture of life:

Some blocks can never be moved, and others must be moved *carefully.*

The Four *Foundational* Blocks

To use this analogy, we should view some aspects of our lives as non-negotiable and others as moderately flexible. Your values are where you invest your most precious resource, your time. A meaningful and intentional investment of your life in the right areas will compound to build something durable.

Through my journey, I have discovered that my foundational four value blocks are faith, family, fitness, and finances. These are critical to the structural integrity of my life. Removing one of these foundational blocks from my Jenga tower will result in its toppling and ultimate fall, fragmenting my life into pieces.

I will explain to you what these four blocks (values) mean for me:

★ **Faith:** Your faith speaks to an understanding that we are all spiritual beings going through a physical experience. As such, it's vital we nurture our spiritual connection with our Creator. I won't be prescriptive about what your practice should look like but for me, faith means time daily in meditation, prayer, and reflection; surrendering to the will of the Divine in the context of our fragile and seemingly insignificant humanity. A lamp can only turn on once it is plugged into an outlet. Likewise it is important that we are plugged into the Source of all life in order for us to shine our true light.

* **Family:** When I refer to family, I mean the people who depend on you and upon whom you depend for physical and emotional support. We all come out of our mothers' wombs craving love and acceptance. The place we should feel the most supported is within our immediate families. I know there are heart-breaking exceptions, and your definition of family might be different. We were born for relationships with others, and as our network grows, it's important to delineate, prioritize, and invest into the vital few connections that you give and get the most value from. Candor and vulnerability are essential for these relationships to thrive: I constantly seek out dialogue with my wife and kids that move us past the superficial and into the meaningful. I've come to learn that people aren't problems to be solved but rather mysteries to be discovered, and the most important people are those you do life with daily.

* **Fitness:** This is your ability to physically perform and includes not only your anatomical shape but ensuring you get the right rest, recovery, and nutrition. I've always had a discipline around physical fitness; however, I didn't always prioritize my food intake or factor in the appropriate rest. Early on I adopted the badge-of-honor mentality for seeing who could go the longest and farthest without needing rest. I used to throw around trite sayings like, "You can sleep when you're dead!" I've since come to believe that we can only be at our best when we feel our best. You cannot give to others what you first do not have within yourself. Our physical bodies are a gift from our Creator that we will temporarily occupy. We should do everything we can to nurture, build, and protect our bodies in order to fully express our vitality and thrive.

★ **Finances:** This is the economic engine that will provide the optionality and choices for you and those you love. More resources equals more choices. Each of us is born with innate passions, a distinct purpose, and a unique set of talents that allow us to contribute positively to the world. By exploring and nurturing these gifts, we can generate resources that will, in turn, support us and our choices. Although our primary goal in life is not to produce blood, it is undoubtedly essential for our survival; similarly, we may not live solely to make money, but we need money to live. As such our finances, and the economic engine that drives them, are a vital part of a life well lived.

Faith, family, fitness, and finances. These four foundational blocks are not only immovable, but they're also interdependent. To live a life of abundance, you cannot focus on two or three of the four. Instead, you must apply your focus and effort in all four areas consistently. They are the cornerstones that underpin who you are and as such I believe they need your attention and prioritization on a daily basis.

The Four *Flexible* Blocks

There are also four flexible blocks of our lives that are important, but not immovable. These four areas I have identified as: refining, friends, fun, and freedom.

★ **reFining:** This means our individual mental and emotional growth. We should be constantly growing personally and professionally. This includes spending time reading from quality books, listening to educational podcasts, attending learning events, and spending time with mentors. While some may elevate refining to a foundational block, I have learned that endless knowledge without application is unhealthy. We should be measuring our content consumption-to-creation ratio to ensure we're giving ourselves space to take what we have learned, apply it, and then develop our own learnings from it. I have discovered that it is easy to get into a place of active procrastination whereby I am too focused on seeking perfection over progress and embrace a ready—aim—aim—aim—aim approach. Once you have learned about a new idea or technique, you need to put it into practice. Knowledge is not power, it is potential power and that potential cannot be realized until you start to actively apply it.

* **Friends:** Time with friends is critical to a fulfilling human experience. The more relationships we create value in, the more abundance and meaningful memories we build. That said, you need to pick your relationships carefully, as you will become the average of the five people you spend the most time with. That doesn't mean we cut everyone else out, but that we learn the importance of association and have different groups of relationships: close associations, limited associations, expanding associations, and dissociations. The latter is reserved for the energy vampires, who by being in your presence suck you dry of life.

* **Fun:** We were designed to be playful, something we express so well when we are kids. Per Shaw's insight, "we do not stop playing because we get old, we get old because we stop playing" and as such pursuing fun is an important part of our humanity. Achieving this can often be accomplished by focusing on the four foundational blocks, integrating activities you enjoy, new courses you want to explore, or adventures you want to embark on with family and friends. I have been fortunate to surround myself with several people who share my enthusiasm for similar outdoor pursuits. That said, there are different seasons of life and with that there needs

to be a check on the time and frequency in the pursuit of fun. Otherwise, you risk becoming the proverbial "playboy." Similarly, there will be instances when you find yourself amidst "the mud, the blood, and the flood,"during which time you may have limited availability for fun pursuits.

* **Freedom:** Ah! My favorite of the Four Flexible Blocks, this is the ultimate capstone of all the blocks harmoniously coming together. Freedom represents the boundless use of your imagination to create the life of your dreams, typically alongside family, finances, fun, and friends. To envision freedom, recall your childhood when everything seemed possible. What were your dreams? As a child, I imagined being a pilot soaring through the clouds and scaling snow-capped mountains, only to ski down pristine, untouched slopes. For many years, these dreams appeared too daunting and distant. However, they are now integral parts of my reality, and through experiencing them, a peculiar and virtuous by-product emerges: I am inspired to think even bigger and explore new possibilities. I love to spend time imagining the brave new future that can develop by using the gifts God has given me, at the same time fostering deeper connections with the people that I have been blessed to do life with.

Refining, friends, fun, and freedom are the four flexible value blocks in our lives. Unlike the four foundational ones, these are not always essential. When necessary, flexible blocks can be moved—carefully and temporarily—while still maintaining the stability of our lives. For instance, we may temporarily prioritize family over friendship. As long as we eventually restore the flexible block of friendship, the overall structure will remain supported. While the flexible blocks do not demand the same daily attention as the foundational four, I do believe it is crucial to incorporate them into our weekly routines.

We can learn more on how to prioritize your values and control your F8 by visiting FullSpectrumLife.com/Resources.

> *"No person would give up even an inch of their estate, and the slightest dispute with a neighbor can mean hell to pay; yet we easily let others encroach on our lives—worse, we often pave the way for those who will take it over. No person hands out their money to passersby, but to how many do each of us hand out our lives! We're tight-fisted with property and money, yet think too little of wasting time, the one thing about which we should all be the toughest misers."*
>
> —SENECA

THE MYTH OF BALANCE

I often say it's hard to know when you're *in* balance, and it's much easier to recognize when you're *out* of balance. As such, I've learned to identify where I'm overinvested or where I may need to reinvest. My best auditing tool is my calendar. It never lies, and very quickly it can reveal when I'm out of balance. My back-up warning system is my wife; we'll discuss more about how we work together later in this chapter. She is an amazing woman, and a valuable auditor of my life, who provides the necessary feedback when she observes that I am lopsided in my priorities.

Getting to balance requires awareness of when you are out of balance and then making adjustments as necessary to realign. It's similar to making small adjustments to the steering wheel of a car, ensuring a smooth and straight drive down the road. We never hold the wheel in the same position for long; we are constantly making small course corrections.

Ultimately, just as we hope to do in Jenga, we aim to create enough balance in our lives with all our blocks that allow us to maneuver, make decisions, and build a towering yet stable structure. As Henry David Thoreau said, "The cost of a thing is the amount of what I call life which is required to be exchanged for it, immediately or in the long run."

Jenga offers this valuable life lesson to us: Moving certain blocks won't affect your tower, while moving the wrong one can bring everything down. This simple concept encapsulates how we must all live our own lives—with the recognition that certain aspects can never fail, or we risk losing everything that is truly meaningful.

THE LIE OF COMPARTMENTALIZATION

While in New York City, I reflected on the architecture of my life. I recognized that I was becoming dangerously close to only focusing on one foundational block—finance—at the expense of all others. This is a common temptation for founders with an achievement addiction. We pour ourselves into work, with our gut occasionally signaling to us that we're neglecting other vital values, yet we often bite into the deceptive idea of compartmentalization. We convince ourselves that even if we neglect one area, allowing it to wither and deplete, that it can be an isolated area of our life we can fix later. This misconception overlooks the reality that we are whole beings, with all aspects of our lives working interdependently. When one foundational block begins to deteriorate, the downward spiral extends into all other areas of life and sabotages the whole.

Famously, the *Titanic* was thought to be "unsinkable" and impervious to destruction, because its builders believed in the ship's ability to compartmentalize. The ship's hull was ingeniously divided into watertight compartments, intended to isolate and contain any damage sustained during her journey. The reality was anything but as on the morning of April 12, 1912, she sank within three hours of striking an iceberg in the North Atlantic. It was long believed that for the ship to have sank so quickly, there must have been a long gash through several compartments. However, when the wreck was discovered, they learned that the engineering was flawed and that in reality the compartments were actually all interdependent. Once a single compartment took on too much water, the load would compromise the next compartment, creating a domino effect until the "unsinkable" ship was at the bottom of the ocean.

Sam Walton, the founder of Walmart and Sam's Club, made a similar mistake. From humble beginnings, he started a small retail business that would grow into a multinational conglomerate, becoming the largest employer in North America. In the process he amassed enough assets to leave his family as one of the wealthiest on Earth. With all his success and the generational wealth he created, one would think he must have died a very happy man. Interestingly, it is reported that on his deathbed, he uttered the words, "I blew it." Admittedly, he had fallen prey to the same mistake that tempts so many entrepreneurs to overinvest into their finances at the expense of all else.

Will we fall for the lie of compartmentalization, believing we can sacrifice the other foundational blocks of our lives in the pursuit of material wealth? We should take Sam's warning to heart and embrace the wisdom his experience offers us. As the ancient text reads, "What benefits a person to gain the whole world yet to lose their soul?"

> *"In my quieter moments I reflect on the fact that we generally take the people we love the most for granted. Until we lose them. Then we take long silent walks praying for a second chance to treat them the way they deserved."*
>
> —ROBIN SHARMA

YOU CAN ONLY JUGGLE A FEW

Any seasoned entrepreneur may be quick to point out that there are moments when every business demands intense time and energy from its leaders and founders. From experience, I know this to be true, particularly for early stage startups. Furthermore, attempting to focus on every block simultaneously is not a feasible approach, given our limited human capacity in any given moment. The real goal is to actively manage all foundational and flexible blocks on a frequent basis, cycling through them as a juggler would cycle objects.

Brian Dyson is a former chief executive officer of Coca-Cola, and he used this analogy of juggling for considering how to manage life's priorities. In his example, he identified that there are some balls made of rubber and others that are made of crystal. Applying this idea to our foundational and flexible blocks, the crystal balls are faith, family, fitness, and finances—you can't ever drop these, or they'll shatter. Refining, friends, fun, and freedom are the rubber balls. You can drop these momentarily and they'll bounce back; however, for the juggling act to be complete, you will eventually need to bring them back.

So the question is, how do you know if you are about to drop a crystal ball? As we stated earlier in the chapter, take a quick look at your calendar and do an honest audit of where you are investing your time. As Stephen Covey wrote, "The key is not to prioritize what's on your schedule, but to schedule your priorities." What's important needs to be scheduled or the busyness of life will quickly creep in and snuff out your availability.

Your Spouse: The Crucial Feedback

A strategy to determine whether your values are in the right priority, is to ask your spouse. Within the right context, your life partner should be your primary feedback loop, and I recommend you do not wait for a crisis in order to begin the conversation. By consistently inviting your spouse to provide supportive feedback, it can help you make ongoing minor course corrections, avoiding the need for larger ones later on.

For over ten years now, my wife and I have scheduled a non negotiable check-in every Sunday morning where we do an audit of our prior week. We start with a self-assessment and go over what worked, what didn't work, and what we are working on in the week ahead. We invite the other to offer critical yet gracious feedback. This has deepened our relationship, provided a trusting place to share intimate details, and provided valuable awareness to blind spots.

Importantly, we begin every conversation with gratitude so that we can enter the conversation with an abundance mindset. We don't start off being critical, pointing fingers at ourselves or each other. Instead, we focus first on how we have been blessed and what has gone *right*. We may bring up a new learning, a financial win or a breakthrough in a parent–child relationship. Most often we simply express gratitude for our health, the place where we live, or memories we cherish. Regardless, starting with gratitude is the key, as it creates a filter so that every piece of feedback focuses on possibility and what we have versus scarcity and what we lack.

I do not want you to assume that my wife and I have always got it right. We have struggled like any other couple; we have had major disagreements and have exchanged harsh words. At one point our marriage was on the rocks and was at risk of failing. What we have since discovered is that intentional time together, with vulnerability and candid communication, is what builds trust, the necessary ingredient for a healthy relationship.

BUILD YOUR TOWER

The strategy to win in both Jenga and life is simple: to build the biggest and sturdiest tower possible. That being said, along the way, we need to recognize that there are some blocks that cannot be moved, and others that must be moved with caution.

Children have the innate ability to think of all the potential and can envision building something spectacular. They want to find the possible limits of that tower, even at the risk of it falling. What if you and I were so bold?

So, the next time you play the game, I encourage you to view each of those blocks in a whole new way and not only rediscover your youth but also discover what I call the *secret* to Jenga:

Build your tower as big and grand as possible without disrupting the foundational blocks!

The fun of Jenga, and the fun of life, is in finding out how far you can push your possibilities. So I encourage you to continue to *kujenga,* and in the process stretch to reach your full potential.

*"We don't get a chance to do that many things,
and every one should be really excellent. Because
this is our life. Life is brief and then you die, you
know? And we've all chosen to do this with our lives
(whatever that is) So it better be damn good. It
better be worth it."*

—STEVE JOBS

CHAPTER 4

SPIDER-MAN VERSUS HIMSELF

"We are products of our past, but we don't have to be prisoners of it. God's purpose is not limited by your past. He turned a murderer named Moses into a leader, a coward named Gideon into a courageous hero."

—RICK WARREN

n the introduction, I mentioned that my favorite toy growing up was a kite, but just one position removed from first place was my Spider-Man web-slinger. I remember strapping the toy to my wrist and then aiming at an unsuspecting target:

"Fire!"

A small dart with a string attached would sail across the room. To an imaginative kid, shooting webs out of my wrist was pure magic.

As an adult, I'm fascinated by the cultural impact of superheroes. Children play with them, adolescents sketch them, and all generations flock to watch the movies. Something captivates us about these larger-than-life personalities who stand for justice and use their individual talents to oppose evil.

The term *superhero* goes back as far as 1908, before the first modern comic book was released in 1933. A few years later, in 1938, DC Comics released "Action Comics #1," featuring an unstoppable character named Superman. With his arrival, the Golden Age of Comics was born.

In 1939, Batman was introduced and in that same year, World War II began. Interestingly, many of the biggest names in comics were children of Jewish immigrants and were hated by the Nazis. In 2016, T. Andrew Wahl stated in the *Humanities Washington*:

> The role that Jewish immigrants played in the origins of the comic book market cannot be understated…Jack Kirby, Joe Kubert, Will Eisner, Jerry Siegel and Joe Shuster…these are some of the legendary figures that were there from the very earliest years, and they were all children of Jewish immigrants.[11]

---

11 "How American History Created the American Superhero," *Humanities Washington* (blog), March 9, 2016, https://www.humanities.org/blog/how-american-history-created-the-american-superhero/.

It is likely that the creation of super heroes was significantly influenced because of the oppression suffered by Jewish people during this era. They were more or less "perfect", devoid of any character flaws and committed to seeking justice. It makes sense, after two world wars, most people had drawn very specific battle lines—there were good guys and there were bad guys, and the good guys were supposed to defeat the bad guys.

During this Golden Age, there was a rising star who was developing different thoughts about how "super" superheroes should truly be. His name was Stan Lee, and he would go on to become the most famous comic creator of all time. Lee was one of the major players in creating the characters in Marvel Comics.

Bucking the conventional wisdom of comic book characters at the time, Lee and the Marvel team took a different path. They introduced a more human nature to the characters—complete with character flaws, troubled pasts, difficult choices, moral dilemmas, and family drama. Here's how Jacob Heilbrunn described it in the *Washington Monthly* in 2021:

> The Amazing Spider-Man, for example, was constantly fretting about his love life, not to mention the health of his Aunt May. The Fantastic Four—Mr. Fantastic, the Invisible Woman, the Human Torch, and the Thing—spent as much time quarreling among themselves as battling their enemies. After going bankrupt in issue nine, the Fantastic Four are evicted from their headquarters at the Baxter Building.[12]

With the introduction of character flaws as a part of the family of Marvel superheroes, Lee had struck gold, or rather silver, as this age came to be

---

12 Jacob Heilbrunn, "The Flawed Superhero of Marvel Comics," *Washington Monthly*, January 10, 2021, https://washingtonmonthly.com/2021/01/10/the-flawed-superhero-of-marvel-comics/.

called the Silver Age of Comics.[13] His take on superheroes was entirely different. Raw, real, human, and nuanced.

Batman and Superman have since adapted and likewise have become more human. They continue to be important and remain in the spotlight; however, Lee and his team would go on to create several of the world's most iconic superheroes, including the most popular of all time: Spider-Man.

On November 12, 2018, Lee passed away. In the days that followed, many outlets wrote about him—some claiming he was the hero of the comic book world. One of those articles, written by Ted Anthony for the Associated Press, described Lee's legacy like this:

> The likes of Spider-Man, the Fantastic Four, Iron Man, the Ghost Rider and the Incredible Hulk composed a catalog of human frailties—schmoes who inadvertently, or negligently, wandered into the traffic of destiny.

> Some moneyed, some working-class, all neurotic, they had powers thrust upon them by misfortune or questionable choices. Their abilities were just as often bane as boon. And sometimes it was hard to tell the heroes and the villains apart. Sort of like real life.[14]

I think that ending line is a perfect place to begin our story.

---

13 Technically, the Silver Age of Comics started in 1956, just a few years before Stan Lee started releasing "flawed characters"; however, virtually everyone agrees that Lee was a major, if not the key, player of this time.

14 Ted Anthony, "A Universe of Flawed Heroes: Stan Lee Was Ahead of His Time," Associated Press, November 13, 2018, https://apnews.com/article/d355ac3dbc154c7abee0e01a998b371d.

DRIVEN TO THE BRINK

Every year just after New Year's, the biggest names in the toy world travel to Hong Kong. Dynatech was primarily a domestic supplier, so early on we skipped attending this annual affair. That said there was a trend for buyers to source more products via direct import. We picked up on this and by the late 1990s, Dynatech was established as an up-and-coming toy company. An increasing amount of buyer's budgets continued being allocated during these trips, so we determined it was important for us to start attending. I planned on joining the January 2000 trip.

It was October 1999 and leading up to the trip, the majority of the world was paranoid and consumed with one singular issue: "Y2K." Supposedly, just after 11:59 p.m. on December 31, computer servers around the world would experience an apocalyptic shutdown that would send the planet into chaos. Everything from widespread power-grid outages to faulty nuclear missile launches were supposedly deemed as possible.

Thankfully, the doomsday predictions were wrong. As the clock struck 12:01 a.m. on January 1, 2000, everyone breathed sighs of relief.

My wife and I had never believed in the hype, and we were busy welcoming in the new millennium with style. We had bought tickets to a black tie event, where we were celebrating the New Year with many of our friends and family. Early in the morning as we left the event and were driving home, I felt a sharp pain in my abdomen. What started as moderate discomfort soon turned into intense pain. Within a few hours, I was supposed to be on a plane traveling to Asia, instead it became clear that I needed to go to the hospital. Shortly after arriving, my greatest fear was realized—I had appendicitis.

It seemed surreal, having just celebrated the introduction of a new millennium and being filled with excitement around the possibilities for my forthcoming Asia adventure. Now it appeared fate had dealt me a bad hand

and instead of looking forward to traveling, I would be bedridden. I was in complete denial and questioning the unlucky and terrible timing of this unfortunate development. I was the CEO of a fast-growing toy company and for the first time in our short history, had planned on making the long voyage to join this vital industry trade event.

I told the doctors about the importance of my upcoming trip and that I had to be on a plane the following day. They flatly replied, "You're not going anywhere tomorrow." What they did not know was that I was driven, and a man of my word. I was raised by a father who had instilled grit and fortitude into me, and I had a stubborn determination that I could overcome any obstacle.

It was strategically important that I attended this industry event as I had made many appointments and had given my word that I would be there. I looked at the physician and calmly said, "Doctor, you may think that it isn't possible, but I assure you, I *am* going to walk out of this hospital and head to the airport tomorrow morning. It's up to you to do everything you can to make my trip to Asia as comfortable as possible." Apparently, he believed me.

To remove my appendix, they performed laparoscopic surgery, the least invasive type of appendectomy. Within a few hours, I was awake and in recovery. I felt like a horse had kicked me in the stomach, and I was groggy. The nurses ensured that I was properly bandaged and gave me a prescription for painkillers. True to my word, I left the hospital and my wife drove me straight to the airport. Little did I know, my problems were just starting.

When I arrived at the check-in desk, they asked to see my passport. I instead provided the agent with a copy of my driver's license and my social insurance number. I know that seems ridiculous, and as I think back on it, it is slightly embarrassing; however, most of my travels had been between Canada and the US. Prior to 9/11 a drivers license was the only documentation needed to enter and leave the US. My only other international trip had been with YWAM when I traveled to Jamaica, and that had been many years prior. In the busyness of preparing to go to Hong Kong, I overlooked the very important detail of ensuring I had the right documentation needed to travel.

The agent at the check-in gate told me that she'd need to cancel my flight and that I would have to try and rebook, once I had my passport.

As I stood there in disbelief, I reflected on my father and what he had taught me about being relentless. He had always encouraged me to fight for what I believed in: to be tenacious and slow to surrender when I had a deep conviction. "You might get knocked down, but it's up to you whether you stay down," he'd often say. I had overcome the health challenge of appendicitis, and I wasn't going to let a documentation issue get in my way!

I petitioned the Air Canada agent to let me travel on the first leg of the flight to Vancouver. I told her that upon arrival, I would head into the city, where I had a plan to get my passport in time to join the second leg to Hong Kong. By some miracle, she agreed and I boarded the plane, all the while wincing from the pain from my recently stitched stomach. The truth is that I really did not have a plan, but I had the conviction that getting my passport was possible and the faith that I would find a way.

While in the air, I carefully strategized my next moves: when we landed, I'd take a taxi straight to the passport office in the city, call the people there who could help endorse me and then race back to the airport and either join the second leg of my flight or find a later option.

At the immigration office, I gingerly hobbled into the building and anxiously waited in the queue. When I finally spoke to an immigration officer, she told me that what I was trying to do was not possible and would take several days to process. I explained my situation to her, and told her the story of all the adversity I'd overcome to get to her desk. I impressed on her the importance of my trip, and yet again I was about to experience another small miracle. She had compassion for me and offered to expedite my application if I could gather all the paperwork needed.

I thanked her, left the building, and began scrolling through my contacts to see who I could reach out to at the last minute. Fortunately, I had a number of contacts in Vancouver and a few of them met the required conditions. It was still early in the day, and I was lucky to get through on my calls. When I explained the situation, they graciously dropped whatever they were doing and within a very short period of time, I had all the signed letters I needed. I proceeded back to the immigration office with all the paperwork and photos in-hand. True to her word, the customs officer pulled out all the stops and within the hour, I was issued a brand-new passport.

I jumped back into a cab and headed back to the airport, with just enough time to board my flight. As I settled into the seat of the aircraft, I reflected on all the challenges I'd overcome in the past twenty-four hours; it was truly miraculous that I was on the plane. My thoughts quickly turned to focus on my state of discomfort as the adrenaline and painkillers were now wearing off. I started to realize just how much agony I was in, which was exacerbated by the fact I was now stuck in a middle seat for the next thirteen hours. A few stitches that were less than a day old held the incisions in my stomach together and I was haunted by the warning from the medical staff that blood clots (as a result of flying) were a real possibility. I took some painkillers and closed my eyes to try and get some much needed rest.

Finally, we landed. As I exited the aircraft, I was instantly overwhelmed by the size and grandeur of the Hong Kong airport. As we traveled from the island into the city, I continued to be wonderstruck by the breathtaking views. The environment was alive and full of energy, with a futuristic flair covered in dazzling lights. I had just arrived at one of the most important commerce cities on Earth, and I was eager to explore the opportunities I could feel were available here.

Suddenly it dawned on me that I'd gone from a small-town kid to an international business traveler, leading a fast-growing toy business. Over the past forty-eight hours, I had overcome the challenges of my appendix, my missing passport, and rescheduling flights. Now I had earned the opportunity to advance my business, and here in this strange new world was yet another moment to prove myself.

First You Run, Then You Faint

"Insecurities are like germs: you can never truly get rid of them, you can just stay ahead of them."
—SEAN STEPHENSON

That trip turned out to be a key inflection point in my entrepreneurial journey. While Dynatech's success would be short lived, traveling to Asia would provide the valuable connections that I would need to help build future business opportunities.

The perseverance I exemplified on that initial trip is what drove me for the next several years. Some of it was good old-fashioned work ethic but there was something else, buried deeper. I was carrying with me an intoxicating motivation: one of tremendous self-doubt. The words *You are not worthy; you shouldn't be here* chased me across several continents, as I was on a quest to validate what I was really made of. This doubtful voice often fueled my stick-to-itiveness as I was determined to prove that voice was wrong. I would outrun, outwork, and outlast anyone in my industry, to accomplish what was seemingly impossible.

The issue is that you can't outrun or outwork your own self-doubt; it will always remain a part of you and only you will decide if it is going to be a defining part of your identity. At some point, you must face it and understand the factors that create it and from there, determine if it will become your slave master or if you will learn to master it.

And, face it I did, in the coming years.

As you read in the opening chapter, Dynatech would ultimately become bankrupt. In 2006, the company had its first brush with bankruptcy through a restructuring. Over the next two years, we tried to save the company and in the end we only went further into debt. Then in 2009, after fighting hard to try and salvage the business, the company finally capitulated.

Until 2006, I took pride in the fact that I was labeled a "young gun" from a farm town in western Canada who had developed a midas touch. The business had become part of my identity, and I had proven that I could outperform many of the bigger players. Meanwhile my self-doubt, as a result of my humble beginning, always haunted me, driving me to prove that I was worthy based on my accomplishments.

This worked well when Dynatech was growing year after year and while the firm was winning awards and accolades from the greater business community. However, when your identity is attached to the results of a business that subsequently comes crashing down, the consequences of shame are brutal.

I want to pause here to make a point as I know many entrepreneurs are dealing with the exact same self-doubt dynamics that I have struggled with. To overcome it, we try to smother it by focusing on our activity. "See what I did" becomes the mantra and that may even fuel temporary success.

Let's face it: business is hard, the mortality rate is high, and the probability for success is low. In an interview with *Success Magazine* in July 2010, Chet Holmes summed up the sobering stats like this:

★ Only 5 percent of companies who start ever make it to $1 million in annual revenue.

* Of that 5 percent, only 1 percent get to $5 million in annual revenue.
* Of that 1 percent, only 1.6 percent get to $10 million.[15]

So, out of one million companies, only fifty thousand will get to $1 million in revenue, five hundred will get to $5 million and only eight companies will get to $10 million or beyond. With that in mind, it would seem irresponsible for us to allow so much of our character definition to be directly linked to achieving business success.

In our pursuit to create companies, we entrepreneurs can move mountains and outwork those around us. My wife and I did just that and along the way shed the proverbial blood, sweat, and tears. We worked tirelessly to build Dynatech from a fledgling startup in our basement into an award-winning multimillion-dollar enterprise. Reflecting on all the effort needed to drive this growth, I now know that my need to extrinsically "prove" myself and satisfy my ego was at the core of my motivation.

Painfully, I've learned that if you value yourself based on performance, when your external proof dissipates, your internal sense of self-worth likewise evaporates. I'm not sure if I ever became the true villain of my story, but with the death of my company and my subsequent battered identity, I certainly had failed at becoming the hero.

SPIDER-MAN'S PERFECT FLAW

> *"Accept that you are imperfect and always will be.*
> *Your quest is not to perfect yourself but to better*
> *your imperfect self."*
> —ERIC GREITENS

---

15 *Success Magazine*, Success Enterprises LLC, established in 1897.

Humans finally connected with superheroes, once Stan Lee created characters who were flawed. We've continued to connect with superheroes whose flaws are so great that the hero has the potential to become the villain. That's why in the movie *The Dark Knight*, Harvey Dent, who is the hero-turned-villain, states, "You either die a hero, or you live long enough to see yourself become the villain."

This phenomenon extends into other historic mythology. The Greek titan gods Atlas and Prometheus have been granted all the title and privilege to thrive amongst the heavenly order; however, they both succumb to temptation, are deemed villains, invoke the anger of Zeus, and are condemned to pay eternal penance. Their stories exemplify something that runs through all our humanity: we are born with incredible capabilities and limitless possibilities, but we also have the ability and propensity of manifesting our worst attributes. To deny this part of our human nature would be naive.

In our storytelling, we have a fascination with the gods and the superheroes within the context of a good/evil dichotomy. It is a reflection of our broken human condition as deep down, we see ourselves in these characters of mythology.

Intuitively, we know that we were meant for big things; however, this desire to accomplish something grand is haunted by an internal voice that points to the flaws in our character, questioning our merit and asking if we have what it takes. We want to write a book, run a marathon, create a work of art, build a legacy, start a company…but the little voice inside casts seeds of doubt that often take root and stop us from necessary actions to discover what is truly possible for us. Whether we admit it or not, or whether we've buried our dreams or not, we all have an internal belief that we are meant for more. This isn't egotistical; it's innate. As C. S. Lewis said:

There are no ordinary people. You have never talked to a mere mortal… It is immortals whom we joke with, work with, marry, snub and exploit—immortal horrors or everlasting splendors.[16]

Even the greatest stories from antiquity showcase heroes with major flaws. Moses is one of the greatest champions of Jewish history; he wrote much of the Old Testament and shepherded the Israelites on their exodus from Egypt to the promised land. However his history is not complete without remembering that he also murdered an Egyptian, repeatedly demonstrated cowardice in responding to God's call to lead the Isrealites, and in a fit of rage, smashed the only living set of the Ten Commandments. Whether in folklore, mythology, religious texts, or comic books, we find the same pattern repeated: a superhero in the making but one who could very well have become the villain. It would seem that C. S. Lewis's words, that we're either "immortal horrors or everlasting splendors," hold some very real weight.

THE TWO WOLVES

"If only it were all so simple! If only there were
evil people somewhere insidiously committing evil
deeds, and it were necessary only to separate them
from the rest of us and destroy them. But the line
dividing good and evil cuts through the heart of
every human being. And who is willing to destroy a
piece of his own heart?"
—ALEKSANDR SOLZHENITSYN

In a popular First Nations tale, a chief tells his grandson that within every human being, there are two wolves, struggling against each other. The

---

16 C. S. Lewis, *The Weight of Glory* (New York: HarperOne, 1949), 8.

white wolf calls us toward a wholesome life of abundance, doing what is good and right and in the process benefiting ourselves and enriching the world around us. Conversely the dark wolf tempts us toward thoughts and actions that are driven by scarcity that ultimately create destruction for ourselves, our families, and our communities. The grandson ponders the story and then asks the chief, "Grandpa, which wolf wins?"

The chief replies, "Whichever wolf you feed."

The slippery slope toward feeding the dark wolf develops in much the same way that it begins for our beloved superheroes. It is what happens when we focus more on our surface-level abilities versus working on the deeper intrinsic motivators of developing our character. When that happens, we are motivated by our egos, and we will chase extrinsic validation by pursuing the four Ps. In this state, we are motivated by fear, and we embrace a scarcity mindset based on the idea that in order for me to have more, I need to take from you; for me to win, you need to lose.

Most superheroes do not suddenly digress to the dark side however. If they succumb to ego, they become increasingly greedy and less focused in pursuing justice for others. If their ability to fly, fight, or run becomes more important than the belief systems that support their values and virtues, they begin to feed the dark wolf.

We see this represented in the mythical journey of Anakin Skywalker, who was developing into an incredibly gifted Jedi before he was seduced by a Sith Lord, on the promise of limitless power. His focus was on what he could do versus who he was to become, and ultimately this became his undoing. He was deceived and ironically was transformed into Darth Vader, becoming the very opposite of what he had pledged to fight against.

In much the same way, entrepreneurs often begin to overly rely upon the strength of their actions to drive their results—their tireless ability, their problem-solving skills, and their ability to persevere through challenging circumstances. These are incredible gifts that can either be used to build incredible business empires or if abused, break the foundation of the most important relationships.

I was at one time an entrepreneur who had become engrossed and driven by my mission to build an enduring company. My intentions were initially to create something that would support myself and my family; along the way I lost the plot and instead became consumed with the growth and so-called success of the enterprise. This was spurred on by my need to overcome my own self-doubts and the internal dialogue that I was an imposter and it was just a matter of time before I was found out. My ego became the enemy as I was prioritizing my finances, feeding the growth of the economic engine while neglecting the other foundational values.

Knowing when you're falling into this trap can be difficult, because relying on your strengths is not inherently wrong. Starting a company is hard work, and it requires an extraordinary effort to get the enterprise off the ground. Without drive, risk, and discipline, nothing would ever be achieved. Initially, that need to prove something creates progress, and humans by nature place an extraordinary amount of value on our personal achievements. However, when all our worth and identity is placed on what we do or what we have, we have started down the path of becoming a villain.

We can see this pursuit of extrinsic validation demonstrated in a modern superhero story, *The Falcon and the Winter Soldier*. Steve Rogers is a weak and scrawny young man who is passed over by army recruiters and ultimately volunteers to receive a secret serum. He is transformed into a super soldier and becomes a multi decorated selfless World War II hero who through a series of events ultimately becomes Captain America. As the story unfolds, we see that he slowly starts to become the very thing he has battled against; he desires to seek out more *power* instead of living out the *virtues* of being Captain America. He suffers from his need to satisfy his ego, to prove that he is better than the stigma from his past.

Many entrepreneurs have similar beginnings—studies show that founders disproportionately come from chaotic homes, driving them to a need to prove themselves. While I had a great upbringing, I had a very disciplined father who set high expectations for me and showed his approval when I performed well. This instilled the same need to show the world (and myself) what I was capable of. What I was really doing was trying to satisfy my ego and to prove to myself that I had the ability to be great, that I was worthy, and I did this by chasing accomplishments.

Today this is commonly described as "the impostor phenomenon" otherwise known as the Imposter syndrome. The term was coined by psychologists Dr. Pauline Clance and Dr. Suzanne Imes in their 1978 paper "The Impostor Phenomenon in High Achieving Women: Dynamics and Therapeutic Intervention." They used this term to describe the feeling of being a fraud, even when you're successful and good at what you do. Since then, the term has been widely used and studied in psychology, particularly in relation to high-achieving individuals of which many are entrepreneurs. At first it fuels us, but if left unchecked, eventually it becomes all-consuming and will lead us to the endless pursuit of more by chasing the four P's. This is the path I was on, where every accomplishment offered only temporary satisfaction that led me to seek out and want more.

In order for us to avoid falling prey to this condition, we must understand the building blocks that make up our internal character and in turn drive our behaviors.

"Wealth is like seawater, the more we drink the thirstier we become, and the same is true of fame."
—ARTHUR SCHOPENHAUER

BE-DO-HAVE

As part of the American Declaration of Independence, Thomas Jefferson included the now-famous words "life, liberty, and the pursuit of happiness." He was trying to express the fundamental values that we humans ultimately cherish. Until that historic inflection point, most of the world lived under oppression and tyranny with no opportunity to seek out self-actualization. With the inception of the United States, the world began a radical democratic transformation, giving everyone the freedom to pursue their passions and create their own future.

The problem is that most of us have gotten it all wrong when it comes to understanding the pursuit of *happiness*.

Happiness comes from a sense of alignment in ourselves. When our actions are in congruence with our beliefs and values, we will in turn use our talents to create value in service to others. Therein we find purpose and meaning, and the result is an internal feeling of bliss.

As an aside, I would refer to this state as *joy*, and not *happiness*. For me, *happiness* better describes a moment in time and is fickle and extrinsic: it can be immediately conjured up and superficially affected by pouring a bottle of wine, licking an ice cream cone, or trying on a new pair of shoes. However, true *joy* comes from a much deeper inner sense of alignment, achieved by living a life consistent with our values and beliefs that is full of meaning. This results in a wholistic self-contentment that radiates through our entire being.

This alignment comes from a "be-do-have" philosophy; let me explain.

If you consider Mother Teresa or Nelson Mandela, it's easy to describe them as individuals who appeared inexhaustibly joyful. They both came from meager beginnings and experienced tremendous setbacks and suffering, yet they had strong beliefs about the way the world could be instead of the way it was. They persevered and had the tenacity and fortitude to live in a way that would bring about the change they envisioned. They were gifted in speaking, writing, and encouraging, and they directed those gifts in the direction of their values and beliefs. Their external actions were aligned with their internal character, and as a result, they inspired others to see their vision of the way the world could be. The results were massive transformations to the social fabric and largely unwanted global fame; however, their facial expressions have become the gold standard for describing true human "joy."

These incredible individuals demonstrate what it is like to truly align ourselves with *being* the type of person who is in line with our values and beliefs, and then *doing* the actions that are meaningful and supported by those beliefs. As a by-product of those actions, we end up *having* the results we want. For instance, if we focus on how we can *be* good parents, we will then in turn *do* what is right to guide our children. As a result, we will *have* a family that has more harmony, respect, and adoration. Or if we consider how we can *become* a good leader in our company, then we will *do* the necessary work to lead in a way that acts in our employees' and company's best interests. As a result, we will *have* the trust of our employees, customers, and the marketplace and ultimately reap the recognition and financial rewards that come along with it.

Alternatively, most reverse the be-do-have philosophy, into have-do-be and in turn corrupt it. The misconception is that if *they have certain material things*, that will give them the opportunity to *do more of what they want*, and that will in turn allow them to *be happy*. These people get caught up pursuing the four Ps (possessions, power, pleasure and prestige) as their priority, to try and satisfy their fragile egos. When they chase possessions, they are valuing things above all else, and in the process, they are willing to use the people within their circle of influence to acquire them. "With a fancier car, I'll have the approval of others, and as a result, I'll feel happy."

Then there are those who chase prestige, which is a do-have-be philosophy. With this mindset, we falsely believe that if we *accomplish something (do)*, we will garner the respect of others (*have*) and it will in turn make us (*be*) happy. "If I *do* well in school and earn my MBA, I will suddenly *have* prestige with this title that my peers will respect, and then ultimately I will *be* considered successful." This is the primary motivation behind those who suffer from the imposter phenomenon. Self-doubts whisper, *You're not a "real" success.* To counter this, we resort to excess activity in hopes that we can *have* some success and then *be considered accomplished.* "See what I did?" they tell themselves. "I now know that I am a successful person because of this activity." The irony is that with every achievement the sweet champagne of victory quickly sours, and the goal markers continue to move further out. You are as good as your last performance, and the only way to seek other's acceptance and approval is dependent on your ability to continue to perform.

Chasing either a have-do-be or do-have-be philosophy is like battling the hydra: when we accomplish success in either of these, it is like cutting off a single head only to find that the problem has come back and actually multiplied. Left unchecked, the thirst for more becomes unquenchable and will ultimately destroy and deprive us of what is most valuable in our lives.

The contrarian idea is to first focus on our state of being and to ask the question, "Who do I need to *become* to get myself to *do* the things that will ultimately allow me to *have* what I want most from life?" You can develop this way of being by coming up with affirmation statements that describe you as that person you want to become. The logical follow on is to then ask the question "what actions and/or habits do I need to consistently perform to become that person? Very quickly you will start to realize that your desired way of being is only supported by consistent deposits made up from the repetition of your actions.

This is not some woo-woo idea; rather, it is acknowledging that we are complex beings with built-in intrinsic motivators that have been formed by both nature and nurture that ultimately determine how we behave. It is also about acknowledging that our state of being is not static; we are malleable and can be shaped. This requires doing the hard internal work of identifying stubborn beliefs, adjusting our worldviews, reassessing our values, identifying the virtues we aspire to, and adopting the right attitude that in turn influences our actions, which produces our results.

Think of it like a wheel. The purpose of a wheel is to turn and propel forward whatever it is connected to. When we are living with a be-do-have philosophy, our beingness serves as the central hub forming our foundation. What we do radiates and extends outward like the spokes that support the outside of the wheel, which in turn produces the results we have.

It is important to recognize that not all wheels are equal. Some wheels move small toy cars, while others drive huge mining trucks. To support bigger wheels, we first start with increasing the hub of our being, which can then support the stronger spokes of our doing. As a result we can have greater impact in our circle of influence, which determines what we have.

THE ROOT OF THE PROBLEM

"Until you make the unconscious conscious, it will
direct your life and you will call it fate."
—C.G. JUNG

For many years, I've struggled with the imposter phenomenon. At first, this condition produced the tough, hard-working entrepreneur who fought through many challenges until there was a breaking point.

On a subsequent trip to Hong Kong, I felt a strange swelling and soreness in my cheek. Over-the-counter painkillers weren't cutting the pain, so I found a local dentist referred to me by one of my colleagues.

When I arrived at the clinic, I found out the dentist that I was supposed to see was away on vacation. He had put an intern in place who was a fill-in for any emergency work while he was away. By then, the swelling was so significant and the pain so excruciating, I had little choice but to get help.

After her assessment, she determined I had an abscessed tooth and would need a root canal to relieve the pressure. Since I previously underwent a root canal, I was familiar with the procedure and understood that it took several shots of Novocaine. This experience was very different as the dentist gave me only *one* shot to which I thought, "Maybe they use stronger medication here than in Canada?"

Five minutes into the drilling, I knew I was in trouble, as a stroke of painful lightning shot from my jaw into my skull. I put up my hands in protest, after which the intern responded by giving me one additional shot; then she kept drilling.

I somehow persevered through the pain as I fought back my instincts to push away. Finally, the drill stopped and the pressure in the infected tooth started to drain. I am not sure what gave it away—the loss of color in my face or the cold sweat beads dripping off my forehead—but she could clearly see that I was in a significant amount of discomfort. She asked my permission to continue and I put up my hand to signal a firm *no*. I paid my bill, and walked gingerly back to my hotel.

Fortunately, I was able to fly home with no issue. When I arrived, I immediately booked an appointment with my dentist to finish the work. Before capping the tooth, he took an X-ray to inspect the prior work. To both of our amazement, while the drilling had relieved the pressure, it had literally gone in sideways leaving the tip of the root still embedded in my jaw. I can only assume that all my squirming from the pain must have thrown her drill off course. Thank goodness he had the foresight to double-check before capping the tooth, as leaving a portion of the abscess root behind would have eventually led to serious health consequences.

Reflecting back on this situation, it seems somewhat humorous and could almost be a plot line for a *Three Stooges* episode. But behind the story, there is greater meaning to be discovered in understanding that we never really solve our problems dealing only with the superficial. Until we are ready to do the deep work of addressing the root of the problem, it will persist, and in some cases, become our undoing.

When striving to improve our results, focusing solely on modifying our behaviors (attitudes and actions) may not lead to lasting change, as it overlooks the real root of the problem which is embedded within our underlying belief system and values.

WHAT LIES BELOW THE SURFACE

Attitudes determine our actions and form our behavior, which in turn produces our results. These elements are what are visible to the outside world and collectively become our external character. It is similar to an iceberg, where attitudes, actions, and results are surface level, but do not fully reveal what lies below.

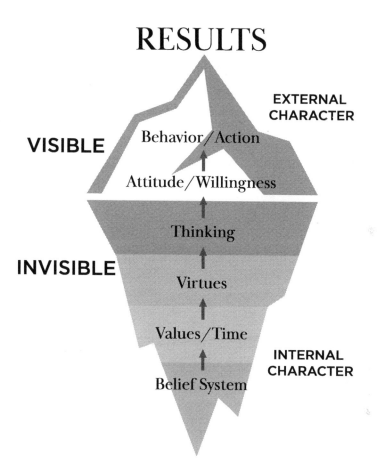

RESULTS

VISIBLE

Behavior/Action

Attitude/Willingness

EXTERNAL CHARACTER

INVISIBLE

Thinking

Virtues

Values/Time

Belief System

INTERNAL CHARACTER

Like the iceberg, the bulk of the icy mass lies beneath and supports what is above the surface. The attitudes and actions that drive our results are supported by a series of hidden layers that in turn make up our internal character.

After spending hundreds of hours with my coach, I have come to learn that it all starts with our belief system, which supports our values, as therein lies the true source code that ultimately drives our behaviors. It is there that we often need to do reprogramming, especially when we are dealing with ego and self-worth issues.

The layers of our internal character are:

Beliefs

Our belief system is the most foundational part of our character, and it supports all other aspects of our being. Through the lens of what we believe, we perceive ourselves and the world around us and together our beliefs form the "why" of our life. Beliefs are shaped through a combination of both nature and nurture and once in place, the primary goal of your belief system is to prove that what you believe is *right*. Some of our beliefs are encoded by design to enable our survival. However, the vast majority of our worldviews (another term for beliefs) are shaped and influenced by external forces, including where you were raised, your specific societal philosophies, your early influences, and how you were valued and cared for as a child. Together, these factors work to shape what we believe to be true, and this in turn forms the operating system for how we run our lives. That does not mean that your belief system is necessarily right; it is all relative and becomes the basis of differentiating between what you believe is your truth and what is the actual truth. As we grow through the seasons of life, oftentimes we need to reconsider and reassess if the beliefs that we are holding fast to are still serving our best interest. If we become stubbornly and irrationally loyal to a set of beliefs, even to the detriment of growing ourselves and supporting others in our circle of influence, we risk becoming outdated or obsolete. It is no coincidence that the abbreviation for belief system also happens to be "BS"! Many times the beliefs that once served us have become nothing more than the BS that is now holding us back.

Values

One layer above the foundational layer of our belief system, we find our values. These represent what you truly feel is valuable in life, and are best represented by where you invest your time and more importantly your attention. We have already invested considerable time learning about values and my personal values (what I call controlling your F8). Your values are the "what" of your life, as in "what do you value?"

Virtues

Virtues are like the guiding principles with which we desire to live our lives. Virtues act like the guardrails that help hold us to a particular path. They become the defining code and make up part of our "how," influencing the way we think and ultimately how our attitudes and actions are manifested. The word *virtue* has Latin roots and originally meant "the excellences of a man." *Vir* means "man," and virtue is a character trait that humans need to express in order to live life well. Virtue is not necessarily something that we have but something that we practice.

We may have different beliefs from others, but we may share the same virtue. We see this during wartime, when men have very different beliefs but a mutual respect for one another because of their shared virtue of honor. Conversely, two people may have the same beliefs but expressed with different virtues; we might have a common belief that we truly thrive when we engage in outdoor pursuits, which in turn supports our value of fitness. For adrenaline seekers, the virtue that they best express this with is courage as they push the envelope of possibilities, while for the conservationist it may be more about stillness as they seek out serenity. Same beliefs, different virtues for how the beliefs and values are expressed and lived out.

"We do not see the world as it is, we see it as we are."

—ANAÏS NIN

Attitudes

Beliefs, values, and virtues, are all under the surface and make up our internal character. Ultimately, they influence what manifests in the three layers that are visible as part of our external character, which starts with our attitude.

Attitude could also be called "willingness" and is exemplified in your eagerness to engage in actions. Your attitude is the style in which you perform your work, live your life, and treat your relationships. Your virtues influence your attitude and together they determine "how" you express yourself.

Our *attitude* is the *style* or way in which an action is performed. In the same way that a virtue helps temper a belief, so an attitude helps alter the outcome of an action. With a kind attitude, giving a gift can bring warmth and love. With an arrogant attitude, the same gift will result in creating misery and contempt. The same action could be performed with two different attitudes, and result in completely different outcomes. Zig Ziglar sums it up like this: "It is your attitude not your aptitude that will determine your altitude in life."

*   *   *

If we put all the layers of the iceberg together, they work together to play out in a symphony that ultimately determines our life: how we behave, interact with others, and achieve results. This layered iceberg exists between our beingness and what we do, which then determines what we will have and, if congruent, results in a sense of joy.

For example, I *believe* that everyone is created with specific intent by a loving Creator who has uniquely equipped us with gifts to fulfill our individual purpose with the highest level of excellence. To support this belief, I *value* time spent in meditation and prayer to invite the Creator's influence into my life, and this value is evident in my calendar. The *virtues* I subscribe to include courage, honor, achievement, and compassion. These guide my attitude, which then impacts my *actions*—I find work that I am specifically gifted in, and I work hard in accomplishing that work.

As a side note, it is my experience that *feelings* follow *action*. As an example, I have never felt the desire to go to the gym to work out. That said, I do the work because of my beliefs around living life with vitality, my value for fitness, and my aspiring virtue of strength. When I complete the workout, I feel incredible satisfaction for being in integrity with my beliefs.

With consistency of aligned actions, you will achieve results and then the trappings of success become inevitable, but they are only a by-product and not the goal. The real prize is in developing your full potential by living in alignment and becoming the best and brightest version of what God intended for you.

> *"A master in the art of living draws no sharp*
> *distinction between his work and his play; his*
> *labor and his leisure; his mind and his body; his*
> *education and his recreation. He hardly knows*
> *which is which. He simply pursues his vision of*
> *excellence through whatever he is doing, and leaves*
> *others to determine whether he is working or*
> *playing. To himself, he always appears to be doing*
> *both."*
>
> —L.P. JACKS

UNCOVERING THE SOURCE CODE

In 1999 I had joined EO (Entrepreneurs' Organization) and became heavily involved with the Calgary chapter, eventually serving on the board. The greatest value of EO is that you join a forum, a small group of individuals who gather frequently and with whom you develop more intimacy, which develops trust between members.

Being a part of EO was always a very enriching experience and when I moved to Toronto in 2003, I decided to continue my membership by joining the chapter and a local forum. When Dynatech went into a financial crisis—and when I probably needed EO the most—I resigned. I had been the "wiz kid" who had only seen upward momentum and growth, and my business and its success comprised so much of my identity that I was ashamed and embarrassed when it started to fail.

For several years afterward, I chose to stay away from EO, questioning how I could offer any value to others as I felt like a failure. Thankfully, Jody, a good friend of mine from my original forum, started a new group and asked me to rejoin. I was hesitant; however, after some persuasive convincing by Jody, I agreed to join.

My first meeting was the day after my return from an exhausting multi-week trip to Hong Kong, which included a sixteen-hour flight back home. I showed up physically depleted, and I was instantly reminded of my low self-worth.

When it was my turn to share, I became overwhelmed and consumed by shame. Covered in the guilt of bankrupting my business and feeling directly responsible for losing a significant amount of investors money, I teared up in front of the other entrepreneurs in the room.

The next several meetings went by in a similar fashion.

It took time and soulful nourishment before my self-worth reemerged. I had to reaffirm my identity on what mattered: developing my internal character. I had to begin the journey of transitioning from a *do*-first mentality to a *be*-first mentality.

While my experience in EO was helpful, it wasn't until the past few years that I've really been able to dissect where my performance-driven mentality had come from.

Awareness is the first step toward change, and therein lies the value of having a coach or mentor who can help you see your blind spots. My coach helped me understand that I desperately sought my dad's approval, and I had created the false belief that my father's love for me was based on my ability to perform meaningful work. "Meaningful work" meant that the results did not count unless the work was hard and the results were exceptional. This was not reality, but it was a construct I'd created.

I know those beliefs once served a purpose, helping me to go long and hard to invest the energy necessary to launch and scale my businesses. That said, the belief was now outdated and it was no longer serving me.

In reflecting on my beliefs that influenced my behavior, I can see a pattern of frenetic work that was exhausting and quite literally making the process hard. With the volatility in the toy business and my lack of trust in my people and systems, my MO had become "ready, fire, aim" and as a result we were often doing and redoing work, with my team running ragged.

I have since updated my beliefs and now focus on how I can build and maintain flow. This has led to a more enduring patient productivity which by definition, also means the enterprise has become more sustainable and scalable. The results have been breathtaking as I have found that I now make fewer but better quality decisions. I have learned slow is smooth and smooth is fast and in that I have learned how to leverage the team around me while at the same time enjoying extraordinary life design. One simple change in my belief system, which initially was hard to accept and embrace, has since made an incredible difference in my quality of life.

Spending time trying to fix the behavior would have been a fool's errand, as my operating system would have eventually defaulted me back to living in a way that was congruent with my beliefs. For change to be lasting, we need to do the difficult deep work of modifying our belief systems.

> *"There are a thousand hacking at the branches of*
> *evil to one who is striking at the root."*
> —HENRY DAVID THOREAU

INFLUENCES: THE WATER AROUND THE ICE

"The man who reads nothing at all is better educated than the man who reads nothing but newspapers."

—THOMAS JEFFERSON

We have the ability to change our internal character which in turn affects our external character and the results we achieve. There is one more element we need to be aware of, and that is the type of water that the iceberg is immersed in. Just as the temperature and salinity will affect an iceberg's shape, so the inputs in our lives affect our thinking, and our thinking ultimately shapes our worldviews. With that in mind, it's critical that we carefully guard the inputs in our life. This includes the people we associate with, the books we read, what we listen to, how we entertain ourselves, and the media we consume.

Choosing the right influences will reinforce an abundance mindset that supports our curiosity, imagination, and creativity. Conversely, if we succumb to the plethora of negative influences that surround us, we'll reap a mindset of lack, scarcity, fear, and anxiety. This in turn affects our beliefs and values, which in turn impacts the decisions we make and what we choose to create. When living in negativity, we lose our spark, our hope, and we will end up consumed by fear. It is part of feeding the dark wolf and when fear becomes the primary motivator, we will start living with a scarcity mindset, focusing us on the four P's and inevitably reaping disappointing outcomes.

Typically, negative influences are much easier to find than positive ones. When you turn on the news, the first thing you hear is what went wrong in the world; when was the last time the news started with reporting something uplifting and beautiful? It surrounds us daily, but unfortunately it does not get your attention. Media knows that if it "bleeds it leads" and our reptilian brains, with their fight-or-flight programming, cannot help but look. Media are motivated by getting you to watch, as that is how they create advertising revenue, and so the more sensational and shocking the better for their bottom line. We must wisely *choose* our influences and constantly seek out what uplifts us. Simple decisions about our inputs will have lasting impact and ultimately become formative to our internal character which ultimately will affect our results.

Think of it from the perspective of a cucumber. If you immerse one in vinegar long enough, it will no longer be a cucumber; it is now a pickle. Beware of the negative influences in your life that will leave you sour and pickled!

CHOOSING ENGINES OVER ANCHORS

Of all the influences in your life, none will be as impactful as the *people* who surround you. You are the average of the five people you invest your time with and with that in mind, you need to go out of your way to find those who lift you up, propel you forward, and act like "engines." Conversely, avoid those who pull you down like "anchors."

Anchors are easy to identify. They live in a state of constant complaint, blaming external circumstances for their lot in life. Typically, they're prone to comparison and jealousy. They may *want* you to succeed…just not more than they do.

On the other hand, engines are rare. When you find these relationships, protect them and consider them sacred. Even when you simply "hang around" these people, you feel more alive. They are grateful and optimistic, and tend to be ceaselessly wonderstruck at the awesomeness of the world we live in and curious to explore new ideas. They cheer you on and never resent you for your success. They have an abundance mindset that believes in our ever-expanding potential by remaining curious and discovering new possibilities.

If you ever want to assess the quality of your relationships, I suggest you start with assessing the quality of your conversations. As Eleanor Roosevelt so wisely suggested, small minds talk about others, average minds talk about events, great minds talk about ideas! Time and attention are precious resources. Stay away from anchors who will belittle your dreams; instead, associate with engines who talk about ideas and who inspire, challenge, and make you better.

COURAGE THE CHIEF CARDINAL VIRTUE

"Life shrinks or expands in proportion to one's courage."
—ANAÏS NIN

Plato describes the original four virtues as justice, wisdom, courage, and temperance. Of all these virtues, I believe courage is the most important. For the other virtues to have relevance, courage must precede as it is the precursor to all action. Courage by definition is to take action despite uncertainty of a known outcome; it is the bliss point between cowardice and recklessness. Without taking action we cannot attain wisdom, we cannot know how to achieve temperance, and we will not have the ability to seek out justice in the world.

The Greeks used the word *arete* to describe fellow citizens who were not only living a life of virtue but also achieving their fullest individual potential. The Greeks understood that, to be fully alive as man, was to be fully virtuous and in the process to maximize your God-given faculty. Courage is the virtue that forces us out of our comfort zone and is the only way we can truly achieve this state of *arete*.

You've probably heard it said that courage is to "feel the fear and do it anyway."[17] In other words, courage is the substantive motivation that allows us to lean into new experiences despite the unknown.

Courage is also like a muscle—the more we use it, the stronger it grows. By definition, we need courage precisely when things are uncomfortable. It's unnecessary to express courage when we feel confident and when everything is in order. Only when we step out into the unknown is courage required to face the unexpected; it is the necessary virtue we need when we face our doubts and when we flirt with engaging potential risk.

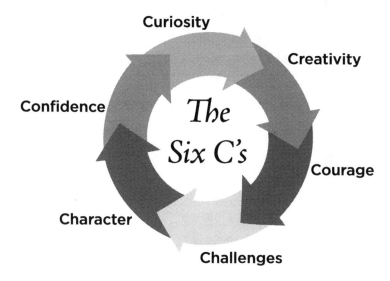

I have observed that in my life there is a courage flywheel that builds momentum with each repetition. It all starts with curiosity. Curiosity is a part of our humanity that longs to explore and discover the unknown. This is then followed by using our creativity to imagine new possibilities. Then comes the difficult task of having the courage to take the initial action. The majority of the time we will face resistance, at which point we then need to continue to embrace courage in order to face and persevere through

17 Susan Jeffers, *Feel the Fear and Do It Anyway* (New York: Ballantine Books, 1987).

the challenges. In order to overcome these obstacles, we must continue to exercise our creativity, which in turn builds our character (we develop fortitude), and that in time is what builds our confidence. With confidence attained, we have the ability to once again explore our curiosities, thus starting the cycle again.

As an example let's use one of my favorite leisure activities, riding a bike. For most of us, riding a bike started with curiosity—we saw other kids riding theirs and we thought, "That seems fun!" Next, we had to have courage to remove the training wheels and take those first few pedal strokes. Inevitably, our bicycles wobbled and we likely even hit the gravel and pavement (if you are like me, you have some scars to prove it). With our bike and our pride overcome by gravity, we faced a challenge and we became fraught with self-doubt: "Can I do this? Should I do this? I'm probably not made to do this. This is too hard. What if people see me fail?"

If we had stayed on the ground, instead of embracing the additional courage required, the challenge would have beaten us back, causing us to shrink and to never realize the full joy and excitement that comes from feeling the rush of momentum and the wind in your face. We had to get back up and try again because as children our default is to live with hope and possibility, and we were easily inspired by the thought of riding a bike with our friends through town. So, we get up, learn from the experience, and then apply a little creativity by keeping our feet continually moving and then repositioning our knees to maintain our balance. Our perseverance, resilience, and tenacity have all increased in that moment, by choosing to push through the pain and in turn helped develop our character. The more we fell and got back up, the more our internal and external character would learn and grow. Eventually, we got the hang of it and were able to ride our bike effortlessly, instilling a sense of confidence in our new-found skill. If you were anything like me, then your next thoughts were back to the curiosity of "Can I do a wheelie? Can I jump? Can I do a tailwhip?"

And all of these curiosities started the Courage Flywheel once again.

Perhaps no story exemplifies this Courage Flywheel in effect better than the tumultuous rise of one of my favorite leaders. This individual famously stated that "courage is going from failure to failure without losing enthusiasm." True to his word, he failed at school, where he performed poorly in every subject (except for history and English composition). He had a speech impediment and suffered terrible nervousness when asked to speak. His goal was to attend the Royal Military College, but he failed to pass the entrance exam. He mustered up the courage to take it again and once again failed. Determined, he hired a tutor, finally qualifying the third time around, but not for the position he desired; rather, he landed in the cavalry.

Eventually, he went into politics, and it took eight years before he gained a cabinet position and three more before he became the first Lord of the Admiralty.

During World War I, he directed a naval and amphibious assault against the Ottoman empire, which turned into one of the greatest military disasters in all of history. Two hundred, fifty thousand lives were tragically lost, and his nation was humiliated. As a result, his reputation was ruined, and he was dismissed from the cabinet and excluded from the war council. At age thirty, it appeared that his political career was over, however this was the same man who would one day say, "Success is never final and failure is never fatal; it is the courage to continue that counts." With his unshakeable courage, he slowly advanced his career forward. Two years later, he became the minister of munitions, then subsequently the secretary of state for war, followed by secretary of state for air, then, finally, the secretary of state for the colonies.

It was this same man of great character and resilience that the British people relied upon during their darkest hours of World War II, when Nazi Germany tried to bomb the country into oblivion. In London's first night of the blitz, two thousand people were killed, and within the first twenty-four days, more than 5,300 tons of bombs were dropped. The formerly proud nation had hit an all-time low, and considering how easily the German army had swept across Europe, there seemed to be little hope of standing up to the Nazi war machine. However, that was precisely the moment that all of his prior challenges had built his character to prepare him for. He had acquired incredible wisdom from his wounds, and he had grown his resolve by pushing through several revolutions of the courage flywheel. He mobilized and rallied his nation with the now-famous words:

> We shall go to the end, we shall fight on the seas and the oceans, we shall fight on the beaches, we shall fight on the landing ground, we shall fight in the field and in the streets, we shall fight in the hills, we shall never surrender.[18]

Without Sir Winston Churchill's audacious courage to fight back, his resilience to push through the pain, and his tenacity to never quit, the political European landscape would look very different today.

* * *

As I reflect on Sir Winston's story and consider my own experiences, the overwhelming reason I got on the plane, even with having recently undergone an appendectomy, was because I had something to prove. That drive, although a necessity at that moment in my life, had an expiration date and I had to have the courage to reexamine my belief systems in order to find a better way to live.

---

18 Winston Churchill, "We Shall Fight on the Beaches," June 4, 1940, reprinted in International Churchill Society, accessed October 20, 2022, https://winstonchurchill.org/resources/speeches/1940-the-finest-hour/we-shall-fight-on-the-beaches/.

"Without courage we cannot practice any other virtue with consistency. We can't be kind, true, merciful, generous, or honest."

—MAYA ANGELOU

SUPERHERO...OR VILLAIN?

Despite having a better understanding, the reality is I've never completely overcome the imposter phenomenon. It's a feeling, and a motivation, that has never fully evaporated. It is part of my internal "dark wolf" that will never go away; it is up to me whether to feed it or to suppress it into a very small corner of my being.

I believe everybody is somewhat haunted by the notion that they don't deserve to be in their tribe. Despite the shiny polished image they portray, no honest person fully believes that they have earned their place. In the words of Bruce Springsteen during an NPR interview: "People see [me] onstage and, [think] 'I'd want to be that guy,' Well, I want to be that guy myself."[19]

Herein lies exactly why we identify with our superheroes, and why Stan Lee's touch of humanity was so significant in the mythological genre's popularity: I believe everyone will struggle with their worth and recognize their potential to be a villain. We know the intimate details of our frail humanity and the worst that is within us, and we are really good at reminding ourselves of the times we behaved at our worst. We are viscerally connected to the fact that within us are incredible possibilities but along with that is the potential to be the worst version of ourselves. We remember the times we were cowards, when we acted selfishly, and perhaps even when our words

---

19 Bruce Springsteen, "Bruce Springsteen: On Jersey, Masculinity and Wishing to Be His Stage Persona," *Fresh Air*, radio show, October 5, 2016, https://www.npr.org/2016/10/05/496639696/bruce-springsteen-on-jersey-masculinity-and-wishing-to-be-his-stage-persona.

and behaviors were cruel. That's why we wonder...am I the hero, or the villain?

And if you reflect on the superheroes we admire, you will note they too are constantly battling the same question:

* Is Spider-Man a superhero, or is he Peter Parker, the timid guy who will never have a real relationship?
* Is Batman a hero who saves Gotham City, or is he the Dark Knight who contributes to the mayhem?
* Is Anakin Skywalker a Jedi Knight, or the prodigy of a famous Sith Lord?
* Is Natasha Romanoff an ex-Russian-spy-turned good, or is she a villain feigning heroism?
* Is Bruce Banner a soft-spoken scientist whose intention is to help humanity or the uncontrollable green monster powered by his rage?

It is within this creative tension that there is the opportunity for all of us to either rise to embrace our heroic potential or succumb to falling to our villain tendencies. To avoid being the immortal horror and to instead become the everlasting splendor, you must nurture your childlike curiosity and embrace the necessary courage to do the work needed to refine your internal character. This is the only way we can make lasting behavioral changes that will bring meaningful results and a true sense of joy that is a result of alignment within our lives.

> *"In the name of the best within you, do not sacrifice this world to those who are at its worst. In the name of the values that keep you alive, do not let your vision of people be distorted by the ugly, the cowardly, the mindless in those who have never*

achieved integrity. Do not lose your knowledge that our proper estate is an upright posture, an intransigent mind and a step that travels unlimited roads. Do not let your fire go out, spark by irreplaceable spark, in the hopeless swamps of the approximate, the not-quite, the not-yet, the not-at-all. Do not let the hero in your soul perish, in lonely frustration for the life you deserved, but have never been able to reach. Check your road and the nature of your battle. The world you desire can be won, it exists, it is real, it's yours."

—AYN RAND

CHAPTER 5

ETCH A SKETCH OF HOPE

"When you're in your 20s, there's all these paint-by-numbers kits to approach life with... You can be a professor, you can be a businessman, you can be a lawyer, you can be whatever... The nice thing about a paint-by-numbers kit is you actually don't have to think about it that much. As long as you stay in the lines when you paint, you're going to end up with a nice picture at the end. But the only way to paint a masterpiece is to start with a blank canvas."

—JIM COLLINS

Some of the greatest inventions are discovered by accident, and Etch A Sketch is one such toy.

André Cassagnes was born in Paris in 1926. He became an electrician, and during a routine light switch replacement, he made a pencil mark on a sticker and was amazed that the graphite magically transferred through the decal. That got him thinking…

Like any good entrepreneur, Cassagnes took his discovery and started to iterate. Eventually, he created a prototype toy and in 1959, traveled to the Nuremberg Toy Fair, calling it "L'Ecran Magique" or "The Magic Screen." Interestingly, not many people were interested in his new creation, including Hasbro, who passed over the opportunity to license the idea.

That changed when Cassanges met the owners of The Ohio Art Company, who purchased the rights for $25,000, and after making some changes to the form factor, rebranded the product as Etch A Sketch. A hit was born as they would sell over six hundred thousand units in the first year and then go on to sell over one hundred million units during the next several decades.[20]

The Toy Industry Association would later recognize the Etch A Sketch as one of the top toys, including it in the "Century of Toys List." Cassagnes's curiosity led to a surprise discovery and his creativity and courage to act would go on to inspire and capture the imagination of millions of kids.

So what is the "real magic" that lies within Etch A Sketch?

THE FINAL KNELL

As you have read in previous chapters, by 2006 Dynatech was in a steep decline. I spent the next two years trying to bail it out of its impending doom.

---

20 Todd Coopee, "Etch A Sketch from Ohio Art Company (1960)," Toy Tales, September 21, 2015, https://toytales.ca/etch-a-sketch-from-ohio-art-company-1960/; Heesun Wee, "Etch A Sketch's Incredible Toy Legacy—and Burden," CNBC, February 22, 2013, https://www.cnbc.com/id/100471234.

I continually found creative ways to temporarily avoid financial meltdown. I threw multiple Hail Marys, and kept refinancing, re-buying, and re-negotiating the company off the precipice of ruin. However when the hull of your ship becomes compromised, you can only displace water so fast and for so long without a fix.

Everything culminated in Q1 of 2008. We'd just returned back from Asia, where we'd met with customers to show them our new lineup of products. Typically after these January tours, buyers place their orders with their selected products for the upcoming season.

However, this year was different. Wal-mart, which represented 40 percent of our company's annual revenues, hadn't placed any orders and had gone remarkably quiet.

My wife, Kelly, managed the Wal-mart business and had met with the buying team during the trip. When she queried one of the buyers for the status of his orders, she discovered that the Wal-mart divisional merchandise manager had instructed his group not to purchase from us. He instead encouraged his buyers to find other ways to source the products. We'd spent years and millions marketing and developing these brands, driving retail results, and servicing the needs of both the end customer and our retail partners. None of that seemed to matter as Wal-mart was now choosing to flex its distribution might to squeeze us out. It was a common theme at that time, as Wal-mart's mandate was to reduce "middlemen," and our distribution company became a target.

When Kelly shared the news, I was in shock, knowing the ramifications of this decision to be cataclysmic for our business. I picked up the phone and called up the divisional merchandise manager. After an initial cordial exchange, I asked if he had instructed his team not to support us? He confirmed that they'd be cutting us out of all their purchasing programs. I listened to his justification, claiming that it was Wal-mart's responsibility to get to the lowest retail price. He was confusing price with value and in the process, chose to ignore the value of our marketing, our team's ability to manage and optimize their inventory, and our localized customer service.

I then responded: "Do you realize I'm going to lay off over seventy percent of my staff today because of this decision? Family breadwinners will be going home tonight without a job!" There was a brief pause followed by his remark, "You will have to do what is in the best interest of your business."

As I reflect back on the conversation, I am sure that he didn't realize the full impact, nor do I think he took any delight in it. He was being a tough merchant and was following a company directive.

I put down the phone and sat there in silence. I had literally given everything I had in an effort to try and save the company. After two years and overcoming a myriad of obstacles, this one decision was now the final nail in our company's coffin. Ignoring the inevitable was no longer possible; the vitality that once underscored our company had long since withered. We'd been struggling to keep the company afloat; however, the attempted rebuild of our fractured hull had failed and now the water was gushing in.

I arranged a meeting with Justin, my direct report and the company chairman. I told him that with the loss of Wal-mart, I didn't see a path forward. Without offering much practical advice, he told me that this outcome was unacceptable and that I needed to find a solution. Justin had been responsible for the syndication of funds from the investment group that handled Dynatech through the original restructuring plan. They had an equity stake as a result, but their main motivator was to ensure that we would return their capital along with fees and interest. I too was motivated in ensuring they were repaid, as I had given a personal guarantee for the loans. Still, in that moment no path forward seemed clear to me, as losing our largest customer seemed too insurmountable an obstacle to overcome.

I felt hopeless and despondent, lacking any clear ideas or inspiration about how I would find a way to salvage the situation.

TECH 4 KIDS IS BORN

"But those who hope in the Lord will renew their strength. They will soar on wings like eagles; they will run and not grow weary, they will walk and not be faint."

—ISAIAH 40:31

In the darkness of what seems to be utter defeat, hope can break through with a righteous vengeance. One of my favorite movies, *Lord of the Rings: The Two Towers* describes this exact moment with poetic intensity:

The battle of Helm's Deep has been raging, and finally, the walls are breached, and the enemy begins pouring into the city. All hope seems to be lost. Théoden feels overwhelmed, but comes to his senses and joins Aragorn in one last stand to face the enemy head-on. As the two ride out to face their foe, the sun begins to rise. Aragorn remembers his last exchange with Gandalf, who implored him to look to the East at the dawn's break.

Aragorn looks up at the mountain and sees a familiar silhouette on the horizon, surrounded by a multitude of horse-mounted warriors. Gandalf and the riders of Rohan come pouring down the slopes, rekindling hope in Aragorn, Théoden, and all the men of Helm's Deep, who in turn press on toward victory over the enemy. The power of hope pierced through what seemed like an impenetrable veil of darkness.

While my experience was less dramatic, I had a similar hopeful inspiration while sitting in a Starbucks trying to reimagine the future of the company. After I left the meeting, at which I was essentially told to *FITFO,* I didn't get far physically—only making it to the coffee shop up the road. I felt worthless as it appeared that all my efforts up to now had been wasted and rendered meaningless. Furthermore, my ability to support my family and the people who worked for me was in question, and that created a tremendous amount of shame.

While our kids were growing up, we had them involved in a number of team sports and my wife and I would spend most of our evenings taking them to their respective sporting facilities. Kelly took our daughter to soccer, while I would take my son to his water polo. I decided to use the couple hours of waiting time to revisit the coffee shop, reflecting and journaling on the business. I started to ask the hard questions to identify what part I had played in creating the situation.

Over the next few weeks, a strange thing happened. I started to experience a revival—emotionally, spiritually, and mentally—I began to sense that there could be a way to turn this tragedy into a triumph.

I discovered some very powerful lessons:

First, we tend to not learn much from what is happening in the moment; rather, we learn by taking the time to reflect on what has happened.

Second, it's often hard to get clear on what you want for your future. The endless white space of open possibility makes it nearly impossible to come up with a perfect vision and plan. However, I find it much easier to get clear on what you don't want anymore and often that can show a new path forward.

I got clear on the mistakes I had made and never wanted to repeat again, and began feverishly writing out a list. It included the following:

- ★ "I'll never again build a company only focused on one small market like Canada."
- ★ "I'll never again have a warehouse full of millions of dollars of inventory."
- ★ "I'll never again let my company be at the mercy of one large customer."
- ★ "I'll never again be a distributor for someone else's products."

* "I'll never again let my pride get in the way of questioning the business model."
* "I'll never again be cash strapped to scale my business, I will create a model that keeps us cash flush."

I had unwittingly started to put together the basis for a new business plan. The guardrails I'd created of what I didn't want had inadvertently created the basis for a future opportunity.

From this baseline, I started to fill in what the new business would look like and with each passing week, it started to take shape. During the next several nights, my pillow talk with Kelly became the foundation of an exciting new venture.

We would no longer be a distributor but instead, we'd *design* and make our own toys. We knew it would be hard to build a brand from scratch, so we decided instead to focus on licensing. While we would continue to sell in Canada, this would no longer be our main priority; instead, we'd focus on the US and other large international markets. We would no longer have a warehouse full of inventory but instead focus on selling products direct from the factory. This would keep us cash flush and ensure that we would never again have the pressure of aging inventory.

As we imagined the possibilities for this new venture, Kelly and I began to experience a renewed hope for creating a better future. We were inspired by the idea that we could have a fresh start and the opportunity to once again build a thriving business.

After developing a product roadmap, I went back to the board and with my newly found confidence presented the vision, mission, and business plan and received unanimous approval. Out of the tragedy and ashes of what had been Dynatech, the phoenix of Tech 4 Kids (our new company) would begin to rise!

A CLEAN SLATE

If you were a toy designer, and you explained to your company that your latest brilliant idea would include an internal mechanism of magnetism, pulleys, glass, and static-charged aluminum, you'd probably get a lot of blank stares. You might pique some interest—at least from your legal department—but most everyone else would tell you the idea sounded like a complicated and precarious toy. What would happen if you explained that, in addition to all of the intricate engineering, the child would "draw," by turning knobs to create dark gray lines on a light gray background? Furthermore, drawing circles and other shapes would be difficult and require immense effort and skill.

The idea would likely sound overly complicated and too difficult to play with. I doubt very few decision-makers would have had the imagination to believe that such a toy would one day become immensely popular. That is exactly the success story of Etch A Sketch. So the question begs to be asked: Why has this toy been so wildly popular?

I propose that it isn't the red color, white knobs, the magnetism, or the static-charged aluminum. The reason Etch a Sketch captures our imagination is this: our ability to start over again.

Something inside of children pushes them to constantly try, try, and try again. The Etch A Sketch illustrates this unending hope like no other toy.

A child turns a knob, and the line frustratingly goes in the wrong direction. They turn two simultaneously and the line jumps around like a frantic bumble bee. Eventually, they learn to move the two knobs in tandem to create a simple square or a staircase.

The genius isn't in the complexity of the engineering, it's in the simplicity of the endless ability to have do-overs. Anytime you make a mistake with an Etch A Sketch, you can simply turn it upside down, shake it, and start again on a clean canvas.

As Tim Walsh said in *Timeless Toys,* "Erasing my mistake is half the fun. After a little shake, my slate is wiped clean and another silvery blank canvas calls out."

ROCK BOTTOM

"If you are going through hell just keep going."
—WINSTON CHURCHILL

There are two primary emotions that drive the majority of our human behavior: hope and fear. We are emotionally motivated by either the hope of gain or the fear of loss and unfortunately, fear is the bigger motivator.

Through fear, our ancestors banded together to defend themselves from a myriad of external threats. Rational fear still serves us today, as it tells us to not cross a busy road, swim a long distance without a safety vest, or take an unnecessary risk in our finances. However, most people default to irrational fears, where they worry and fret about the worst case, seeing the obstacles and not the opportunity.

Irrational fear is rooted in a scarcity mindset, and it is what holds us back from exploring all the possibilities that we are capable of. When we operate out of this type of fear, we won't take a risky step because we perceive we may lose something we already have. We don't start a business because we don't want to lose our respected position in our day job. We don't invest in an opportunity because we don't want to lose our savings. We don't travel because we are afraid of flying in airplanes. We don't want to talk to the pretty girl at school because we are afraid of the pain that would come from possible rejection.

While fear is a *natural* emotion, it's not the *optimal* motivator; the greatest motivator of our humanity is hope. Hope sees every obstacle as an opportunity and springs up from an abundance mindset. I have come to learn that an idea empowered by hope can withstand any opponent or adverse situation at any time.

If you're an avid sports enthusiast, you've seen this dynamic play itself out in rinks, stadiums, and coliseums around the world. We have all watched games that throughout the match one team has completely dominated. Then as the game comes into the final period, quarter, or extra time, something happens. The winning team begins *playing not to lose* in order to *protect* their lead, instead of trying to *increase* it. Meanwhile, with nothing left to lose, the losing team begins to rally and decides to suddenly play harder to try and win. Often the outcome is that the once-losing team closes the gap and in many cases goes on to win the game.

There's a difference between playing not to lose and playing to win. Playing not to lose is playing out of fear, and frequently the fear you focus on is manifested. When you are playing not to lose, whether in sports, business, or life, it often results in the very thing you are trying to avoid: *you lose*. The team that's playing to win almost always does, because they're playing with *hope and have an abundance mindset that in turn sees the possibilities to win.*

Fear is a difficult motivation to overcome and ironically, it often intensifies as you feel you have more to lose. However when there's nothing to lose, the only real choice you have is hope, which is why the Etch A Sketch is so much fun: if things look bad, you can choose to shake it up and start over.

When I refer to J. K. Rowling, most imagine a highly influential woman whose *Harry Potter* series has made her one of the wealthiest women in the world. Most don't know her backstory and that, when her marriage fell apart, she subsequently found herself as a single mother, holding a four-month-old baby and living on government assistance. Her life as she had originally imagined it, looked more like a messy scribble of sketch marks than a masterpiece. However in interviews, she now considers those moments as an opportunity to take an eraser to her canvas to start again. In her words:

> I was set free because my greatest fear had been realized, and I was still alive—and I still had a daughter whom I adored. And I had an old typewriter and a big idea. And so rock bottom became the solid foundation on which I rebuilt my life.

At rock bottom, we can choose our attitude, and with that, our response. We can either resist the change, longing for a return to the *good 'ol days*, or we can submit, learn from the circumstances, own our mistakes, and then choose again.

Submission may seem like a negative word, but in this case, it's simply a willingness to confront the reality of our present circumstances. Submission is not to surrender. Submission, rather, forces us to realize that what we are doing is no longer working, and we need to stop and pick a new path forward. When we *surrender* there is no future, as we give up altogether.

When we don't submit, we choose to resist by default, and resistance leaves us in a spin cycle based on anxiety, aversion to change, and a longing for what used to be. This leads to what I call the "F state": being fearful, frustrated, frazzled, frenetic, and uttering other "F" words.

What is the most powerful antidote to this F state? Hope in our ability to imagine and create a better future.

The amazing thing about hope is that it cannot be part of our past. Hopes of the past are regrets. Hope also cannot be part of our immediate reality; if it's already happened, it's not hope, it's accomplishment. Hope can only exist in the *future*, as vivid imagery of what we long for, but have not yet realized.

The key to inspiring hope is that we must be curious and be willing to use our imagination to re-envision a better future. Everything is really created twice: first in our minds, and secondly, in reality. This second occurrence happens only because of the first—we hope, and then find the courage to create.

Yet, we often refuse to see rock bottom as our opportunity for hope, because that sort of perspective requires a deep change in our attitudes.

We hate change. As Mark Twain said, "The only person who likes change is a baby with a wet diaper." We'd rather hang onto what we know, even when it's obvious that our old ways or mindsets are no longer serving us.

As a survivor of the German concentration camps, Viktor Frankl provides some insight into surviving and thriving through adversity.

In his book, *Man's Search for Meaning*, Frankl famously stated, "Everything can be taken from a man but one thing: the last of the human freedoms—to choose one's attitude in any given set of circumstances, to choose one's own way."[21] Frankl discovered that despite the restriction of his external freedoms and the unbelievable suffering that surrounded him, he still had a locus of control over his *response*.

In life, as we face uncertainty and ambiguity, we will be predisposed to default to a scarcity mindset that is driven out of fear. It is having awareness of this that gives us the opportunity to recognize when it is happening and

21 Viktor E. Frankl, *Man's Search for Meaning* (Boston: Beacon Press, 1959), 88.

as per Frankl, to then choose our response. Once we've chosen hope, we can see how our terrible circumstances are not happening *to* us but rather *for* us, and the rock bottom foundation can become the basis of starting something new.

STEP BY STEP, LINE UPON LINE

"Strength and growth come only through
continuous effort and struggle. On the other side
of pain and hard work is the reward of a stronger,
more capable version of yourself."
—NAPOLEON HILL

The ancient book of Hebrews defines faith as "the substance of things hoped for, the evidence of things not seen." I love the interplay between the words "faith" and "hope," as they are intrinsically linked in how we can create a better and brighter future. Faith is having trust that the good that we have witnessed in the past can and will happen again if we are consistent in actions. Hope is the emotional longing for the yet unseen to become reality.

When a trapeze artist performs in a high-flying act, there's typically a moment when they must release one bar, "flying" through the air to grasp the arms of another. In the process they require a great deal of both faith and hope. They have faith that as part of the act, the bar with their companion will continue to swing in cadence as they have seen demonstrated before. They have hope that when they do release from their bar and stretch for the arms of their companion, they will be caught. If they *don't* release the bar, they are simply just swinging; another version of the rocking horse syndrome. While they certainly would be playing it safe, they would never show us the incredible possibilities we witness in acts like the Cirque du Soleil.

Likewise, in business it is easier to simply hang onto our current comfortable bar and just try and maintain our ability to swing. That said, I believe all opportunities have a "best by date"—remember, all racehorses go lame. There comes a time to admit that something has reached its end of life and we need to let go and move on. Only by letting go can we create the space needed to embrace new opportunities. Often, we won't let go because we confuse *failing* with being a *failure*. *Failing is part of succeeding and is a normal part of pursuing a path toward success.* Failing is getting knocked down, after which we can choose to get up and go again. Being a failure is when we get knocked down and choose to stay down because we have given up hope for the future.

Creating success and significance in our lives is a compounding process that comes as a result of a series of small steps. Confucius famously stated that the journey of a thousand miles begins with a single step. The child who learns to walk cannot make progress without taking the first few baby steps, falling down, and then building on them step by step. It is literally failing forward.

And that leads us to the second lesson the Etch A Sketch brings us: *we don't get to skip lines.* Every beautiful design is created by stacking "line upon line." Children will never stop trying to walk. They will fall, they will scuff their knee, they may cry to a parent, but they will always get back up and try again, using every experience as an opportunity for betterment.

As we become adults, we often find ourselves losing the ability to embrace adversity. Instead, we go out of our way to try and skip the pain, seeking "success without sacrifice." Who could blame us, it's so much easier to choose safety over risk and comfort over pain.

You may never fail in business to the level that I failed with Dynatech, but it is important that you are aware that failing in life is inevitable. You will never achieve anything great without experiencing setbacks, hardships, making mistakes, and failing forward. The alternative is what most people do, which is to play it safe and not explore what is possible by pushing the boundaries of their comfort zone. Hopefully you do not succumb to living a life paralyzed by fear, inadvertently becoming a bystander, and squandering your precious life; in which case you will become a failure by default by never realizing all the potential of the God given gifts that are within you.

"Life is a journey that looks like a detour. It seems like only by looking back we can see a way to untangle the mess. This whole journey is disappointing me at a rate I can stand. It never works out exactly the way we had originally planned or hoped. With clear direction we can weave a future of Hope. The difference between tangled and weaving is intention."

—JOHN MARSH

WRITE AND REFLECT

"We rejoice in our sufferings, knowing that suffering produces endurance, and endurance produces character, and character produces hope."

—ROMANS 5:3,4 (ESV)

The Etch A Sketch offers unlimited chances to turn it upside down and try again. However, the first step to any change starts with awareness. Entrepreneurs notoriously pass through successes without pausing to celebrate or learn from them because, as entrepreneurs, we're *supposed* to be successful.

The blessing that comes from failing and hitting the "proverbial wall" is that it typically forces us to stop and take a moment to reflect. Wounds create scars that can become lessons and teachings of what to emulate and what to avoid. Scars symbolize our resilience by marking the challenges we took on. They should also serve as a reminder that you were stronger and survived what tried to kill you!

My most valuable learnings have come from writing and reflecting. Not only is it a cathartic and healing experience, but by journaling, we begin to unpack the lessons and can glean the wisdom from our wounds. Furthermore I find writing helps me understand myself better. The benefit is self-discovery and revealing where I made choices that created poor outcomes. Writing also helps to learn from myself and illuminates more of what I really think. In both cases this leads to the opportunity to reflect, learn and then choose a better path forward.

Modern thinking attempts to convince us that we're simply victims of circumstance, a seemingly freeing thought. However, real freedom comes from recognizing that we *do* have control in our lives in our ability to choose and influence the path forward.

STOP-START-CONTINUE

As I write and reflect on painful failings, I try to contemplate my involvement in co-creating the experience through three lenses:

* What do I need to *stop* doing?
* What do I need to *start* doing?
* What should I *continue* doing?

Similar to the process of reimagining the future of Dynatech and the subsequent launch of Tech 4 Kids, I find it easiest to start with imagining what I don't want anymore. Through reflection, I focus my energy on identifying the things I must eliminate so that the pain I just experienced doesn't repeat itself (stop). Next, I can consider what actions I need to proactively take to avoid the situation from happening again as well as new choices that I believe will lead to better outcomes (start). And finally, this focused reflection then helps me identify what behaviors are serving my best interests and supporting the vision and mission so that I can keep doing them (continue).

All of this process culminates into reinforcing one philosophy: I choose to never be a victim. I have the ability to submit to what happened, be accountable to my involvement and choose again, with hope to create a better future.

Reflection = Forgiveness

Not only does reflection allow us to change the course of our own paths, but it gives us an opportunity to seek out forgiveness where needed.

Nelson Mandela famously said that "resentment is like drinking poison and then hoping it will kill your enemies." When we perceive ourselves as victims—whether it's true or untrue—poison begins to formulate. We may have been really wronged, or we might just be looking to shift responsibility and blame. Regardless if perceived or real, the antidote to wrongful treatment is the same: first pause, reflect, and write. It is especially important that as part of the process you are accountable for the part you played that led to the events. This process helps heal the wound, releasing the poison of resentment.

Difficult experiences create fractures that, in many ways, are similar to what you see in broken bones. Without proper medical care, a broken bone will become gangrenous, with the potential of the whole infection ravaging the body. Conversely, a broken bone that is nurtured and cared for heals back stronger than before.

Brokenness, then, can either make you bitter or better. Being broken, whether physically, mentally, spiritually or emotionally, is an inevitable part of our human journey. How we respond will determine whether we remain helpless or become the hero of our life. The first step toward that healing is to pause and reflect, followed by forgiveness. In many cases, that may be simply finding forgiveness for ourselves.

> *"The first to apologize is the bravest. The first to forgive is the strongest. The first to forget is the happiest."*
>
> —NICKEY GUMBLE

HOPE FOR RELATIONSHIPS

> *"Everyone says forgiveness is a lovely idea, until they have something to forgive."*[22]
>
> —CS LEWIS

Hope isn't just about restoration for our own lives and business ventures. Most importantly, the Etch A Sketch teaches us that we should be hopeful in the restoration of broken relationships.

Remember the Wal-mart divisional merchandise manager who instructed his buying team to stop supporting us? His name is Don and I was initially very resentful of him and held him directly responsible for delivering the final death blow to my business. I believed that his direction led to us letting the majority of our people go, leaving millions unpaid to creditors, and eventually resulting in us shuttering the business. Of course this was a false explanation as there was no accountability for the role I played in building a bad and broken business model that I had tried to make work through my sheer force of will.

As time passed I became aware that Don had also lived through heartbreak and tragedy, having lost his daughter due to a medical accident. It

---

22   C. S. Lewis, *Mere Christianity* (New York: HarperOne, 1952), Kindle.

helped me gain perspective: I had lost my business, but Don had lost one of his precious children.

I read a fable once about a pilgrim who was disgruntled about carrying his "cross" (the burdens and troubles of life). A sage convinces him and others to throw off their crosses into a pile and to then proceed to choose a new one. After examining all the other crosses within the pile, the pilgrim suddenly realizes that his problems by comparison were relatively trivial. He then desperately searches to find the original cross he had previously discarded.

The lesson is simple: everyone is suffering at some level. As difficult as we believe our journey is, we must remember that everyone is going through challenges and often, they are worse than what we are enduring.

Stephen Covey famously cited one of his seven habits that we need to seek first to understand before trying to be understood.[23] Once I was able to understand the gravity of what Don had lost, I experienced empathy and compassion for him that would ultimately lead to a place of forgiveness.

Several years later, I ran into Don at a fundraiser. By this point he'd retired from Wal-mart, but still, seeing him created anxiety. I was reminded of his tragic loss which created a desire in me to show kindness, and curiosity for how time had helped us both heal. Perhaps this was an opportunity to choose again and rewrite a better ending to our story.

While the situation remained the same, I had changed. I had submitted to the events of the past (but not surrendered). I had chosen to glean the wisdom from my wounds, and was now inspired by the future we'd created at Tech 4 Kids. When I saw Don, instead of lashing out with resentment, I reached out with my palm. We shook hands, and that one act planted the seed of what has since become a beautiful relationship.

Don had a wealth of experience, incredible industry knowledge, and many influential connections. Most importantly, I began to understand

23 Stephen R. Covey, *The 7 Habits of Highly Effective People* (New York: Free Press, 1989).

more of his character and learned that his beliefs and values were in fact very similar to my own. Fast-forward through several meals together and hours of enjoyable conversation, the man who was once my enemy had become my friend.

In 2016, I invited Don to join the board of advisors for Tech 4 Kids. That's the power of hope and of finding forgiveness, of being willing to shake the Etch A Sketch and rid the screen of the past messes so that we can begin again.

Don and I continue our friendship to this day. I am so grateful I opened up to him, as his wisdom has enriched my life, and his generous and giving heart has amazed me. He has a continued passion and desire to stand in the gap for marginalized kids and he still leverages his influences in the toy industry to garner support for the charities where he generously invests his time.

CHOOSE HOPE

No matter how deep our despair, no matter how challenged and pressed we feel, there is always an opportunity to restart. There is always hope.

With every twist and turn of the knobs, children create lines on the screen of their Etch a Sketch in their attempt to create something remarkable. Not every picture is beautiful, and oftentimes they are riddled with mistakes. Still, hope is always available for a fresh start and the opportunity to find a better way forward. Every line we've drawn, every entanglement and every mistake, is simply an opportunity from which we can learn, if only we take the time to reflect and unpack the lessons.

In the moments we experience our greatest tragedies, we can begin to learn our greatest truths. When we reach our lowest point and confront our greatest fears, adopting the right mindset allows us to not simply "go through" the situation, but to actually "grow through" it. We will often come to recognize that our obstacles are in fact unique opportunities; they did not *happen to u*s but rather *for us*. It is up to us to reflect, to learn the lessons, to embrace hope for new possibilities, and then to choose again.

So, whenever you find yourself at the bottom, take heart, give your life a little shake, and choose the power of hope to inspire you to start over again.

> *"We can make the best or the worst of it. I hope you make the best of it. I hope you see things that startle you. I hope you feel things you've never felt before. I hope you meet people who have a different point of view. I hope you live a life you're proud of, and if you're not, I hope you have the courage to start over again."*
>
> —F. SCOTT FITZGERALD

CHAPTER 6

ASSEMBLE THE PERFECT TOY BOX

"The single most important thing you need to do is to pick the right people and keep them. There is nothing more important than this."

—JIM COLLINS

I f a child's toy box could speak, it would tell tales of swashbuckling adventures, mythological discoveries, and unending playtimes. The toy box, while seemingly nothing more than a container, is really a platform for all things creative and imaginative. That's why some parents pass their toy boxes down through the generations; it's as if they're giving a piece of their imagination to their children.

But there is one toy box that actually *can* speak:

Andy's toy box.

I'm not sure we will ever forget the first time we saw Pixar's original *Toy Story.*

The movie opens with the catchy song "You've Got a Friend in Me" playing in the background, and for a few moments we see young Andy playing with his favorite toys. Nostalgia fills every scene as Andy moves from one toy to the other, until he lays Woody down on his bed, and excitedly exits, leaving a seemingly empty bedroom.

Moments later, the toy cowboy springs up on its own accord, and we discover that the playthings are actually alive.

The toy box opens up and out comes a motley ensemble of animated toys. It soon becomes clear that Sheriff Woody is the leader and shortly after the eccentric cohort emerges, he decides to host a meeting. Woody uses a toy karaoke machine as a microphone, a Tinker Toy container as his podium, and eventually orders the Green Army Men to "establish a recon post downstairs." On their mission, they use the toy walkie-talkies to relay messages back to Andy's room full of toys. Pure toy magic!

My favorite scene from the Toy Story universe actually comes from *Toy Story 2,* when the toys set out on an adventure to save Woody, who's been stolen by the film's antagonist, Al of Al's Toy Barn. The mission is one of seemingly impossible odds, forcing these charismatic toys to leave the familiarity of their toy box to rescue their comrade.

Time and again, they overcome obstacles in the pursuit of their worthy goal. At a crucial point in the story, Buzz, Rex, Mr. Potato Head, Slinky, and Hamm must cross a busy street. To disguise themselves, they use traffic cones as they meander from one end of the busy street to the other. As the cars see orange traffic cones in the middle of the road, they attempt to drive around them, and hilarity ensues as the toys unknowingly create a barrage of traffic accidents.

Throughout the series of movies, there are many fun scenes and adventures that these toys embark on together. Behind the humor and entertainment they provide, most of us miss the greater lesson to be learned: they each have unique skills that collectively support the goals of the team. Slinky can stretch to fill gaps, Etch A Sketch can draw a map to guide them and Lenny the binoculars can help them see far distances. Each toy brings a unique superpower to the team that supports the mission they are pursuing. The group takes advantage of their diverse abilities, using them to miraculously achieve the seemingly impossible.

What we also learn is that it is not just about each toy's unique abilities but also their character. These toys are committed to a mission and set out in pursuit of it, working as a unified team and risking their own safety to achieve success. Woody is their friend, and their loyalty to each other gives them the courage to act. Whatever these child playthings lacked in size, power, or ability, they make up for with an optimistic attitude and a unified resolve to succeed. They want their friend back, and that singular motivation unites them to attempt the impossible, and achieve the improbable.

This just so happens to be a lot like running a business. The same positive attitudes and diverse skills that we see exemplified in these fun characters are what is required of a team when pursuing a worthy business endeavor.

TALENTED TERRORIST

In building a business, having a unified talented team is what creates the magic to help accelerate the company towards a common goal. Most importantly, the internal character of each team member must be in alignment with the company's values. Conversely, when organizational members lack alignment in their character, the company's cultural foundation erodes, and the business becomes compromised. I've been in both situations, separated only by a short time; what I learned paints both a painful warning of what to avoid and a powerful vision of what can be achieved.

The person leading the Dynatech's development team was someone named Arnold and he was incredibly competent within his role. When he walked into a room he was very persuasive and had the ability to move his audience to make purchasing decisions. From the moment I met him, I was in awe of his ability to sell, and he played a significant role in helping to achieve our spectacular growth.

In early 2008, Arnold approached me and made what appeared to be a magnanimous gesture: he resigned. The company was failing and Arnold reasoned that we could no longer afford him. As a goodwill gesture, he would sacrifice himself for the benefit of saving the jobs of other team members. Our first reaction was one of shock; we were going to lose our top sales producer. That quickly turned to appreciation as we knew in light of our situation that layoffs were imminent, and we applauded what seemed to be his selfless act. Meanwhile my wife felt curious (and even a bit uneasy) about his resignation: it seemed overly generous and out of character for how Arnold usually behaved.

Within a few weeks of his departure, suspicions were validated as deception started to surface. We learned that as Dynatech struggled, he had gone into self-preservation mode and in the background he had been doing deals on the side. He also had reached out to several of our suppliers, and convinced a few of them to work with him directly.

To reveal the extent of his deception, we started a forensic audit of his computer and email. In the process we discovered that he was having an affair with one of his staff members, someone whose job he supposedly "saved" when he resigned. As we dug in further, what we uncovered got even worse. Arnold, along with his mistress, had set up a pornography website. They had registered domains for a number of popular toy brands that we were distributing, with the intent to display explicit content. As far as we could tell, the plan was an attempt to extort us.

I'm not sure we ever found out the totality of Arnold's ethical failures. What we did conclude was that despite Arnold being incredibly talented, he had chosen to become a terrorist as the company experienced difficulties. When you allow talented terrors to join your team while the business is experiencing "good times," then you usually only see their positive attributes. However during times of crisis, that is when your team member's true colors are revealed.

"WHO'S COMING WITH ME?"

Times of crisis can also reveal the very best on your team and those who will rise to the occasion.

Small- and medium-sized toy companies often work with third-party agencies, who help to coordinate all the procurement and on-the-ground logistics at the factories in Asia. This arrangement allows Western companies to have physical resources on the ground, working at the source to ensure manufacturing and shipping run smoothly. Dynatech was working with a Hong Kong agency in this type of relationship when the business finally capitulated. Due to our good relationship, we had expected to continue working with them as we transitioned into Tech 4 Kids.

At our agents office we had a dedicated team which included Kyle, one of our Canadian team members who had moved to Hong Kong to be more hands on with the product development process. Late one evening while I was on a family vacation, I received a surprise phone call from Kyle. He informed me that our agency was uncomfortable with our recent history and had intended to terminate their agreement with us. I tried to arrange a call with the principal running the agency, but he insisted that any conversations would have to be in person. The risk of termination created an existential threat. Our new startup could not survive without having agency support for our product development and factory relationships. I booked the next available flight to Hong Kong, kissed my family goodbye and embarked to face yet another looming threat to our business.

A few hours later I arrived, checked into my hotel and went straight to the office. There was a sense of uneasiness amongst our team as video cameras had been installed to monitor our activity. I asked to speak with the agency principal, but for several days in a row I was told he was not available. Finally later in the week, the agency principal showed up in our office surrounded by an entourage. He looked directly at me and said: "We're here to escort you out of the building." I was stunned, wondering why he did not choose to meet with me first to discuss the situation so we could come up with a solution. In the moment I tried reasoning with him but it was to no avail. He was resolved in the decision which had come directly from his board.

In a bold act of desperation, I appealed to some of the agency's employees, urging them to walk out and join our soon to be formed Tech 4 Kids Asia team. I knew that to carry forward we would need help, and that it would be particularly beneficial to start with seasoned talent. This was a real Jerry Maguire "Who's coming with me?" moment. Incredibly, two agency members packed up their desks and decided to join. We were then escorted out of the building and into an uncertain future.

A few moments later, the gravity of what had happened started to set in. I now had three employees and zero idea about how to run an Asia office.

We walked to a café where I sat down and ordered everyone a coffee, and then stared off into space trying to muster up the right words to reassure my newly formed team. We had put our faith into this new opportunity; however, its fate now seemed precarious. I was weary and fatigued and felt gut punched at losing the confidence of our agent and potentially our manufacturing partners as well. In that moment of hopelessness, Kyle stepped in and boldly stated, "We can get through this; we will figure it out."

Kyle was an extraordinary individual who was exactly the right leader we needed in that moment. At Dynatech he worked in graphics and supported our leader in product development. When we parted ways with our head of product development, Kyle stepped forward and asked to take over the role. He recognized the opportunity we were going to create with Tech 4 Kids, was a great cultural fit, and offered to relocate to Hong Kong. His physical presence in Asia would give us an incredible advantage in our ability to use, speed to market with new product development.

Fast forward to this disorienting moment in the Hong Kong cafe. We had been abruptly severed from our lifeline in product development and manufacturing, yet Kyle's words inspired hope amongst our fledgling new team. Kyle's plan was to offer up all four hundred square feet of his Hong Kong apartment and convert it into a temporary office. We would lean on the experience and connections of our new team members to operate out of this makeshift setup. We all agreed and began putting a plan in motion to convert Kyle's tiny living room into our Asia head office. Kyle had just enough privacy to sleep, use the toilet, and cook. He had graciously allowed the rest of his apartment to become our office.

We operated this way for almost a year, and reflecting back, it was a key inflection point buying us enough time to build on our early momentum.

Kyle's hope and courage became the deciding factor between the certain death of our nascent startup and what would eventually become a thriving enterprise. He remained hopeful, developed a clear plan and with his confidence, he coached our team to do exceptional work. They were just ordinary people who through great leadership had been inspired to produce extraordinary outcomes.

At Dynatech, my primary focus was to hire based solely on talent. This approach ultimately led to adverse outcomes, including the fallout from Arnold's character failure and betrayal. With Tech 4 Kids, we were given a chance to start over. However this time, I was committed to creating a toy box that would be filled with the right team players. People who not only fit our culture and brought with them the right attitude and complementary skill sets, but who would also challenge each other to achieve the best outcomes.

ATTITUDE > APTITUDE

If you and I were to sit down and write a list of who we thought were the most successful people of all time, we'd likely come up with similar names. Describing these exceptional people, we might use adjectives such as: courageous, disciplined, resilient, convicted, trustworthy, loyal, friendly, humble, kind, and compassionate.

Nearly all of the attributes we'd write down would include virtues and *character traits*, not *abilities*. When we pause to consider what we truly value in remarkable people, it isn't their ability to handle workload, which prestigious school they attended, or even their previous job experience. What we truly admire is an *attitude*.

With history's greatest leaders and change makers, we value attitude over aptitude.

Yet, when it comes to recruiting to build out our teams we usually do the exact opposite. We say we want a multitasker, a detail-oriented self-starter, or someone with such-and-such education or experience. During the search, interview, and hiring process, we prioritize aptitude, nearly at the exclusion of attitude. Furthermore, potential employees market themselves almost exclusively based on aptitude. This becomes a game that experienced professionals learn to master—organizing one's resumé, instilling power words, and positioning their experiences to appear as accomplished as possible.

If we believe that what matters most is one's attitude, why not adapt our hiring and onboarding practices to align with our beliefs?

Having had a front row seat, I have witnessed the impact of both approaches firsthand. At Dynatech, I hired nearly exclusively for aptitude, seeking out individuals with the right education or most experience. By the time I had started Tech 4 Kids, I had learned some tough lessons. As a result, I became increasingly aware of the importance of looking for signals that ensured there was an alignment in the candidate's attitude that would fit with our company culture.

Nothing great in our world was achieved as a solo act. Most of the world united to defeat Hitler, we ended slavery through the collective efforts of abolitionists and Jesus rallied twelve disciples to create a movement.

One person may invoke an idea and inspire others, but to see that inspiration develop into reality requires a team who's aligned. When you can find people who share the same vision and work together, there's very little you can't accomplish.

HUMBLE, HUNGRY, SMART

If we're hiring for attitude, and want to avoid recruiting people who might become "talented terrorists," then what, specifically, are the characteristics of a good fit?

Patrick Lencioni is the bestselling author of the *5 Dysfunctions of a Team, The Advantage,* and *Death by Meeting.* His work has had a profound impact on the way I think about building sustainable, and durable teams. In his book *The Ideal Team Player,* Lencioni offers three attributes that he believes are necessary for a candidate to exhibit:

* *Humble:* Simply put, someone who consistently demonstrates humility by caring as much about others and the organization as they do about themselves. While it is harder to identify humility, it is easy to diagnose if a candidate is arrogant as they will tend to talk about themselves and their accomplishments over that of a team. Most importantly, Lencioni points out that a humble person not only deflects taking the sole credit for a good outcome but will actively edify the efforts of all members of a team.
* *Hungry:* In the workplace, a hungry person is someone who has a serious work ethic. They aren't workaholics who find their identity in work. Rather, they prioritize and when required apply a focused effort and strive to do everything with excellence.
* *Smart:* In Lencioni's view, "smart" doesn't just refer to technical acumen, but also emotional intelligence. This team player understands how to perform their role and has the experience to prove it.[24]
* Lencioni's beliefs are based on his twenty-five years of working with

---

24 Patrick Lencioni, *The Ideal Team Player: How to Recognize and Cultivate the Three Essential Virtues* (Hoboken, NJ: Jossey-Bass, 2016).

multiple businesses in helping shape and build high-performing teams. His conviction is that organizations should look to hire someone who has this trifecta of rare and valuable attributes.

Warren Buffett has a similar list that he refers to as the three Is: integrity, intelligence, and initiative. He insists that all three must be present and warns that if any candidate has only two of the three, they will not last and will ultimately create some sort of dysfunction.

As an easy hack, Lencioni suggests that you can have everyone you are considering (and perhaps existing members of your team or in your family) rank the order in which they excel at these attributes. By forcing someone to rank themselves, they'll have to put something as their worst attribute. Be wary of candidates who rank humility as their lowest trait and be mindful that people are putting their best foot forward in interviews. If you are doing this exercise with your existing team, then it becomes helpful in providing a reference point for areas of improvement in their personal growth plan.

As leaders, when we know what to look for in identifying these important characteristics, then we increase the odds of getting the ideal team player while reducing the chances of hiring bad cultural fits.

FIT CULTURE

"Culture eats strategy for breakfast."
—PETER DRUCKER

It is critical to seek out the hungry, humble, and smart attributes, but while doing so also look for characteristics that align with your company's culture. A company that is remarkable at doing this is Zappos.

In 2013, I visited the Zappos headquarters in Las Vegas, Nevada, and met the company's founder, Tony Hsieh.[25] Tragically, Tony passed away in 2020, but he left behind a masterclass in building a cohesive company culture.

Before he founded Zappos, Hsieh got really clear on the culture he desired to create. Hsieh had exited Link Exchange and in the process got clear on the type of culture he did not want.

When you arrive at the Zappos headquarters, you'll find office workers running around in costumes, banners and mascots adorning every cubicle, and meeting rooms that look like a grade school birthday party. The entire operation aligns perfectly with Hsieh's cultural vision: he wanted to remove the distance between an employee's play and their work.

If you don't work at Zappos, you may think the atmosphere is just one nut short of a peanut butter and jelly sandwich, but if you *do* work there, you love all the wackiness. Hsieh created a culture with a clear set of beliefs and has used it to attract the right people. The culture champions in the company are then responsible for attracting and hiring people who share similar beliefs.

Preserving the integrity of the Zappos culture is so important to its strategy that the company offers up to $2,000 to new employees to *quit*. The genius of this strategy is that it flushes out the decoys who would be "mercenaries" versus true "missionaries" who are passionate about the vision and mission of the business. Hsieh knew what only a few seasoned founders understand: that $2,000 is the best and cheapest off-ramp for bad cultural fits.

---

25   Hsieh is pronounced "shay."

THE DIVERSE TOY BOX

As children grow, their preferences for toys may change, and they often develop an appreciation for having a variety of options to play with. For instance, even though Woody held a special place in Andy's heart, he was just one of many toys in Andy's toy box. Other beloved toys included Buzz, Rex, Bo Peep, Slinky, and several others, each with their own distinct features and characteristics. Together, these toys offered an array of playtime possibilities for Andy, leading to the engaging and dynamic storytelling that has made the Toy Story franchise so beloved.

Sheriff Woody uses his leadership skills to host meetings and build out the team strategies. Rocky Gibraltar uses his physical strength to lift and move things easily. Slink stretches to help others climb, and RC uses his speed to transport other team members. By leaning on each other's strengths, they are able to overcome individual weaknesses, and when their strengths are combined, they achieve extraordinary outcomes.

These brave toys provide an excellent example that teaches us the principle: *none of us are as smart as all of us.* Likewise, diversity means strength and it is imperative that founders find talent that complements their weaknesses. What is work for you, is likely play for someone else. Based on my past experience, I know that I *can* create a budget for a business plan or build a Gantt chart to track product development…but I also know I would really need to work at it. I've found people who are gifted at this type of work, and who also love doing it. My goal is to build a holistic toy box with a variety of team members who share common values and virtues but possess different superpowers. This is an essential ingredient to creating a truly sustainable, scalable, and ultimately saleable enterprise.

The benefits of diversity play out not only with skill sets, but perhaps even more so with differing worldviews. Suppose there are four of us sitting around in a circle and a beach ball with multiple colors is placed in the middle. When asked to describe the color of the ball, I might say that from my side, it appears blue and white. The person sitting opposite of me may just as accurately describe it as red and white, and another could say that it's only yellow. Diverse thinking is seeing the same world with different perspectives and lenses. When considering problem solving and strategy, if you invite diverse thinking into your work environment, and empower people to speak out, you foster a fuller picture of the marketplace. Different perspectives help uncover blind spots. Given in humility, (focused on doing what is right versus trying to be right) they provide the needed input to produce the best outcomes.

In the current marketplace, we've confused diversity to focus on skin-deep issues such as ethnicity, gender, and sexual orientation. I am neither discounting nor trivializing that there is real-world discrimination and inequality against these characteristics. The diversity I am referring to is diversity in thought, experience, and skill sets. Hiring for only surface-level diversity will never provide the true differentiation in thought that a successful enterprise really needs. We must consider the topic more holistically, examining what are the blind spots in our businesses, what skills are we missing and who will provide the contrarian points of view that we need to avoid the trap of groupthink.

At Tech 4 Kids, my second-in-command was a woman named Willy who is from Hong Kong. She was a terrific fit for our culture as she perfectly personified the company's core values and virtues and was completely committed to our vision and mission. She was humble, hungry and smart, and her strengths complimented my weaknesses. As a result, she earned the right to become the integrator for the company and became the COO leading our operational teams.

Willy and I continue to work together today but in a different venture. This leads to another important point which is to never lose your best people. There will be some rare relationships you need to protect, where the chemistry is unique and your combined efforts become exponential. What I truly appreciate about Willy is that despite having an incredible work ethic, her humility and empathy towards the needs of others is world class. She is a treasure, and I am grateful we continue to do life together.

COMMON HIRING ERRORS

Kelly and I were part of the small group of leaders at Tech 4 Kids that would interview all potential candidates together. I would often walk away excited to hire the person as I could see their potential. My wife on the other hand was often much more cautious, noting some obvious and sometimes not-so-obvious deficiencies that I had overlooked. Like most founders, I have two potentially fatal hiring flaws: I'm overly optimistic and I'm prone to hiring people that I like.

Similar to seeing opportunities in the marketplace, entrepreneurs tend to see the possibilities in every person they meet. They also tend to hire people like themselves, because of common interests. Unfortunately this inadvertently creates groupthink.

My coach often states to me "A skilled hunter knows how to hunt, a masterful hunter knows how he is hunted." To protect myself from myself I had to develop a system that would help me make better decisions on selecting the right talent. I studied all of the best content including: the hiring module from Darren Hardy's Business Master Class, Patrick Lencioni's *The Advantage,* and Brad Smart's *Who.*

Now, every hire must first pass through a multi-interview gauntlet with other high performers in our company, *before* a final interview with one of the company's executive team members. Very few make it through, as along the way any interviewer has the right to veto the candidate. Each step leans on the insights and intuition of the other trusted leaders, flushing out decoys and protecting the organization from my tendency of being overly optimistic about any one candidate.

A nuanced shift in our approach is that our interviewers play the role of guardians of the company culture. The right qualifications for the role are simple table stakes. As they consider each potential candidate, their default position is that the person they are meeting is not worthy and does not qualify. It is only through a series of thoughtful and challenging questions that the candidate is given the opportunity to prove them wrong. If successful in doing so through several interviews, only then are they presented the opportunity to join the team. Most companies do this the opposite way, placing too much weight on previous aptitude and only then considering the possibilities of the potential candidate for the role.

If you're the typical optimistic entrepreneur, I encourage you to create a similar gauntlet: build a system that protects the company from your biases and includes your best leaders as part of the selection process. Once in place, trust the system to help identify and recruit the right talent.

WHAT DO *THEY* WANT?

Part of finding the right people is knowing what they're looking for. Overall, there is a misconception by most founders that people are looking for opportunities that have the highest compensation. While compensation is an important factor, it's not the most important point that attracts the best talent.

When I attended Darren Hardy's Business Master Class, I was surprised to learn the truth about the key drivers for attracting top talent. For the right candidates their motivators in order of priority are as follows:

★ **People:** They want to belong to a special community and culture with great and talented people.

- ★ **Challenge:** They are inspired by bold ideas, big goals, and the chance to do something meaningful.
- ★ **Opportunity:** They want to be part of a movement that is going somewhere.
- ★ **Growth:** They thrive from growing their skills and capacities.
- ★ **Money:** They want to feel they are compensated fairly for their contributions.

Compensation is a crucial part of recognizing value, however, many entrepreneurs focus on compensation exclusively. What the right candidate really wants is a chance to work with great people, be part of an exciting growth story, and the ability to increase their influence. When compensation is the primary motivator for a team member, there is a good chance that they are really a talented terror.

Your job as the leader is to find the people who are already living your values and who fall in love with your vision and mission. That likely means there's a very good chance they are already hired and working somewhere else. In my experience, most high performers are not sitting around searching postings on job boards. They are actively employed, committed to a cause and in their role achieving results. Once you've identified them, your goal is to attract them to your bold vision for the future. You will need to first find out what their goals are and then ensure there is a goal match. Your job is not to convince them to join the cause but rather to inspire them by demonstrating how the success of the enterprise will also support their ability to achieve both personal and professional goals.

THE NECESSITY OF FIRING FASTER

"The toughest decisions in organizations are people decisions—hiring, firing, promotion, etc. These are

the decisions that receive the least attention and are
the hardest to unmake."

—PETER DRUCKER

I've been fortunate enough to be involved in a number of business forums and masterminds. I was invited to join a very special group that also includes Dave Liniger, the co-founder of RE/MAX. During one of our gatherings, someone asked him about the biggest mistake of his career. I leaned in—I didn't want to miss the juicy nugget from a billionaire who'd founded both an iconic brand and real estate empire. I expected that he'd drop some sage financial advice about the learnings from a deal that went really bad. Yet, Liniger said, "My single biggest regret is that I did not fire people fast enough."

Liniger had boot-strapped his company, going through many trials with a small team that he felt a sense of loyalty towards. He further explained that the original team didn't grow as the company grew, causing blockages within the business. Liniger had turned a blind eye to obvious performance issues because of the loyalty and devotion he felt for his founding team.

Liniger went on to say that when a founder does not fire fast enough, you're letting three people down: yourself, your team, and the person you're failing to fire. He then further unpacked the lesson.

First, when you keep an underperformer in a role, you are letting yourself down. This person misses timelines or produces shoddy work and requires your constant oversight. This distracts you from what you need to be focused on and creates mistrust, where you become apprehensive to delegate work. This results in you becoming reluctant to delegate tasks to them, meaning you are only increasing the amount of extra work you are accountable for.

Second, you are letting down the others who work with the person. The unsaid truth amongst the team is that they all recognize that there is a weak performer in their ranks, and ultimately you are increasing their workload as they have to pick up the slack. Furthermore, when you don't fire poor performers, your real risk is that the other team players will lose trust in you as their leader. The leader may *say* they care about high performance, but their actions, tolerance, and ultimately failure to remove poor performers would say otherwise.

Finally—and this one really blew me away—Liniger noted that when you refuse to fire someone, you're letting *them* down. A struggling employee knows they're struggling, but what they probably don't know is that there is another place where their talents and gifts can better serve them. By not releasing a struggling employee, you're actually being selfish; you are thinking you are protecting them. The reality is you are only protecting yourself from dealing with a difficult situation and you're holding them back from finding *their better future.*

I took a deep breath, as Liniger finished sharing his "fire-faster" philosophy. "Ah, that's what's going on," I thought, as I reflected on my company. At the time, I was living the exact scenario he was describing. Many of my employees who'd been the right people for the early days of the business were no longer what the business needed. I had been selfish as I was trying to avoid having the hard conversations. That selfishness had eventually led me to believe that these employees were generally incompetent and needed my help. This created dysfunctional, codependent relationships, where I believed these employees needed me. Worse, I was even creating that belief in them, and I'd become the limiting factor in scaling the company.

Now I know, as Liniger learned: part of building the right toy box is removing the *wrong* team members faster. How much more effective would it have been if Woody, Jessie, or Bullseye had removed the toxic influence of Stinky Pete early on in *Toy Story 2*? The movie may not have been as interesting, but it certainly would have been less dramatic.

It is true that perhaps you have someone who is the right fit, just in the wrong seat, and in other cases some employees just need some coaching or assistance to overcome temporary obstacles. Yet, for those who've hit their ceiling of possibility, and they can no longer grow with you, the most compassionate action is to release them back into the marketplace.

I get it—most entrepreneurs I've met genuinely care for their people. Over time, they grow personally attached to those employees as if they were extended family members.

But in reality, you're born into a family, and they will always be your family. You're "stuck" with them, and your loyalty to them is innate and unquestionable. Many organizations act and feel this way toward their staff members, extending loyalty based on time and tenure. As long as both the employee and the organization are growing and creating value, the relationship works. However, when that's no longer the case, continuing the relationship is harmful for both.

THE RIGHT PLAYERS PUSH EACH OTHER

The idea that a company is not a family sounds harsh, but think of it in terms of winning a championship in sports. We accept that the coach should be entirely focused on building a championship-winning team. There is no better example than Netflix's *The Last Dance*, the documentary about Michael Jordan's last season with the Chicago Bulls. Both Phil Jackson and Jordan were obsessive about not just winning, but creating a dynasty team. Jordan held each of his teammates accountable to perform and if not, he would verbally accost them, and at one point he even got into a fistfight with Steve Kerr!

Of course I'm not endorsing physical force as a way to try and inspire your fellow team members. However, you should look at your company's vision and mission as sacred and pursue them with all the passion and drive possible. Achieving them will only be possible by curating and empowering the right team.

If done right it will actually raise the output performance of the other players. Most know that Usain Bolt won the 100-meter dash during the 2012 Olympic games, but few stop to consider the results of the other athletes competing. Prior to the Games, the record for the 100m was 9.84 seconds. When Usain won, he ran the race in a staggering 9.63 seconds! Equally as impressive, Yohan Blake came in second place and ran it in 9.75 seconds and the third-place finisher, Justin Gatlin, ran it in 9.79. Incredibly, all three men beat the previous Olympic record!

High performance is contagious. If you want to run faster, run with *faster people.*

THE WRONG PLAYERS
TEAR EVERYONE DOWN

The converse is also true, and tolerating poor performers and bad cultural fits is a greater risk to the enterprise.

William Felps, a professor at UNSW in Sydney, studied the effect of poor performers by placing an actor, Nick, on teams of undergraduate students who were working on a project. Nick was instructed to be a deliberate saboteur and while working with the team to exhibit bad behavior.

When Nick was on the team the performance was dragged down by 30 to 40 percent. Astonishingly, the others on the team usually emulated Nick's bad behavior. That's the subversive effect of one bad apple.[26]

In business, you are fighting for your life! It is both figuratively and literally true because your competitors are trying to do anything to run you into the ground. More importantly, your most precious asset is your time.

---

26 Ira Glass and Will Felps, "370: Ruining It for the Rest of Us," *This American Life*, Chicago Public Radio, December 19, 2008, https://www.thisamericanlife.org/370/transcript.

Your company and the people who make it up are all a representation and manifestation of how you have invested that time. Give yourself the best chance of success by surrounding yourself with team members who act as engines (not anchors) and whose talents you can leverage to achieve your vision and mission.

THE 1:3:1 RULE

> *"Plans fail for lack of counsel, but with many*
> *advisers they succeed."*
> —PROVERBS 15:22 (NLT)

There is something that often happens in scaling companies, when, not addressed early on, becomes the limiting factor for the business. I call it the Wizard of Oz syndrome, where the founder becomes the all-knowing center of information as well as the supreme decision-maker for the entire organization. Initially, this may feel empowering and rewarding but as the company grows, it becomes a debilitating and unscalable trap.

Escaping this trap is a two-part process. The first step is to ensure we hire the right people. Secondly, we need to ensure that we empower these people to make good decisions.

At Tech 4 Kids, I had spent too much of my time falsely feeling important by being the chief problem solver. Finally I realized that I was not scalable. Instead, I decided I needed to surround myself with people who were clearly smarter than me in their respective areas of expertise.

I went on a mission to find leaders to fill the roles in operations, finance, product development, sales, and marketing. When I looked at the compensation for these roles, and some of the talent I wanted, I realized that I needed to pay them more than what I was paying *myself*. At first this did not feel right, as I was the one working sixteen-hour days and taking all the risk.

I am sure you have heard the definition of insanity is to continue doing the same thing and expecting different results. If I wanted things to change, I needed to make some changes. So, I took a leap of faith and hired top performers in each of these roles, in many cases paying them more than I paid myself.

Then, I worked with my coach to develop a specific tactic to empower them, called the 1:3:1 Rule. The idea is simple. If someone has a problem, they aren't allowed to present that problem until they have first come up with three possible solutions and after carefully considering them to make one recommendation.

1:3:1 Rule

When you come to your leader with an issue or problem you can't solve, you must:

1. Define one problem.

2. Offer three possible solutions.

3. Recommend one of those solutions.

Your goal is to go from being the author to becoming an editor. You want to encourage and activate the creative problem solving skills of your team. With that said, you always reserve the right to be the editor and review their initial idea and find ways to improve on it.

Fast forward eighteen months, the bold decision to hire top talent and to empower them with strategic decision-making skills turned out to be transformative for the business. By leveraging their competencies and expertise, I was able to buy back some of my time, and I no longer had the pressure of trying to be the Wizard. In our leadership meetings, I was clearly no longer the smartest person in the room, as I'd hired people that were not only terrific cultural fits but were much more competent and capable in their respective disciplines. While I may not have paid myself the highest salary, the collective efforts of this high-performing team were now creating incredible value in the business, resulting in exponential growth to the company's profits. As I was the largest shareholder, my equity was growing, and knowing this made me feel pretty smart.

GOODBYE TO ANDY'S ROOM

A successful enterprise comes down to the right arrangement of people who are focused on the same outcome, have the right attitude, and bring their diverse worldviews and skill sets to the table. As the CEO and leader of the enterprise, you need to set the vision and then your most vital role is to find the talent, inspiring, equipping and empowering them.

One valuable strategy for identifying and recruiting top performers is to leverage their networks. As the saying goes, "birds of a feather flock together," so it's likely that high achievers associate with others who share their level of excellence. To harness the power of these networks, consider empowering your current leaders to help expand your organization by actively seeking out and attracting other talented individuals they know. You can incentivize this behavior by offering a finder's fee. This approach can ultimately save you significant costs compared to using agencies or hiring human resources personnel to sift through countless resumes. Most importantly, it will help ensure that you have the right people in place to drive your organization's success well into the future.

As you fill your toy box with team members of high character who are unified around a common mission, you may notice something: you start to gain momentum; and that's exactly what we'll talk about in the next chapter.

> *"If you could get all the people in an organization*
> *rowing in the same direction, you could dominate*
> *any industry, in any market, against any*
> *competition, at any time."*
>
> —PATRICK LENCIONI

CHAPTER 7

NEVER WASTE HULA-HOOP MOMENTUM

"The flywheel, when properly conceived and executed, creates both continuity and change. On the one hand, you need to stay with a flywheel long enough to get its full compounding effect. On the other hand, to keep the flywheel spinning, you need to continually renew, and improve each and every component."

—JIM COLLINS

The advent of what has since become known as the Hula Hoop, can be traced back as far as 1000 BC. The simple ring was originally made from vines, and eventually molded out of plastic. Over the years it has had various resurgences in popularity, but none quite so insane as the Hula-Hoop craze from the 1950s.

In 1958 Wham-O launched the first branded Hula-Hoop, borrowing the idea from an Australian company. It was an instant hit and became an iconic brand due to the memorable alliteration of the name that was inspired by dancing in the Hawaiian islands.

Around the world, children and adults flocked to join this international craze, which garnered attention and even created some controversy due to the provocative movements resulting from the "hip gyrations" required to play.

According to Tim Walsh of *Timeless Toys,* the craze was one of the fastest short-lived fads in toy history.[27] Wham-O sold nearly one hundred million units of the Hula Hoop in the first twelve months, leading to plenty of knock-offs and imitations. As many toy fads have experienced, there was a sudden drop off in sales however the Hula-Hoop frenzy never died completely. Eventually, Wham-O would reintroduce hoops with a number of innovations, including decorative swirls and ball bearings to help maintain momentum. Each new iteration would temporarily boost sales, but they never again reached the volume levels of the initial '50s launch.

MASH'EMS MOMENTUM

Many of the best ideas come from our curiosity and then our willingness to explore, build, learn and iterate. That's exactly how Tech 4 Kids discovered

---

27 Tim Walsh, *Timeless Toys: Classic Toys and the Playmakers Who Created Them* (Kansas City, MO: Andrews McMeel Publishing, 2005).

Mash'ems, a soft and squishy water-filled collectible featuring thousands of licensed characters.

In 2010, just a couple years after the inception of Tech 4 Kids, I was sitting in our Hong Kong office with Kyle. We had booked some time for one of our "blue sky" sessions where we would brainstorm new product ideas. The toy business is driven by constantly developing new and fresh innovation, and during this session we were pushing ourselves to imagine new possibilities for our product development road map.

It was both the proverbial best of times and worst of times. The worst of times because we were just coming out of the great recession; markets were still very uncertain, and retailers were being very conservative about their purchasing decisions. The best of times because most other toy companies were sitting on the sidelines and not investing into new product development, being primarily driven by fear and scarcity. This was a unique opportunity for our company to stand out by investing into new innovation and introducing fresh ideas.

We reviewed a rolling list of ideas and kept tossing them back and forth, weighing out the pros and cons for each. As a new start up we had to be very conscious of how we invested our development dollars, as we had limited resources to work with. From the list we reviewed, no single concept stood out; we seemed stalled in finding our next big idea.

I paused long enough to catch Kyle stretching and squeezing a stress ball. The conversation seemingly drifted from the topic at hand…only to reveal what our subconscious was already leading us towards. We began discussing how squeezing a stress ball gives great satisfaction to the user. We considered that kids had historically enjoyed toys such as Water Wigglers and Stretch Armstrong; toys that you could squish, pull, and deform. We had learned from experience that the most popular toys tend to take simple play ideas that kids love and combine them into a fun and creative concept.

With that in mind we asked the question: what if we could create collectible stress balls for kids that are shaped like popular children's entertainment characters? Unexpectedly, the stress ball that Kyle had been subtly playing with had become a big idea.

We did some research and confirmed that there was nothing like it in the market. We then leveraged our connections with licensors, convincing them to join us in creating this unique "white space" and creating a new category of squishy collectable toys.

Our first iteration of Mash'ems were of Marvel-licensed characters. As a result of limitations with their master toy licensee, Marvel allowed us to only make the product in the shape of the character *heads*. This certainly was not our original vision, but it was a start. To try and make up for the awkward form factor, we developed a hand launcher to be able to catapult the characters. Beyond using Mash'ems as stress balls, kids could flick them at targets.

Unfortunately, the results were lackluster as it turns out squishing superhero heads and flicking them around just wasn't as fun as we'd anticipated. The toy business has very short patience, so typically when you see poor results, you fail fast and "kill" a project quickly. That seemed to be the fate of Mash'ems, chalking it up as just another failed experiment. That is when an unexpected and incredibly *lucky* turn of events came our way. (We will discuss the importance of luck in a future chapter.)

In December 2009, a small, obscure Finnish company called Rovio launched an app game that would soon become the cultural phenomenon known as Angry Birds. The entire Angry Birds brand was built upon round-shaped birds, launched from a giant slingshot, flying through the air to smash structures in an attempt to take out the pesky pigs. Furthermore, when they landed, they would often playfully bounce around and in the user's mind they appeared to be soft and squishy. It couldn't have been a more perfect fit for how we had originally designed both the Mash'ems and the launcher.

We connected with the Rovio licensing agent and put together a proposal for creating a line of products. They loved the idea, and in very short order we were welcomed as one of the original Angry Birds licensing partners.

This move proved to be a game changer!

The app game had become huge globally and fans had been eagerly awaiting Angry Birds merchandise. We were one of the first companies to bring Angry Birds products to market and with it a floodgate of opportunities opened up. Retailers from around the world came knocking on our door and in a short period of time we were able to sell tens of millions of Mash'ems. As the Angry Birds app kept evolving and coming up with new versions of the game, we continued to develop new products in lockstep. Children were thrilled to be given the opportunity to bring a physical play experience with these adorable digital characters.

That is when we decided to double down on product development, taking advantage of the moment to make Mash'ems based on other characters. From the Marvel experience we already knew that the heads of characters did not have appeal. So we created a new design that added a short, stocky body to an oversized head. This became the iconic new form factor that all Mash'ems became known for.

We successfully secured a number of additional license agreements and launched Mash'ems characters based on: Smurfs, Power Rangers, WWE, TMNT, and DC Heroes. We even went back to Marvel and with the momentum we had we were able to convince them to let us make Mash'ems, based on the new look.

With the success of Angry Birds Mash'ems and a slew of new licensed characters in our portfolio, we felt confident we now had the necessary ingredients to turn Mash'ems into an evergreen property. It didn't happen…

the new versions hit the market and the resulting sales were disappointing. We had "stars in our eyes" and did not see the obvious truth that so much of the initial Mash'ems success was directly linked to the Angry Birds game. To make matters worse, the Angry Birds craze had started to slow and as a result our company's overall sales started to soften.

We were dumbfounded, as we were confident we had all of the right ingredients for building a new category of squishy collectables. We knew from our experience that once kids discovered Mash'ems that they loved playing with them. The problem was our ability to get the message out to the masses and we had become too reliant on a single licensed property to help fuel demand. Mash'ems were now at risk of becoming a fast fading fad and if we wanted to preserve the potential, we had to move quickly to find the right medium to market the message.

The toy business has historically relied on large TV advertising budgets in order to reach your target audience. These tend to be very expensive and are more of a shotgun approach at trying to reach your target demographics. At that time our company was too small to make the investment needed to successfully market a product through a TV campaign. We were looking for other options, and we became fascinated with the possibilities of YouTube. We noticed that there was a popular trend emerging of "unboxing videos," where people would post a video of themselves opening up new products. To our amazement, the number of views that these unboxing videos were getting was massive, and we soon learned that toy unboxings were among the most popular types of videos.

We saw an untapped opportunity as YouTube influencers had not yet become prolific. A key inflection point in our marketing strategy is when we found Evan and his father, Jared, the creators of EvansTubeHD. They were huge fans of Angry Birds and produced really clever videos about the game that had garnered millions of views. We contacted them and they agreed that they would produce some creative videos if we were to supply them with free products. Not only did they do an incredible job of creating a unique unboxing experience, but they added in some fantastic storytelling using the product. Their first video of Angry Bird Mash'ems received over twenty million views! They too were amazed with the success, so we sent them more products and they produced a second and third video which both went on to achieve over thirty million views each! Kids loved watching the clever Mash'ems storytelling; as Evan would squish, pull, stretch, and distort the toys. It was a win-win; we were providing the props for them to create unique content, and they were creating fun videos and getting paid based on the number of views.

We set up a marketing team focused on executing on our newly found YouTube strategy and started to target and send out packages to other influencers. We also started to send out samples of other Mash'ems characters. These influencers also created unboxing videos and to our amazement they too would generate millions of views. Within weeks of the YouTube unboxing videos airing we started to notice a stark increase in Mash'ems sales. It was incredible to see that as the view counters climbed, so did the demand for the product.

There were other advantages to being on the YouTube platform. We monitored the comments in the video chats and were able to engage directly with fans. We were able to let people know where to buy the product, learn what their favorite features were and get real-time feedback on what characters we should next introduce.

It was an incredible and novel marketing "hack." Leveraging the proliferation of UGC unboxing videos allowed us to massively extend our audience reach for virtually free. We were receiving the benefit of hundreds of millions of impressions that if we had tried to pay for using traditional media, would have cost us tens of millions of dollars. A massive flywheel was created that drove both the squishy collectable category and Mash'ems brand awareness, increasing overall demand.

We would go on to sell over half a *billion* Mash'ems worldwide and in 2017, the Mash'ems brand was honored to receive the Novelty Toy of the Year Award by the British Toy & Hobby Association.

Mash'ems are still available today and the brand has achieved something very uncommon in the toy business—longevity. Today Mash'ems is part of Basic Fun's portfolio of products which offer an expanded collection including: Care Bears, My Little Pony, Toy Story, Harry Potter, and other popular characters. (You can see more at www.basicfun.com).

Certainly there was some luck involved (there always is) but thankfully, we never gave up and stopped believing in our simple squishy idea. The success of Mash'ems was transformative for the business and became a key contributor to our ability to scale and ultimately the future exit of Tech 4 Kids.

"A river cuts through rock, not because of its power,
but because of its persistence."
—JIM WATKINS

GET THE HOOP GOING

The first time you try to spin a Hula-Hoop across your waistline, you're likely to walk away thinking, "This is much harder than it looks!"

The first several attempts at getting the movement just right are quite frustrating. It's easy to spin too slow or too fast and the rhythm required can seem difficult to master. However, if you continue to practice (perhaps with a little help from a YouTube instructional video) then somewhere along the line, you're bound to swivel your hips in such a way to keep the ring spinning. It is mesmerizing to see the hoop go round and round your waist, reaching a synchronicity that becomes second nature and is almost hypnotic! Once the ring is spinning, it's easy to keep it going.

With practice, you can even add multiple hoops to your routine and have them independently spinning around your waist or other limbs. In 2005, Marawa Ibrahim of Australia broke the Hula-Hoop record for the fourth time, spinning two hundred hoops simultaneously!

I think the simplicity of the Hula-Hoop is what makes it so compelling. On one hand, it's just a giant simple ring, but when in motion it defies gravity and creates a rhythmic wave that magically orbits your body. Like Mash'ems, the product's simplicity is what creates the foundation for its ability to capture our imagination.

KEEP IT SPINNING

Just as with the frustrations of learning to spin a Hula-Hoop, within every business opportunity there's a similar pattern; in the beginning, it takes time and effort to get an opportunity going. Often it does not work, so you need to iterate, pivot, and adjust to find the right rhythm. Once you do, a potential huge payoff ensues; you will have achieved momentum and it takes less energy to then maintain it. You can now slow down and add just the right amount of energy to keep the hoop spinning. You can even leverage your momentum and introduce other hoops to get them going.

Business works the same; once you have momentum, it is easier to leverage your success to introduce new products. Once you have established trust, your customers are more likely to support you as you introduce additional products or enter into new categories. This becomes a key ingredient for your ability to grow sales and scale your business.

Momentum in the marketplace—just like the momentum in a Hula-Hoop—is difficult to capture, and often, like in the fad-driven toy business, easy to lose. The trick is that it's so much easier to stabilize an already-spinning hoop than it is to get a static Hula Hoop up and spinning.

Looking back, it would have been easy to discard our original idea after the failed launch of the Marvel version of Mash'ems. Even after the initial success with Angry Birds, the trend slowed and we started to see a "wobble." We could have called it quits and moved onto something else, having to then muster up from scratch the precious energy required to get a new hoop spinning. However, we were convinced we had something special and so we kept trying, as we believed that the squishy play pattern was compelling. We creatively iterated in our product development and in parallel sought out a clever marketing solution, leading us to develop symbiotic relationships with YouTube influencers. That proved to make all the difference, re-energizing our wobbly hoop and ultimately having it spin faster than before.

Change management leader Price Pritchett once stated:

> Everything looks like a failure in the middle. You can't bake a cake without getting the kitchen messy. Halfway through surgery it looks like there's been a murder in the operating room. If you send a rocket to the moon, about ninety percent of the time it's off course—it 'fails' its way to the moon by continually making mistakes and correcting them.[28]

For entrepreneurs, it's that "messy middle" that can really get us. After spending an immense amount of time on a product or service, we sometimes experience an initial "pop" of success. Then, when the energy starts to wane, we are prone to just quickly move on. One of the key lessons I learned is that in order to reap the full rewards of your efforts, you need to add in a bit of well-timed energy to keep the idea fresh and momentum going.

---

28 Price Pritchett, *You 2: A High-Velocity Formula for Multiplying Your Personal Effectiveness in Quantum Leaps* (Dallas: Pritchett LP, 2012).

One of my realizations for myself is that I am a good starter and/or finisher; however, I struggle in the middle. I tend to thrive off of the endorphins and energy that is found when something is first being launched or brought to a conclusion. I like the feeling of doing something that is new, big and exciting, but this can lead to a constant state of frenetic movements. It's similar to only gathering the gold scattered on the surface, without ever pausing to realize that by digging a mine, I could extract even more value out of a property. Working in the messy middle is a difficult discipline to master.

Consider a Coke bottle: If you place your finger on top, shake and release, you'll be rewarded with an explosion of foam. Clouds of sugary goodness will energetically spill out from the top and run down the sides of the bottle. Now that the initial release of energy has subsided, it would be easy to simply reach for another bottle to shake it for the same explosive outcome. However, the original bottle still has an immense amount of untapped cola in it, and we now need to implement another strategy to extract it with a straw (compostable, please). We have already put in the bulk of the effort—instead of moving on, we just need to be smart to ensure we get everything out of the opportunity.

In business, a similar gush of energy occurs when a product or idea is initially well received, and most entrepreneurs *live* for that moment. They want to see their ideas explode into the market. Then, either because the initial excitement is gone or because the category becomes more difficult to harvest, they leave and move onto something else.

FIND YOUR RHYTHM WITH 1,000 FANS

Finding the rhythm of your Hula-Hoop can be a daunting exercise. Most great business ideas start as a contrarian insight and very few launch with the right iteration. Typically, a viable business concept needs further refinement before it finds product market fit.

James Dyson is worth over $5 billion today, but it took him fifteen years and over five thousand prototypes to perfect the Dyson vacuum. How many of us have the stomach to innovate in a category like home vacuum cleaners, which is considered dull and commoditized? Talk about persistence and staying power!

Many entrepreneurs never find their rhythm, because after they face initial difficulty they give up. They move on too soon, never realizing that they left their great idea as a premature still-born. So, how do you ensure you don't give up on your great idea?

Kevin Kelley produced a now-famous essay called "1,000 True Fans," where he suggests that a relatively small number of true fans can help you build, iterate, adjust, and refine your concept.[29] Ideally, this original group will believe in your product enough to stick with you, become emotionally invested in your success, and will start evangelizing on your behalf.

We found our first 1000 fans for Mash'ems on YouTube. Once they were identified we leaned on them for feedback, gleaning the best ideas in order to allow the brand to evolve. These people can be your first and best feedback loop and your informal board of directors. They test marketability, add or subtract features, and help shape your concept into something that could eventually appeal to the masses.

NEXT STEP: CROSS THE CHASM

Geoffrey Moore refers to these "1000 true fans" as your innovators, which in time with care and fostering lead to the early adopters. In his book *Crossing the Chasm,* Moore explains the challenge for most new ideas is to gain

---

29 Kevin Kelly, "1,000 True Fans," *The Technium* (blog), March 4, 2008, https://kk.org/thetechnium/1000-true-fans/.

sufficient traction to appeal to a larger consumer group called the early majority.[30]

Most ideas never make it as most entrepreneurs, retailers, and VCs lack the patience and diligence required. The greatest factor influencing an idea's success comes down to the right timing, which I also believe is the true definition of luck.

Timing is everything and I firmly believe that the right idea at the wrong time is still the wrong idea. Occasionally, it could be decades before the marketplace shifts so that you can move your product from an obscure, off-beat group of early adopters to be able to cross the chasm and appeal to the early majority. This requires diligence and patience.

Imagine being Catherine Hettinger, who in 1993 filed a patent for a spinning fidget toy that was shortly thereafter rejected by Hasbro when submitted as a toy concept. The patent expired in 2005 and faded into nothingness. Then in 2015 a version of the fidget spinner was re-created followed by Antsy labs launching the fidget cube in 2016. The timing was perfect as there was a growing global awareness of mental health issues such as ADHD and the new fidget toy category exploded in popularity.

In 2016 we decided to jump into this product category using our strength in licensing relationships. With that we created and launched the very first line of licensed fidget toys with Star Wars, Minions, and Power Rangers. By 2017 fidget toys in all various shapes and sizes had become the hottest selling products in toys around the world and from what we know, Hettinger never benefited from this phenomenon. It was the right idea, just introduced at the wrong time, making it the wrong idea for the moment.

I had a similar situation in 2005 with the creation and launch of a product line called Atomic Blox. It was an innovative light-up construction system but our timing was off and we didn't have the patience to nurture

30 Geoffrey A. Moore, *Crossing the Chasm: Marketing and Selling Disruptive Products to Mainstream Customers* (New York: HarperBusiness, 1991).

our early adopters. We initially garnered critical acclaim during our 2004 launch, attracting a group of excited toy enthusiasts who were thrilled about our idea. They were compelling blocks that snapped together and would light up as a result of completing a successful circuit.

Developing a safe electrical light-up construction toy was difficult, re-quiring more R&D than most of the other playthings in our portfolio. We started shipping the product in fall of 2005, and after some initial success with specialty retailers, we tried to move into the mass market. Unfortu-nately, sales never materialized beyond a niche group of innovators and early adopters. So, after three years and hundreds of thousands of dollars invested, we killed the project and moved on. Yet, if we'd paid close atten-tion to the macro trends of the marketplace, we might have adjusted our strategy to have more patience.

When you think of how prolific LEGO is, it is hard to believe that in 2004 the company almost went bankrupt. It is reported that in the early 2000s LEGO had become distracted from their core business and started investing into other initiatives. These included theme parks and an attempt to launch an action figure line accompanied with a TV series that ulti-mately failed. With all of the additional investments, the company had become $800 million in debt and by the end of 2004, reported a loss of $225 million.

It was at this low point that the family-owned business decided to make a change in leadership and brought in Jørgen Vig Knudstorp. Jørgen had worked as a McKinsey consultant for LEGO and was named the CEO in 2004. He made some drastic changes to refocus the company back to its core competencies and started to move the Danish toy maker onto a firmer financial footing. LEGO reoriented back toward growing the construction category versus trying to extend the brand into new speculative opportuni-ties. As a result of LEGO's refocus, building sets would become one of the largest and most durable evergreen categories of toys. This transformation would lead to LEGO being recognized as a top ten global brand (we will learn more about the Lego Legacy in a future chapter).

LEGO's success also meant that with the growth of the construction product category, there would be opportunities to open up subcategories such as magnetic or light-up construction toys. We did not have these insights nor the patience to continue to support Atomic Blox beyond the initial product launch. Another company did however, and they picked up where we left off. They took our idea and created a brand called Laser Pegs, dubbing their blocks as "the original light-up building bricks." They weren't the first in fact, but they were the intelligent followers who timed their launch just right.

If we had had the patience to work alongside our one thousand true fans, we could have been in a position to take advantage of the moment when the construction category was in expansion. Crossing the chasm to reach the early majority of customers requires having the patience to foster the relationships with your early adopters, while also refining the value of the product. All of this must happen within the context of exceptional timing.

"MASH'EMS" ULTIMATE QUESTION

Of course, there is a time to let a project go. The road to business success is littered with heartache from founders who believe that entrepreneurs should never, ever quit.

I don't believe that—there *is* a time to quit, to bow out and to save your dry powder and move onto your next idea.

Knowing when you should persist and iterate or when you should kill a project is a finessed skill that doesn't come without experience. I don't have a perfect scientific answer to help differentiate between the two, but there is a guiding question you can use to find your way. If you have a project that is struggling to find its market fit, ask yourself this question:

"Based on what we know today, does this product/service have the potential to reach mass-market appeal?"

follow this up with

"What would need to be true for this to happen?"

The second question is the most important as it helps you lay out the roadmap for how you can build towards a successful outcome.

If, upon reviewing your answers, you feel that your idea has the potential to appeal to a mass market, but the timing may not be quite right, then it may make sense to stay the course. While waiting for the timing to line up, you can continue to refine your value proposition by nurturing your dedicated group of early supporters, who can help prepare your product or service for a larger audience in the future. However, this approach requires securing the necessary financial resources to provide the runway you need.

The other option is that you learn from the challenges of your initial product launch and from these insights there is merit in considering making a pivot. What many people fail to recognize is that successful pivots have been a vital part of the evolution for many well-known startups. In the spirit of Eric Reis's build, measure, learn, founders are constantly coming up with a thesis, testing it out, and then analyzing the results to decide whether to persist or pivot. Pivots are not about quitting but rather about using your learnings to take a different direction. As Will Rogers stated, "If you find yourself in a hole, the first thing to do is stop digging."

One of my personal favorites is the story of Nintendo. Nintendo began as a playing card company in the 1880s. The demand waned in the mid-twentieth century and they pivoted into a taxi company and then instant rice makers—both failed. They chased the appliance market in the '60s by making vacuum cleaners. They pivoted again to become an hourly hotel chain, which eventually was wound down. Finally, in the '70s, they negotiated the rights to distribute the first video game console. From that, they introduced the now-famous pudgy Italian red plumber and his skinny green brother.

Netflix started out as a mail-order DVD service and then progressed to downloadable films, then to streaming films, and now 85 percent of their new spending is going to original TV shows, films, and other productions. That is more than any other studio (including HBO, Disney, and Warner Brothers).

Slack was started as Glitch, a video game platform. They developed a communication channel while working on the game that proved more valuable than the game itself.

IBM was the big blue giant for what seemed like an eternity. Then the "IBM-compatible" personal computers were offered for a fraction of IBM's prices, so they could no longer compete. The blue giant was brought to its knees and it seemed their fate was sealed following other former giants like Kodak and Blockbuster. Then they made perhaps one of the most difficult pivots as they literally tossed their hardware legacy and committed fully into IT consulting services. It was a stroke of genius and today they are worth over $100 billion.[31]

YouTube started out as a video dating site, launched in 2005 on Valentine's Day with the unofficial slogan "Tune In, Hook Up." After five days no one uploaded a single video, so the founders pivoted and the rest is history. Without them, I would not have had the marketing tool I needed to evangelize the world about Mash'ems and we might never have discovered Justin Beiber.

These are all examples of fantastic pivots that resulted in creating iconic enterprises. Many times, a small pivot is all the difference you need to achieve product market fit. If, however, you are facing headwinds and your

---

31 "IBM Market Cap 2010-2022 | IBM," Macrotrends, accessed October 20, 2022, https://www.macrotrends.net/stocks/charts/IBM/ibm/market-cap.

gut tells you that your concept will never have large-scale appeal, perhaps it's time to call it quits and save your resources for better opportunities ahead.

W.C. Fields summed it up well: "If at first, you don't succeed, try, try again. Then quit. There's no use being a damn fool about it."

PRIMING THE PUMP

In his book *The Compound Effect*, Darren Hardy uses the example of a pump to discuss the importance of momentum.[32] Many older campgrounds have old water pumps with pumping handles for extracting the water from the ground.

Before any water appears, you must first "prime" the pump, which requires an immense amount of effort, without any apparent results. However, once water does begin to flow, pumping becomes much easier. To keep the water flowing, you only need to exert a fraction of the original energy required.

But imagine if you quit halfway through priming the pump. All the effort would have been for naught and you'd never find water at all.

Similarly, if you stopped pumping after the water started flowing, it would flow for just a moment but then suddenly dry up, losing the momentum you'd worked so hard for.

When a rocket is launching from Earth, 90 percent of its fuel is burned up just to get into orbit. Likewise, you should expect that as a founder, the majority of your energy will be invested heavily into the beginning of your venture. It is the price you need to pay to start something great and what is required in order to build momentum.

---

32 Darren Hardy, *The Compound Effect: Jumpstart Your Income, Your Life, Your Success* (New York: Vanguard Press, 2010).

Too many entrepreneurs start well, but then do not see the results hoped for, only to fizzle out and apply their energy elsewhere. They bounce from idea to idea, never putting in enough effort to get the idea off the ground. If they do get it off the ground, they often take the initial burst of business, then move on, again losing the momentum and leaving much of the value behind.

Marketplace momentum is incredibly difficult to achieve; once you do experience it, don't rush to that next great idea without tapping all the value you can out of your current endeavor. If you achieve momentum, prevent the wobbles by continuing to iterate, pivot when needed, and kill it only when absolutely necessary.

It's a lot like a Hula-Hoop: often hard to synchronize your motions to get it moving, but once you do, the plan is pretty simple…keep it spinning.

"People with momentum can get so much done. Momentum is easy to lose and almost impossible to fake."
—SHAUN KING

CHAPTER 8

STAY PLIABLE
AS PLAY-DOH

"If we don't trust one another, then we aren't going
to engage in open, constructive, ideological conflict.
And we'll just continue to preserve a sense of
artificial harmony."

—PATRICK LENCIONI

The creativity that Play-Doh can inspire is one of the greatest of any product to emerge from the toy business. Children can mold and shape it into anything their minds can imagine. An early advertisement for Play-Doh featured a young boy who'd made what appeared to be an elephant. The ad quoted the child saying that he'd made a dog whose nose had grown so long because he lied so much.

With a touch of imagination, a mound of Play-Doh turns into buildings and then moments later becomes a tree or an animal. It's no wonder the product has sold billions of cans and in1998 was inducted into the National Toy Hall of Fame. The origins of this magical ever-shape-shifting compound are as fascinating as the product itself.

Originally, the product was introduced as a wallpaper cleaner by the Kutol Products Company. It was marketed as a safe, nontoxic cleaning agent that could be used to remove coal buildup. After World War II, the market started to shift away from coal toward petroleum energy and the soot-buildup problem was becoming less of an issue. Demand for the cleaner plummeted and Kutol's revenue trajectory went into a steep decline.

Joseph McVicker was hired into the family business to try and save it. He had a sister-in-law named Kay, who was a school teacher. After several discussions between the two, a new purpose for the nontoxic wallpaper cleaner was born: it would become a toy.

In 1956 McVickers launched a new product, called Play-Doh, and it became a smash hit, selling millions of cans. Shortly thereafter the rights were sold to General Mills and eventually acquired by Hasbro.

The product has since sold over three billion cans globally. Luckily, the co-creators of this wonderous product were just as pliable about pivoting their business model as the product itself.

ONE THING ON HIS AGENDA

"The ultimate measure of a person is not where they stand in moments of convenience but where they stand in moments of challenge, moments of great crisis and controversy."
—MARTIN LUTHER KING JR.

It had been ninety days since we had officially consummated the merger of Tech 4 Kids with The Bridge Direct to form Basic Fun. Tech 4 Kids was having a great run, experiencing significant momentum as a result of the success of Mash'ems and growth was being perpetuated by several new product launches.

On paper, a merger with The Bridge Direct made total sense: we had similar-sized businesses, we had complementary product lines, and the consolidation of our operations would eliminate redundancy, allowing us to grow faster and more efficiently. Once we were merged, we would have formed one of the largest toy companies in North America, and we believed this would give us an advantage in the market.

I had started my original journey in the toy business almost by accident. After several years working to overcome many challenges, it had become my passion. During my career, there had been several tumultuous moments that had forced pivots and restarts. Now, twenty-three years later, I had not only survived as an entrepreneur, but the company I was leading was now thriving.

Merging Tech 4 Kids into becoming part of this new "bigger and better" business model was going to require a lot of change in how we had previously operated. Initially I was hesitant but I saw it as part of a necessary evolution for the business, and I was determined to apply my full agency towards the new opportunity. In reflection I now realize that I had rushed into this partnership somewhat haphazardly.

After a few bankruptcies in the toy business, I was ready for some financial stability. I had my two kids, and an overly patient wife who deserved some security. Kelly was not only one of the co-founders of Tech 4 Kids but also my faithful life partner and my chief business strategist. From humble beginnings we'd bootstrapped, creatively problem solved, climbed the ranks, fallen, dusted ourselves off, and then willingly started all over again. Any profits we had generated in the company were being reinvested into supporting its ongoing growth. This was all on the premise that someday in the future it would pay off and we would eventually reap the financial rewards. The merger not only made scaling and operational sense but it would also provide us an opportunity for some liquidity.

The Bridge Direct was founded and led by Jay Foreman. Jay is a larger-than-life personality, well known and highly regarded in the toy industry. Over a few decades, he was successful in launching several iconic products and brands. I'd gotten to know Jay through industry events and more than once we'd contemplated the idea of how we might work together. I was drawn to his gregarious and magnetic personality and I respected what he had accomplished during his storied career. As ten years my senior, I believed that by working together, I would benefit by learning from his experience and connections. With that in mind, I helped draft a plan to merge Tech 4 Kids with The Bridge Direct, linking arms with Jay in creating Basic Fun; supposedly a bigger and better opportunity.

We were well into the process of putting the companies together, when friction started to bubble beneath the surface. I recognized almost immediately that the cultures of our two companies were not meshing. We had different philosophies on how to manage and lead teams, as well as what the hierarchy for decision-making looked like. Our leadership styles were not compatible, creating tension which started to weigh on the whole enterprise.

Soon, the relationship between Jay and I became nothing more than civil grinning and nodding, giving the false impression everything was OK. The truth was that we had created a dangerous artificial harmony between us that was leading to mistrust and growing animosity.

Every year I go on a retreat with my coach and it is an opportunity for me to sharpen the saw, reveal blind spots and get clear on my intentions for personal growth. When I explained to him the dynamic of what was happening, he instantly recognized the dysfunction that I had co-created. He called me out for not having the courage to speak openly and candidly with my future business partner. He challenged my fears and apprehensions, asserting that I would never be able to build a durable business unless I was willing to have authentic conversations with all the leaders, and most especially, my co-founder.

He was right and I knew that in order for our business partnership to be functional and healthy, I needed to take action to clear the office air. I also knew that we were being watched by our team, who could easily sniff out the disharmony and dissension. With our behavior, Jay and I were setting a bad precedent for the whole organization, and it was creating unhealthy factions.

I returned back to the office and sensed the brewing tension. I couldn't take the disingenuous smiles and small talk anymore and finally worked up the courage to confront Jay. I booked a one-on-one meeting with him, bracing myself to delve into difficult conversations and to lay out everything from my point of view while expressing my feelings and concerns. I attacked the problem and not the person and in doing so, acknowledged my own role in creating the dysfunction. I explained that while we had merged our companies, I knew our philosophies were not aligned and I admitted that I had been afraid to "rock the boat." I explained that I was willing to turn over a new leaf and was committed to doing the work necessary to try and make the relationship work.

After listening, Jay thanked me for sharing my thoughts and then explained that while he was committed to making the newly merged company work, he was unsure if our relationship could ultimately work. While his response was somewhat unnerving, it felt good to have had the difficult conversation. In the process I had believed we'd come to a new understanding and it was my hope that we had reached a fresh starting point. At the very least, a new precedent of candor had been set, and I was certain we would continue to engage in this way going forward.

The following week, we both flew to Hong Kong to attend a trade event. On the surface, our dialogue was friendly and cordial; we were collaborating well. The tough conversation appeared to have been an important turning point in our relationship. Ten days later, we ended the trip on a high note, by co-hosting a celebratory dinner with our team and playing pong together late into the evening.

The following morning I left Hong Kong, and after arriving back in Toronto, I went to a recurring monthly meeting with our chairman Justin. Our newly merged business was now about 90 days old and Justin had been very aware of the ongoing relationship challenges between myself and Jay. What he was not aware of, is that I believed that significant progress had been made, and I was excited to update him on what I thought had been a meaningful breakthrough.

We sat down to eat breakfast, and I laid out my agenda and then turned to him asking if there was anything he wanted to add. That's when he looked me in the eyes and with a slight smirk uttered the words:

"I only have one thing on my agenda. Today will be your *last day* working for Basic Fun."

My initial reaction was one of shock, followed by sadness and quickly turning into anger. Justin was my long-standing business partner and someone who had mentored me. He had earned my trust by investing his resources to bail out Dynatech and when that failed, he helped put together the seed capital to launch Tech 4 Kids. Justin had believed in me when no one else would, and he had journeyed with me through some very difficult times. Due to his trust in me, I had felt indebted and gave him my unwavering loyalty. Time and time again, he had stepped in the gap when no one else would.

While the gravity of Justin's words started to sink in, I realized that I was having yet another Jerry Maguire moment. I was being fired while sitting in a public restaurant, limiting my ability to truly express my emotions. I sat there in disbelief as he muttered a few more words and then handed me an envelope filled with documents.

I walked out of the restaurant bewildered by what had just transpired and noticed something strange: my phone, which was normally very active, was now dormant. I soon discovered that all my devices were no longer accessible and my remote access to email, messaging services, and cloud storage had been disconnected. Adding insult to injury, I had been physically locked out of my office building. With a few words over breakfast, I was suddenly and unceremoniously fired and completely cut off from the very company I had co-founded!

Throughout my adult life, I had been deeply involved in the toy business, founding several companies that have consistently ranked amongst the fastest growing ventures in the industry. My name had been in magazines and publications, I was a frequent speaker at various organizations, and my business awards were numerous. Sure some mistakes were made, but I was a fighter who had overcome significant challenges and had gone on to build a thriving company.

Despite the journey we had been on together, Justin's actions shouldn't have come as a surprise. Over the years of working with him, I got a closer look at his working style. One word had formed in my mind:

Ruthless.

Justin was an expert in restructuring businesses, and I had witnessed his aggressive nature several times throughout our working relationship. This was especially evident when he was negotiating with creditors, letting go of staff, or negotiating financial terms with banks. Our relationship had been cordial, and I had justified his actions as being necessary in doing restructuring work. I knew he had the ability to be extremely callous, I just never imagined that it would ever be directed towards me.

Mike Tyson is famous for saying that the punch that knocks you out is the one that you don't see coming. I had a false perception that I was insulated from Justin's ruthless style. My naivety had blinded me, and little did I know that I was about to receive a gut punch that would leave me lying on the mat.

I have since come to learn that if someone behaves poorly *for you*, it is just a matter of time before they will direct that same bad behavior *against* you. I should have heeded the advice Maya Angelou offered: "When people show you who they are, you should believe them."

There is an ancient parable about a scorpion and a frog. The story goes that a scorpion asks a frog to carry him over a river. The frog is afraid of being stung, but the scorpion argues that if it did so, both would sink and the scorpion would drown. The frog thinks about it, agrees with the logic, and invites the scorpion to jump on his back. Midway across the river, the scorpion indeed stings the frog, dooming them both. When the frog in desperation inquires "why?" the scorpion responds "that is just what scorpions do." Justin had shown me who he was, and I had falsely believed that I was immune. Instead, I became the target of his sting, and my career in the toy industry was about to come to an abrupt end.

"Every storm is a school. Every trial is a test. Every experience is an education. Every difficulty is for your development."
—RICHARD C. WHITCOMB

TRUST: THE MAGIC INGREDIENT

When Play-Doh starts to dry out, simply by adding some water, it can regain its moldability. Likewise in relationships, trust is that magic ingredient that keeps connections healthy and malleable.

When trust is present, we will allow vulnerability and transparency to exist. This leads to a willingness to engage in conflict, focusing on what is right and not who is right, in an effort to achieve the best outcomes. When trust is absent, we become guarded in how we engage in relationships, and as a result our interactions will be superficial.

The Play-Doh metaphors for human relationships could not be more pertinent: the truest high value within human connections is our ability to love each other and within that context, show vulnerability and candor in our willingness to help each other grow.

During our lifetimes there will be very few relationships that achieve this potential, because trust is fragile, often taking years to build but only seconds to destroy. When we love others, we're making deposits into growing the trust in our relationship. With consistency over time, that trust strengthens and our relationship deepens. We gain greater confidence in speaking truth to one another as we value the relationship.

Tough feedback can be difficult at first, as it's often highlighting a blind spot we were unaware of, or offering a unique point of view that is diametrically opposed to how we think. Either way, we're likely to initially resist. Remember the Courage Flywheel we discussed in chapter four—challenges provide an opportunity for us to apply creativity that in turn builds character, leading to confidence and the curiosity for new discoveries. Tension in relationships is the perfect moment to engage in constructive conflict. *Constructive* means we are looking to build value into the relationship, reinforcing the focus on *what's* right, not *who's* right.

Play-Doh only becomes something interesting or beautiful through force and pressure. We roll it and squeeze it and pound it to form a shape. We use utensils and dies to cut out patterns. We pull and stretch it to smooth out the corners and edges. As we push, pull, and form the clay, it transforms from a lump of colored nothing into a wonderful creation. Only with tension and pressure does true beauty emerge. Likewise, this is the same process with how we will build meaningful relationships.

A well-known verse in Proverbs says, "As iron sharpens iron, so one person sharpens another," reminding us that our most valuable relationships are where meaningful trust is developed and where we will then do the hard work to sharpen each other, in the process helping each other achieve our highest potential.

The difference between humans and Play-Doh is that we have a choice. We can *choose* to avoid the discomfort that comes from healthy conflict and remain a lump of colorful dough. We would be full of potential, but with lack of use, we grow old, stale, and eventually useless. Or we can seek out a few highly valuable and trusting relationships, where we actively engage in healthy conflict, with the intent to help chisel, shape, and mold us into the best and brightest versions of ourselves. If we remain pliable through the process, are open to feedback, and submit to where we need to make the necessary changes, we will emerge as more competent creators, more imaginative minds, and more insightful individuals.

It is important to remember that molding and shaping is difficult work, for both dough and people. From the Play-Doh's perspective, none of it is a fun experience. If the dough could speak, it would surely object: "Ow! Please stop!" But stopping the process would cause the dough to miss out on its real potential. Similarly, healthy conflict in our relationships help mold us into the people we are meant to become. On the other side of temporary pain is always a better version of ourselves and the constructive feedback of others is often the required medicine.

Of course, no one is another's final authority. We are not in a position to judge but rather we are there to help each other in the molding process. The rules of engagement are simple: we are to first ask ourselves the question, "What does love require me to say or do?" and then act accordingly. Secondly, when we are providing feedback to the other party, we should ensure that we *attack the problem* and *not the person*. Too often we get this wrong and start down a path of personal attack, which will only result in creating resentment and mistrust, depriving our relationships of the very thing it needs to remain pliable.

If we're fortunate enough, we'll have a half dozen truly meaningful relationships throughout our lifetime that contribute to the majority of our growth.

The two most important relationships in your life also happen to be those that you should have developed the highest level of trust with: your spouse and your business partners. You must ensure you select these relationships carefully as in both, you will entrust a large portion of your well-being, and that always makes us vulnerable. Be wise in these critical decisions, as if you get it wrong, it will lead to much misery.

TRUST VERSUS ARTIFICIAL HARMONY

If Jay or I had looked past the numbers and paused before diving into our merger, we would have recognized that our leadership philosophies and management styles were incompatible. This would have allowed us to remain colleagues and friends but wiser for coming to the realization that we were just not a good fit to be business partners. Instead I ignored all the signs early on, solely focusing on the financial rewards and not questioning the durability of the new partnership.

The fact of the matter is that business isn't simply numbers; more importantly, the business of business is about *people*. The health of the relationships will ultimately determine the health of the enterprise, and the key ingredient to all meaningful relationships is trust.

Great ideas are only birthed through the labor pains of conflict. Not conflict for the sake of conflict, but rather soliciting diverse points of view to shape an idea from different angles, with the intention of creating the best results.

Where trust does not exist, artificial harmony moves in: people grin, nod, and agree (even if they quietly disagree) simply to not "rock the boat." Artificial harmony is perhaps one of the most insidious sicknesses that can infect any business. It causes parties to pretend everything is OK, when they know, deep down, there are problems.

If you've ever wondered how an awful idea gets approved by a round-table of intelligent executives, you can point to artificial harmony as the culprit. When people won't speak up, they become the proverbial lemmings marching toward the cliff of disaster, and companies have paid billions for making such mistakes. Walt Disney World invested heavily into their supposed state-of-the-art Magic Bands. These wristbands were touted as the future of the theme park industry, supposedly increasing efficiency and affording game-changing, personalized experiences throughout the park. Unfortunately, they never lived up to expectations and the company only discovered the mistake well after the investment was made, with the bands now serving as simple park passes. Disney is tight about the numbers, but many analysts believe the wristband project cost more than $2 billion. By comparison, the first Disney theme park cost $188 million dollars to build, *after* accounting for inflation.[33]

Preventing these sorts of blunders are why companies such as Google have purposely created a culture that invites dissension. They go so far as to *yell* at each other at meetings when they're passionate about a particular project. They openly invite dissension and disagreement as they want to hear all the differing perspectives. They subscribe to the belief that healthy human conflict will help them avoid making billion-dollar mistakes.

* * *

For candor to be effective, it must be given out of love, and it is important to let the other person know how much you care about them. I often ask the question "If I saw something that I thought was holding you back, would you want me to let you know?" This is a way to provide friendly feedback and a word of warning, that if received well, will create a deeper level of trust in the relationship.

Ed Catmull is the co-founder of Pixar, the most celebrated animation studio in recent history, having earned over $14.5 billion at the global box office.[34] They've created some of the most iconic animated franchises, including *Toy Story, Cars*, A Bug's Life, and *Nemo*. In his book *Creativity Inc.,* Catmull reveals the secrets behind their firm's uncanny track record of success. They've formed a committee called the "Brain Trust," where a hand-selected group of individuals gather to critique all the company's creative work. In Catmull's own words:

---

33 The cost was about $17 million in 1955, which works out to about $188 million in 2022 after accounting for inflation. "CPI Inflation Calculator," U.S. Bureau of Labor Statistics, https://www. bls.gov/data/inflation_calculator.htm; History.com Editors, "This Day in History: July 17," History. com, last updated July 15, 2020, https://www.history.com/this-day-in-history/disneyland-opens.

34 Frank Pallotta, "Which Pixar Film Has Rocketed to the Top of the Box Office?" *ABC 12 News,* June 16, 2022, https://www.abc12.com/which-pixar-film-has-rocketed-to-the-top-of-the-box-office/ article_b24025f8-8850-5fcf-b033-2cb8b1a57bd7.html.

Lack of candor, if unchecked, ultimately leads to dysfunctional environments... [So,] we created the Braintrust...which meets every few months or so to assess each movie we're making...

Its premise is simple: Put smart, passionate people in a room together, charge them with identifying and solving problems, and encourage them to be candid with one another. People...feel freer when asked for their candor; they have a choice about whether to give it, and thus, when they do give it, it tends to be genuine...

Films only become great when they are challenged and tested. In academia, peer review is the process by which professors are evaluated by others in their field. I like to think of the Braintrust as Pixar's version of peer review...

The film itself—not the filmmaker—is under the microscope. This principle eludes most people, but it is critical: You are not your idea, and if you identify too closely with your ideas, you will take offense when they're challenged. To set up a healthy feedback system...focus on the problem, not the person.[35]

Companies such as Pixar, that foster trust and candor, are those that will create the future; they have rigor in their feedback which promotes longevity. Companies with artificial harmony quickly lose their edge. These companies become nothing more than a hollow office filled with "yes people" who are surrounded by confining walls, temporarily propped up by an artificial and constrained culture. Choose to be like Pixar.

---

35 Ed Catmull and Amy Wallace, *Creativity, Inc.: Overcoming the Unseen Forces that Stand in the Way of True Inspiration* (New York: Random House, 2014).

*　　*　　*

If you ask someone if they want to hear the truth, they'll *likely say yes.* But feedback, especially when it's "negative", is hard to give and even harder to receive. For one, we're scared of tribal rejection. Our reptilian mind whispers, "If I speak up, will they reject me?" That certainly was the motivation preventing me from early-on engaging in the difficult conversations with Jay and Justin.

The second reason we forgo difficult conversations is selfishness. We put ourselves on a pedestal, thinking the other individual can't possibly handle what we have to say. This self-focused dysfunction is a result of our susceptibility to pride.

Feedback from people we trust is not only required but necessary for us to continually grow by becoming aware of our blind spots. What is important to remember is before speaking up, the person receiving the feedback needs to know that you care. While having difficult conversations often feels unnatural, cold, or even harsh, letting someone make a preventable mistake is worse.

"ARE YOU OPEN TO FEEDBACK?"

Several times when engaging with my coach, I will sometimes start to resist what he is saying to me. When that happens, he has a special trick to overcome this. He pauses and asks, "Are you open to feedback?" This simple question serves to get me to reflect on my current state of receptivity while de-escalating any built up tension.

Of course, there is the possibility of saying no. That's usually a good indicator it's time to end the session as no meaningful progress can be made; as the saying goes, "A person convinced against their will is of the same opinion still."

QUALITY OF LIFE QUADRANT

*"People are always blaming their circumstances for
what they are. I don't believe in circumstances. The
people who get on in this world are the people who
get up and look for the circumstances they want,
and if they can't find them, they make them."*
—GEORGE BERNARD SHAW

Once I mustered up the courage to confront Jay, my fear of rejection actually came to pass, as shortly thereafter I was fired. I Left feeling bewildered and betrayed, I had a choice to make—I could either choose to become bitter, or decide to get better.

Here's the rub: even if we play the game of life correctly, we can't guarantee those around us will. Even if we play fair, they may not, and furthermore, there is a huge part of our lives that we have no control over.

Circumstances influence outcomes; however, if we focus too much on what we can't control, we risk becoming a victim at the mercy of external factors. Real-life heroes tell us a different story:

* The biological parents of Steve Jobs gave him up for adoption, and his adoptive mother even struggled parenting him, believing that she'd made a mistake by taking him in.
* When Elon Musk was a kid, he was continually bullied and treated as an outcast before becoming a prolific entrepreneur.
* Maya Angelou was abused as a child before becoming a world famous poet.
* President Lincoln is considered the greatest leader in US history, yet he rose from obscurity and faced several defeats during his years in politics, while being afflicted with a debilitating depression.

Over and over again, we find that the most successful people overcame significant setbacks and difficulties. They could have surrendered and decided the circumstances were greater than their ability to respond. Instead they chose to use their challenges to refine their character, developing the resilience and courage to eventually create lives of significance.

We have the same choice.

If we believe that the trajectory of our life is entirely dependent on how others treat us, or that luck is the only factor that brings success, then we are choosing to live "in effect," by giving up our power and agency to external forces. There is a better path. While we cannot control what happens to us, we have the ability to choose our response; and in so doing living "at cause," knowing we can influence the outcome.

Warren Coughlin is a very talented coach who worked with our executive team at Tech 4 Kids and introduced us to an idea called the Quality of Life Quadrant. He used this model to explain our progression along a career path and how our choices could ultimately lead to a life of misery or meaning.

Quality of Life Quadrant

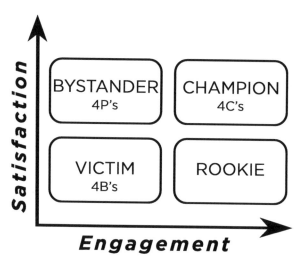

Within the quadrant, *engagement* is the horizontal axis and *satisfaction* is the vertical axis. Engagement is recognized as the level of effort that is applied into one's career while satisfaction is the level of fulfillment we experience.

ROOKIE: THE STARTING LINE

We all get to start out life in the bottom right of the quadrant as rookies. As we begin to embark on our chosen paths, our *engagement* is super high. However, our *satisfaction* is low, because we haven't yet realized any meaningful results.

As we progress through life, we face adversity; our first job does not work out, our business fails, or a relationship ends. These headwinds become a turning point that will push us into one of three types of people.

VICTIM: "OUTSIDE FACTORS DETERMINE MY QUALITY OF LIFE"

When we allow external resistance to diminish our engagement, we move from being a rookie to becoming a victim. We are initially excited about the future prospects and we use our skills to attempt to build something meaningful. Along the way we run into challenges. Initially we might persist and start to build character and resilience. However if we lose our vision for the possibility of creating a better future, we will stop fighting, submit and eventually surrender. With disengagement, we are choosing to believe that external factors are determining our destiny and what we do, can have no real impact on our lives.

We live in a culture in which victimization has become a plague. The masses are seemingly being drawn to the idea that it is so much easier to blame someone else for their circumstances rather than being accountable.

The blame is directed at parents, a bad boss, the government, or some other force beyond their own control. They point to external factors as the reason for their condition and make excuses as to why they are not living up to their potential.

There's power in being a victim, because you get to blame someone else or some event for your circumstances and relinquish accountability for yourself. Ultimately you are surrendering control of your life to external factors, living a life in effect. The legal profession certainly has figured out the profitability that comes with victimhood. We see billboards along every major highway proudly proclaiming that if you have had any number of mishaps, then you could have just won the lottery by simply dialing their memorable 800 number.

Certainly, resistance, difficulties, and obstacles that people don't deserve happen all the time. If you are living a bold life then eventually someone *will* victimize you. But as Paul Coelho wrote, "You drown not by falling into a river, but by staying submerged in it." Life is going to deal us challenges and we have a choice to either be defined by what happens or refined by it. As long as we remain focused on the past, we diffuse our energy from being able to imagine and create a better future. While being a victim is temporarily satisfying it is ultimately a trap, as you create a prison of limitations within your broken belief system. Choosing to be the victim is a choice to fail at life as you will never discover your true possibilities and potential.

I certainly had a choice to become the victim after being fired from Basic Fun. In fact, that was my initial and natural reaction, being disillusioned by what had happened. Eventually, I came to the conclusion that it did not happen *to me*, but rather *for me*. I had a chance to take the lessons from the experience and the opportunity to choose again. I realized that when you choose to become a victim, you are saying that this external element—the person or the circumstance—has power over you and your life. You surrender and for a moment feel satisfied and safe: it's easier, because you've abdicated responsibility for yourself. Now, you're no longer accountable for your own future and fate.

Victims suffer from what I call the four Bs: blindness, bitterness, blame, and begrudging. Consumed by anger and frustration, they become blind to the reality of their situation. They are bitter about the proverbial tough "cards they were dealt.", They are blaming others and events for the circumstances they are in, and ultimately resort to comparison and become begrudging of others who supposedly had it easier.

BYSTANDER: "I'LL PLAY IT SAFE"

These are people who start off with high engagement and initially achieve a modicum of success and with it achieve a certain level of satisfaction. However, they decide to play it safe (playing not to lose), engaging at the minimum level, staying within their comfort zone, and drifting unintentionally through life. They may not have all the bitterness of the victim, but they have a similar level of disengagement and are likely to settle for a life of mediocrity.

The bystander grows into a profession and gets on a career ladder; making enough to meet their basic needs and setting themselves up to retire comfortably. However, they stop there and start coasting, lacking the motivation that pushes them out of their comfort zone.

They feel insecure as they know they are not living to their full potential. Instead of developing their talents and skills to build a beautiful life, they chase superficial desires in an attempt to find happiness and a sense of worth. While pursuing the four Ps (power, prestige, pleasure and possessions), they seek to dull the nagging sense that they are less than what they could be, making up for their insecurities with quick dopamine hits and trying to impress others. They become the proverbial people who know it all, show it all, and ultimately owe it all.

Being a bystander is enticing because it's comfortable. Once someone achieves *some* success, it's easy to go into autopilot, and allow their dreams and hopes to wane. The allure of being a bystander is that it appears comfortable and safe, however it leads to an insidious outcome of a life of wasted potential. People who chose this path let their *resources get in the way of their resourcefulness*, never discovering their true possibilities and taking the best within them to their grave.

There is no stasis in life; you are either growing or decaying. By choosing to remain comfortably disengaged, you will eventually be haunted with the unsettling realization that you never truly explored the full potential of *what you could have been*.

> *"The definition of hell is: Your last day on Earth,*
> *the person you became meets the person you could*
> *have become."*
> —DAN SULLIVAN

CHAMPION: "I AFFECT MY OUTCOMES"

The champion is a person who is truly making the most of life's journey. They are the people who are playing to win, striving to live on the edge of their comfort zone, and as a result, they're highly engaged and highly satisfied by their growth. They believe that in order to have more, they must become more. They take action when there's uncertainty, and they're accountable for what they do. They forgive themselves and others when victimized; they submit to the external conditions that affect them, learning the lessons and then integrating the newfound knowledge to choose again.

They are people on the never-ending quest to discover all the possibilities and potential within them. When they face resistance, they do not simply *go through it* but rather *grow through it* by adapting, changing, and when necessary pivoting.

Champions have high satisfaction and experience real joy in life because they are chasing after the four Cs. They pursue challenges, use creativity to solve problems, are charitable with their resources, and use what they have to create meaningful connections with others. They choose to be the heroes of their own story.

Joseph Campbell, describes the hero in this way:

> The journey of the hero is about the courage to seek the depths; the image of creative rebirth; the eternal cycle of change within us; the uncanny discovery that the seeker is the mystery which the seeker seeks to know. The hero journey is a symbol that binds, in the original sense of the word, two distant ideas, the spiritual quest of the ancients with the modern search for identity, always the one, shape-shifting yet marvelously constant story that we find.[36]

Your Choice

Of course, bad things happen that are out of our control. However, it is in moments like these that I like to recall the formula taught to me by my friend Darren Hardy:

$$E+R=O \text{ (event plus response equals outcome)}$$

In other words we don't control E, the event. But we *do* control the R, our response. Ultimately this will determine the outcome. We cannot choose the cards we are dealt, but we do choose how we decide to play them.

---

36 Joseph Campbell, *The Hero's Journey: Joseph Campbell on His Life and Work* (New York: Harper & Row, 1990), 46.

One of the greatest modern-day examples of someone who has lived this principle to its fullest is Oprah. By many accounts, Oprah is considered the most influential person alive. However, let's consider her life for a moment. Being a black woman from a disadvantaged family who was abused as a child and had difficulty starting her career in journalism, Oprah could have easily claimed the victim storyline. Had she taken this path, she would have missed out on discovering her true potential. Instead she *chose* to get better instead of being bitter; overcoming her circumstances and ultimately creating a life of prominence, influence, and meaning that has inspired millions of people around the world.

Buddha famously stated that "life is suffering." We will all experience *pain and we can choose to either let the pain build the strength into us or beat the strength out of us.* In the moments of trial we have a choice to make, knowing that with our response we are choosing to become a victim, bystander or the hero of our story.

> *"You must get involved to have an impact. No one is impressed with the win-lose record of a referee."*
> —NAPOLEON HILL

BIRTH OF SOMETHING NEW

I was fired and hated the callous and careless approach that had been used, but I now had a choice to make on how I would choose to respond. To the outside world, it appeared I'd suffered yet another spectacular failure in the toy business but as I pondered the possibilities, I could see a different narrative forming. Thankfully, I remained pliable, and instead of playing the victim, I took time to reflect, learn from the experience, and then to chart a new course.

While they could take away my company, they could never take away my ability to *choose* my attitude and response. I remained optimistic knowing that my experience and connections would serve me as long as I remained open to new possibilities. Bruised but not broken, I started to contemplate a new future.

Asking myself the question of what I really wanted to do in my next venture, I began to journal and reimagine the possibilities of building a business from the ground up:

* ★ What problems do I want to try and solve?
* ★ Who would I want on my team?
* ★ What values and virtues would I advocate?
* ★ What impact did I want to make?

Prior to that fateful day of being fired, I was confident that I wanted to build a large company in the kids entertainment space. The plan was to create an enduring and durable enterprise by merging my toy company and then scaling it by following the M&A rollup playbook.

I have since learned that sometimes, God saves you from *what you want* to give you *what you need*. I had just been given the gift of time: time to reflect, to recalibrate, to reimagine, and to rebuild. It was an opportunity to prepare myself spiritually, emotionally, and mentally for my next adventure.

"To dare is to lose one's footing momentarily.
Not to dare is to lose oneself."
—SØREN KIERKEGAARD

STAY PLIABLE

In the 1950s, when Kutol Products discovered that their wallpaper cleaner could be used as a plaything, a new toy was born. Originally, they wanted to call it the Rainbow Modeling Compound. Thankfully, relatives of the owners suggested a much better brand name: Play-Doh.

To this day, it is uncertain who was the person who came up with this simple and memorable name, and I'm not sure it even matters. The point is that the owners of Kutol were open to constructive feedback. I can't be sure, but I'm certain that if someone hadn't been willing to speak out and the original name remained, the product might have never achieved its incredible level of success.

When we engage in healthy conflict and allow candor and feedback to mold us, we make better decisions and become stronger as a result. When we speak up, we act in courage and we are doing a service for others. Just as Play-Doh needs water to remain soft and pliable, relationships need the magical ingredient of trust. If our hope is to be shaped into something beautiful we must water our closest relationships with trust, and then be willing to be molded by the interactions.

In the end, the difference between people and Play-Doh is that we have the power to choose. We can allow what happens to us to turn us into brittle victims or hardened bystanders. Instead I encourage you to remain pliable, fostering trust within your most valuable relationships. In doing so you will choose to become the champion of your life, being at cause and ultimately determining how your hero's journey will unfold!

> *"You cannot go back and change the beginning*
> *but you can start where you are and change the*
> *ending."*
> —C. S. LEWIS

CHAPTER 9

SURF LUCKY WAVES

*"I have seen something else under the sun: The race
is not to the swift or the battle to the strong, nor
does food come to the wise or wealth to the brilliant
or favor to the learned; but time and chance
happen to them all."*

—ECCLESIASTES 9:11 (NIV)

The history of the surfboard is ancient with accounts of surfing dating back as far as 2000 BC. According to Matt Walsh in *The History of Surfing*, the modern iteration likely started in the thirteenth century (AD), when Tahitians brought the sport to Hawaii.[37]

For centuries, boards were long, sometimes up to twenty feet and weighing two hundred pounds. You could tell someone's rank in Polynesian society by the length of their board—the ruling class used the larger boards, called the *olo*, while the working class used the *alaia*, a much shorter board. If you are a modern-day surfer you likely understand why this makes sense, as the bigger boards make it much easier to catch the waves. (Although maybe not as fast and fun).

Captain James Cook "discovered" the Hawaiian Islands in the late 1700s after which Westerners took their first attempts at trying to surf. For many generations thereafter, the traditional surfboard remained relatively unchanged and, for most, difficult to master.

Mark Twain even wrote about surfing in *Roughing It*:

Each [native Hawaiian] would paddle three or four hundred yards out to sea, (taking a short board with him), then face the shore and wait for a particularly prodigious billow to come along; at the right moment he would fling his board upon its foamy crest and himself upon the board, and here he would come whizzing by like a bombshell!... I tried surf-bathing once, subsequently, but failed. I got the board placed right, and at the right moment, too; but missed the connection myself... None but natives ever master the art of surf-bathing thoroughly.[38]

---

37 Special thanks to Margaret Rhodes for this analysis, from her February 25, 2016, article in *Wired* titled "The Fascinating Evolution of the Surfboard," which was originally about Jim Heimann's book, *Surfing*. https://www.wired.com/2016/02/fascinating-evolution-surfboard/.

38 Mark Twain, *Roughing It* (1872), reprinted in The Project Gutenberg, last updated September 23, 2022, https://www.gutenberg.org/files/3177/3177-h/3177-h.htm.

It was not until Duke Kahanamoku, a two time Olympian and the "father of modern surfing" that the sport was brought to the masses. "The Duke" was an Hawaiian American swimmer who took back-to-back golds in the 1912 and 1920 Olympics.[39] While he was "riding the wave" of popularity in the pool, he also had the opportunity to introduce the world to his favorite hometown sport.

In 1926, another competitive swimmer, Tom Blake, hollowed out his board, creating a much lighter version. In *The History of Surfing*, Matt Warshaw writes that "Blake's hollow style board was the main reason that California experienced its first surfing popularity spike. Blake would continue to innovate and later introduced *the* game-changing single fin, giving riders better stability and control of their boards.

Today, you can buy a board that weighs less than ten pounds, made from a polyurethane foam and likely, it will have three fins and a tapered tail (two other innovations that would soon be introduced). If you think surfing is hard *now*, consider what it must have been like when your board was finless, two hundred pounds and twenty feet long!

TWO WEEKS, ONE DECADE
AND LOTS OF LUCK

"Expect the best. Prepare for the worst. Capitalize on what comes."
—JIM ROHN

Tech 4 Kids was birthed out of the tragic demise of Dynatech and just a few years later, it would be merged with The Bridge Direct to form Basic Fun as part of a scale up strategy. Very thin threads connected all these opportunities together, creating what seemed like much bigger and more impactful

---

39 The 1916 Games, slated for Berlin, were canceled because of World War I.

possibilities. However it was not to be and 90 days after the completion of the merger, I would find myself displaced from the toy business.

As I look back on my journey and take time to reflect, I come to realize that my life is a series of happy accidents—otherwise known as luck. You might be wondering how this can be true, given the numerous financial and business challenges I've experienced. To better understand and before moving on to reveal my next business adventure, I would like to share the story of the final few weeks of my time associated with Basic Fun. To truly appreciate the significance of *that,* we must first visit the *beginning* of Tech 4 Kids.

Dynatech was failing and headed towards capitulation. When it became clear that we should sunset the company, I came up with a new business model that would eventually become Tech 4 Kids. In the summer of 2008, I went back to the investment group and presented a business plan, asking for $1 million to support the launch.

At the time, Canada, like much of the developed world, was enjoying what appeared to be a great economy. Investor money was flowing rather easily to anyone who was able to present a credible plan. All that said my track record had become mired, having already burned through nearly $4 million of cash trying to salvage Dynatech. Nonetheless our investors were looking for a new plan to recoup these losses.

I pitched the group, demonstrating that I had learned from my mistakes and I would now grow a new meaningful opportunity. I explained how we would not only build a business that was profitable, but I also offered a solution to return their original capital. Fortunately they agreed and we were able to secure the funds, however the conditions were extremely onerous with a one year term and a very steep 24 percent interest rate. While the terms were tough, we were out of options and so the paperwork was completed, with the $1 million of new seed money hitting our bank account the first week of September, 2008.

Fourteen days later, Lehman Brothers filed the largest bankruptcy in US history, dropping the Dow Jones by more than five hundred points in one day. The shockwaves sent the entire market into a tailspin which ultimately resulted in the 2008 global financial crisis.

The timing of our funding was incredibly lucky. Reflecting back, if I had not pitched the new business plan during the summer months of 2008 or if the investment committee had delayed their due diligence by a week, there is a high probability that Tech 4 Kids would never have launched. By mid September the entire market had fallen off a cliff and along with it drying up investment capital for new ventures.

Fast forward 10 years to when I had been unceremoniously fired from Basic Fun. When I was let go, my business partners at the time had not offered severance or a plan to purchase my shares. They explained that I would have to sit on my common stock and that one day it might become valuable if there was a future liquidity event. In light of how I had been treated, I was not comfortable with this outcome, as my level of trust in my partners was very low.

I sought out legal counsel to figure out my options. I interviewed a number of possible litigators, most of which stoked my hopes of suing and seeking retribution for what had happened. That was until I met Mike Tamblyn.

Mike is a seasoned lawyer with a calm, cool, and collected demeanor. He let me rant about all the wrongdoings and mistreatments before helping reveal to me the brutal facts about my predicament. After carefully reviewing the legal agreements, he explained that I had signed away all my rights because I'd not sought out proper ILA (independent legal advice) ahead of signing the merger agreements. He predicted that a court would likely have little sympathy for me and he believed that I would be viewed as a sophisticated executive who knew what I was doing and simply fell out of favor. Furthermore, he revealed that I had unknowingly signed documents that gave the board the right to fire me without notice or recourse. While that was sobering news, there was a bright spot in that he did not find anything that could restrain me from selling my shares, if I could find an interested buyer.

Mike's practical advice and approach resonated with me and I decided he was the right advisor to help guide me. Following his recommendation, I approached my partners to let them know that if they would not make a reasonable offer, I would go and find another party. They seemed disinterested, throwing me lowball numbers, which I subsequently declined. I started up discussions with a number of private equity (PE) groups and found a number of interested candidates. Basic fun was profitable, had a great growth story and PE was familiar with the rollup model with the arbitrage that could be made on enterprise multiples.

When my co-founders became aware that I had outside interest from PE, they suddenly had a change of heart and became interested in purchasing my shares. Beyond them not liking the idea that I might be able to choose a new equity partner for them, I believe that Justin was inspired by what I was doing. He could see an opportunity to buy and then re-trade my shares to their own PE sources.

Their share purchase offers were now much more compelling and realistic. In late January 2018, after some back and forth, they came back with an updated offer. It wasn't what I was asking for, but it was not far off—and this time, it was fair. The term sheet put forward had one caveat: after signing, they would have a one month window in which they could rescind the deal.

I carefully considered the new offer but as I reflected on the overall situation, bitterness started to seep into my thoughts which led to a feeling of wanting revenge. I believed I could play this out to get more. Furthermore, I was confident that behind the offer, Justin had plans to use my shares for his own personal profiteering. It irked me that he would be benefiting at my expense.

I wanted Justin to pay for the wrong he had committed by betraying me, and that meant I wanted to suck every penny I could out of him. I stared at the piece of paper that represented the financial outcome of the last two decades of my career. It provided economic freedom, but it also had a steep price as once I signed I would be committing to a future outside of the toy business for the next several years.

My wife, the only person who'd been there with me through every step of this ride, came in and sat down next to me. She looked me in the eyes, and said something I'll never forget:

"Brad, if you'll simply sign the offer, you can move on. They only get the best of your worst, as they only have a piece of your past and none of your future." She was right. I needed to let go and instead imagine and embrace the possibilities for a new and better future.

I signed the document, scanned it and sent it back. I remember instantly feeling a weight lifted off my shoulders. I had made the decision to move on and with it I experienced a new found sense of freedom. Within the day the offer was returned back to me countersigned, and the one-month clock (with the option to rescind the offer) started ticking…

30 days passed and we had not received notifications of any change. The window of withdrawing the offer was now closed and my partners were committed to buying my shares at the agreed price in the signed term sheet. Two weeks later on March 14, 2018, Toys"R"Us filed for liquidation. They were not only one of the largest toy retailers in the world but at that time Basic Fun's largest customer! To say that it would have been hard to raise money for a toy company during the uncertainty of that time would have been an understatement.

Presumably, this created some difficult dynamics for my partners as the payments that were now due, did not show up. When we inquired as to their whereabouts, initially there was no response and when we did finally hear from their council the messages were confusing. Mike and his team continued to press on the status of the payments letting the otherside know they were at risk of being in breach of the agreements. Eventually, wire transfers showed up, however they were different from how it was originally planned.

If I'd chosen to push back and waited *two more weeks before* signing back the offer to purchase my shares, the news of Toys R Us would likely have thwarted the deal by giving them the opportunity to withdraw the offer. Furthermore, in light of the losses that Basic Fun would have experienced with Toys R Us, my shares would have been worth considerably less and almost impossible to sell to anyone else.

Once again, two weeks of lucky timing had made all the difference. This was the lucky 2 weeks on either side of 10 years. There are 521 weeks in a decade and to think that only 4 of them (0.76%) made all the difference in the extraordinary outcomes I have experienced.

Zones of Racing and in Life

Mike Tamblyn is not only a great lawyer but also is a Porsche race instructor. He taught me the following analogy from racing that I think is appropriate for both business and life.

Races are won or lost in the corners. There are three phases: the prep zone, the work zone, and the reward zone. When you come into the corner of a race track it is important to scrub the right amount of speed so you can work smoothly and not frenetically as you go through the corner. Most drivers come in too fast, struggle through the corner, and then have a sloppy exit.

> The key principle is you can only accelerate quickly out of the corner to the extent you are willing to slow down going in. Do not get too greedy coming in, focus on slow in and out fast...just as in life we need to learn to go slow in order to go fast; slow is smooth and smooth is fast.

SURFING THE MARKETPLACE

Living in Canada, I don't get to ride ocean waves as much as I'd like, but when I do, *I love it.* (we make up for it with wake surfing.)

Something about the feeling of acceleration and the momentum when you do catch a wave is tantalizing and addictive. Surfing isn't an easy sport to learn however despite its harsh treatment of beginners, once you catch your first wave, it's hard not to be hooked. The rush that you feel once the surging water propels you forward is unmatched.

Interestingly, mastering surfing is more about how to *predict* the waves, being in the *position to catch* the wave, and once in motion, to then maintain one's composure on the board to ride out the wave. Everything in surfing has to do with timing: being in the right place and making the right movements at exactly the right time. I think there's a lot that entrepreneurs can learn from this unique sport.

Let's further explore all the different elements that are necessary for a good ride to come together:

★ **Lucky waves:** You learn quickly that a wave on the North Shore of Maui is not the same as a wave in Jupiter Florida or Baja California. Maui has legendary waves, but when they are pumping, they also come with high consequences. Some waves are a slow swell and others move so fast that a surfer needs to be towed into them. The key point is that no two waves are the same and not all waves are equal in terms of the skill needed nor the thrill of the ride.

★ **Board:** The board is what propels you across the surface of the water and makes a difference on the ease and speed of your ride. There are long boards, short boards, and boards with different configurations of fins. The board is your vehicle that you choose to surf the wave, and the choice of the board matters in your ability to surf.

★ **The Surfer:** Of course, the human element comes into play. How fit are you to be able to paddle out? Can you move quickly to position yourself? How is your agility, coordination and balance? Experience, athleticism and determination all matter.

If you've ever caught a swell you know the rush that comes from getting the timing just right, standing up on the board and then carving down the face of the wave, feeling the splash of salt water on your body. You are a conductor and if you orchestrate the timing just right, catching the wave feels like a symphony of music reverberating through your body.

In business, this musical feeling comes when you build a company that does *repeatable* innovation and *continued* excellence. If you can somehow coordinate all the right elements, you can create a sustainable, scalable, and ultimately saleable business. Just as in surfing, it's easier to write about it than to actually do it.

Most companies start off by doing one thing great, driven by a skilled founder who has a unique idea and then executes well. They get lucky by being perfectly positioned when the wave builds and successfully capitalize on riding out its potential. However, when it comes to scaling beyond that, most founders do not know how to build redundancy in the company or have the ability to replicate the initial innovation. It is the difference between being a one-hit wonder in music or striving to become a legacy band that over many years continues to produce fresh and innovative music.

In surfing, the board, the wave, and the surfer all matter. In starting a business, there are four critical elements needed that allow for a scalable venture.

They are:

1. A bright founder with a great idea
2. A smart and different strategy
3. A high-performance team
4. Disciplined execution

It is also important to note that not all elements are equal in terms of the impact on your efforts on the results of the business.

It all starts with a budding entrepreneur who has a great idea; however, on its own it is not enough. As they say ideas are like noses in that everyone has one; on their own they are relatively worthless. It is only when a founder has a worthy idea and has the courage to *act* on it, does a real opportunity begin to take form.

Next, you must develop a smart and *different* strategy. As Steve Jobs once said, "You can't look at the competition and [simply] do it better. You have to look at the competition and, [instead], do it differently." If your description of what you are doing starts off with comparing yourself to another company and offering a "better" solution, I don't believe you'll ever build anything significant. By comparing yourself to another company you are already giving deference to them as the market leader and now you are competing over the small remaining market share. The best promotion for Coke has been Pepsi's advertising using them as a reference point. That does not mean Pepsi is not a significant competitor however as long as they maintain this positioning, they will never lead the cola category.

Next are the people. Nothing great can ever be built with one person. If you want to operationalize your smart strategy, you must attract, recruit, and retain a talented team. It is then up to you as the leader to inspire and unleash their potential, empowering them to achieve the goals that will fulfill the company's mission and vision.

Finally, it's all about execution. Of all the elements within your control, this is the most important and impactful ingredient to determine the outcomes. You could have all the other ingredients added into the recipe correctly, but the cake won't bake on its own. Only in the "oven of execution" will the ingredients transform into their possibilities.

As a point of reference to the importance of execution, I would like to reflect back on the 1998 Nagano Winter Olympics. My home country (Canada) is known as a powerhouse in the world of hockey. That year happened to be the first that the NHL would allow players to compete in the Olympic Games. Canada sent their best, with a team made up of legendary players such as Gretzky, Yzerman, Messier, and Lindros. Canada was predicted to be the easy favorite for the gold medal, but unfortunately it didn't happen; in fact, they were not even contenders as they never made it to the gold medal game. How is it that the team with the most talented lineup of players, who were expected to dominate, did not win? There are lots of theories about poor coaching and the adverse effect of individual ego's however the simple answer is a lack of execution. They had all the skill, but they lacked the necessary will needed in order to combine their efforts to create the synergy to produce the winning results.

As a part of this list of 4 things within your control, I want to introduce a 5th element: *Luck.* Luck has the potential for more exponential impact than any other factor for influencing the outcome of your efforts.

Essentials to Startup Success

```
                    Luck x 10,000

                ┌──────────────┬──────────────┐
                │     #1       │     #2       │
  L             │   Great      │              │        L
  u             │  Founder     │  Different   │        u
  c             │  and Idea    │  Strategy    │        c
  k             │              │              │        k
                │    x 1       │    x 10      │
  x             ├──────────────┼──────────────┤        x
                │     #3       │     #4       │
  1             │   High-      │              │        1
  0             │ Performance  │  Disciplined │        0
  ,             │   Team       │  Execution   │        ,
  0             │              │              │        0
  0             │   x 100      │   x 1,000    │        0
  0             └──────────────┴──────────────┘        0

                    Luck x 10,000
```

If you weigh the importance of these five elements, they have a growing magnitude in terms of their impact on your results. If you're more of a math than a visual person, here's the formula:

1x Founder/Idea + 10x Different Strategy + 100x Team + 1000x Execution + (1 − 10,000) × Luck.

Each element is critical—a talented entrepreneur can have a great idea but poor strategy and never get the company off the ground. You can have a great idea and a smart strategy but without a highly skilled team, you'll be unable to execute at scale. You can have an idea, a smart strategy, and a skilled team who executes, but without *luck (the right timing)*, your outcomes will be disappointing.

LUCK = TIMING

I love the interviews Guy Raz conducts on his podcast *How I Built This*. The show features hero's journey stories from fascinating founders. Guy does a great job of keeping the conversation naturally flowing, asking great questions and eliciting incredible stories from his guests.

If you listen to enough episodes and lean in close enough, you'll hear a recurring question. Raz repeatedly asks the founders about how luck impacted their success. Nearly without fail, every founder admits that luck has been an important ingredient in their success. Some may describe luck as a contributing factor while others come straight out and admit it was foundational in their ability to build a company of consequence.

In business, luck is simply about *timing*. The right idea, introduced by the right people at the right time. When Steve Jobs introduced the first iPhone in 2007, the world was ready. Over the prior decade the development of the internet and the proliferation of mobile devices had created an ever-more-connected world. These mega trends were converging and swelling to create the perfect wave upon which the iPhone could be launched. That timing created an exponential factor that when combined with Jobs's vision and the execution of his team, created a global phenomenon. A decade before, and it would have been too soon and might have suffered the same fate as the Newton device. A decade later, and likely Blackberry would have become too dominant.

Victor Hugo stated so well, "Nothing is more powerful than an idea whose time has come." History is full of examples of great ideas, smart strategies, and amazing teams that simply did not time it right. I cannot help but think of eToys. They had a visionary founder, a different strategy for distribution, and hired some of the best talent in the industry. Yet they are now a distant memory, as the way people were shopping and the distribution systems for delivery were just not yet ready when they were launching in 1997.

Luck constantly surrounds us. It's an ever-present force that we cannot control and the rate of change is accelerating. Marketplaces move, governments change, and popular opinions evolve. While we can't control luck itself, we *can* control what we do with it. Jim Collins calls this the "return on luck." How you respond to the luck you find is what will determine the returns you will make.

THE FOUR TYPES OF LUCK

Dr. James Austin has defined various types of luck in his book *Chase, Chance, and Creativity.* According to Dr. Austin, there are four types of luck.

Dumb Luck

This is nothing more than the wholly undeserved luck that falls upon all of us at one time or another in life. We do nothing to earn it, and yet, dumb luck shows up and grants us incredible good fortune.

I was born in Canada, a free, wealthy, and well-developed nation. Nothing I did merited this outcome, and anyone born in a similar free democratic country enjoys the same dumb luck. Furthermore, I was born with all my limbs, I had two loving parents, a good education, and an opportunity to start my own business. Again, this is just a result of where I was born and raised and when I consider this against the odds, I understand I am breathing rare air.

Fortuitous timing continued to follow me into college as I happened to walk down the right hallway, at the right time, and noticed a beautiful young lady walking towards me.

Later that week, I had my chance to meet her. I saw her speaking to someone I knew, so I quickly ran up, pretending to be interested in my acquaintance. I acknowledged them both, and then turned my attention to the lovely young lady who'd captivated me. To date, we've been together for three decades, and this relationship has been the single greatest blessing in my life.

Dumb luck will happen to us without our input at all. Some things, like where we are born, we cannot control; however, when we identify luck, it is up to us to respond in order to *capitalize* on it. When my now-wife first caught my eye in the hallway, I could have let her slip by. I could have been too intimidated by her big boyfriend (a fashion model and captain of the basketball team) and lacked the courage to find a way to meet her, but I didn't. I was presented with a lucky opportunity, but on its own it would have slipped like sand through my fingers; I was still required to do my part.

Grit Luck

This type of luck requires intentionality. Entrepreneurs experience grit luck after they've been grinding it out over time. They lose money, they face regulatory changes, a partner backstabs them, they go out of business; despite getting knocked down, somehow, they just keep getting back up. They're tenacious in their pursuit of success, resilient in their ability to learn from difficulty, and no obstacle seems enough to keep them from trying at least one more time. Along the way, an idea happens to pan out, if for no other reason than they just kept at it and at some point, the law of averages takes effect.

It is easy to focus on the stories of those like Mark Zuckerberg, who, seemingly overnight and on his first attempt, hit a grand slam in business. The reality is that over the course of a founder's life most entrepreneurs will experience multiple upsets, pivots, and failed business ventures.

In his book *Super Founders,* author Ali Tamaseb noted the results from his four-year study of every unicorn startup from 2005 to 2018. He found that, on average, most of the founders had a *decade* of work experience.[40]

One-in-a-billion founders like Zuckerberg are just that—one in a billion. More than likely, if you're going to be in business, you're going to need a healthy dose of long-term perseverance, which, when the right timing occurs, can result in lucky outcomes.

Grit luck, by nature, is simply the execution of perseverance. Try enough times, and luck will eventually find you. Thankfully, perseverance is entirely within our control; however, it is up to us to do so smartly. We need to learn the difference between when we are in the right spot to catch a wave or when we need to change locations. We need to know when to persist, when to pivot and when it is time to call it quits, saving our efforts for another beach on another day.

Seeing Luck

An entrepreneur develops seeing luck after standing on the shore of the marketplace and observing wave after wave. Seeing luck is acquired by observing the horizon and developing the ability to sense changes in the tides and identify the swells of opportunity where the next wave is building.

Consider baseball for a moment. If you give yourself enough at-bats, you'll hit some pitches purely by chance. That's grit luck. But after some time, you begin to time your swings better; you begin to read the pitch, and you start to hit more balls with fewer at-bats. The more balls you hit, the more you learn *how* to read the pitcher and that informs how and when to swing. That's seeing luck in action.

Seeing luck is only achieved by progressing through grit. If we pause long enough to learn from our mistakes, we can develop the muscle memory

---

40 Ali Tamaseb, *Super Founders: What Data Reveals About Billion-Dollar Startups* (New York: PublicAffairs, 2011).

to sense a wave when it's starting to swell, sizing up how big it will be and what path it may take. We can't control those waves, but we can ensure that we are positioning ourselves to be able to surf all its potential.

Seeing luck means that we learn from our prior experiences, we get into the water, paddle to the right spot, and in a moment leverage our speed and strength to stand up and ride at exactly the right time.

Attraction Luck

As the term suggests this is when you attract additional lucky opportunities. This type of luck occurs when you become so good at what you do that not only do you have the ability to spot opportunities, but the world *brings the opportunities to you.* Only a handful of people are so lucky: Warren Buffett, Bill Gates, Jimmy Iovine, Sir Richard Branson, and those like them. They are people who have become the best in their industry and as a result attract others, who have their own brilliant ideas and wish to seek them out as partners.

Attraction luck is simply a level of luck that is very rare as it is built on reputation. It is a result of repeated success of continually riding epic waves with excellence. If you become the Laird Hamilton of your industry, other surfers will take notice, bringing their opportunities and ideas to you and asking if you want to join them in surfing the new waves they have discovered.

"The world runs on luck. The question is what you are doing with it. Are you aware enough that you are getting lucky? Are you talented enough to take the advantage and run with it? Do you have enough grit and resilience to stick with it when it gets hard?"

—KEVIN SYSTROM

LEARNING TO SURF

I think there is another important lesson that surfing can teach us. My buddy Dan Martell often says that "learning to run a business by going to school is like learning to surf by reading a book." I couldn't agree more.

I get asked all the time by kids who are looking for career advice if they should go to school and get an MBA prior to starting their entrepreneurial journey. I know the question is driven by a nagging sense of a lack of self-worth. In addition, our society has somehow conditioned us to believe that we need a formal education before we can attempt anything meaningful. From my perspective, most of our Western education system is an antiquated remnant of an old industrial complex designed to train factory workers. The main purpose of school is to teach you how to organize, learn, and solve problems. It can also serve as a hub of social connections...such as meeting your spouse!

Most of my peers who are successful entrepreneurs have little to no postsecondary education or are doing something very different from what they went to school for. However, they've developed a wealth of knowledge from their own experiences in attending the School of Hard Knocks.

Tim Ferriss wrote about the MBA dilemma in a famous blog post called "How to Create Your Own Real-World MBA." Ferriss was struggling with spending $120,000 for a two-year education. After several meetings with mentors, he instead decided to create his own fund, and he would use that money to set up a series of experimental investment bets that he would then learn from:

> I went into the "Tim Ferriss Fund" viewing the $120,000 as sunk tuition costs, but also expecting that the lessons learned, and people I met, would be worth that $120,000 investment.

The two-year plan was to methodically spend $120,000 for the learning experience, not for the ROI.[41]

For Tim the bet paid off as Ferriss is now a bestselling author, blogger, and admired thought leader in the world of personal development and business.

Running a business is really a lot like learning to surf. The best learning will not come from studying the board, the beach, or the waves. Rather, the real learning will only come by experiencing it firsthand and when you hit the water, you must be prepared to struggle.

You will be exhausted from the paddle out. You might experience sea legs as you bob in the unsettled water, waiting for the swells. When you attempt to paddle in, you will often mistime the waves and either get dropped or get tossed, resulting in a tumble in the white water. All of this is expected; in the beginning you have to be willing to suck at any skill that is worth learning.

Malcom Gladwell calls this learning curve the ten thousand hour rule, which is the required investment of time in any area of life in order to achieve mastery. If that's what it takes to become a master of surfing, why would you expect your entrepreneurial journey to be any different?

As the saying goes, you miss 100 percent of the shots you never take. With that in mind, if you want to catch some waves of luck, then the best place for you to be is with your board out in the water. Don't be like the majority of people who will remain timid souls and choose to be spectators on the beach. Muster up the courage to grab your board, to dive in, and start paddling!

---

41   Tim Ferriss, "How to Create Your Own Real-World MBA," *The Tim Ferriss Show* (blog), June 28, 2010, https://tim.blog/2010/06/28/mba/.

Mentorship: The Only Shortcut

If you are looking for a shortcut, the only one I can recommend is mentorship. Find people who have what you want in life. You can learn from getting tossed around in the waves on your own, or by jumping in the water with someone who knows how to paddle the waters. For instance, if your long-term goal is to start your own company, it makes sense to find someone who has already successfully done so and ask for them to teach you. Another form of mentorship can come from working for someone else. Working at another company can provide you with the relevant experience and connections. During my entrepreneurial journey, I have often thought that I could have saved myself much time and heartache by learning the ropes at someone else's company. I highly recommend mentorship. It's the better, cheaper, and less painful way to learn.

Many who seek out mentorship hold this strange notion that there's a Yoda-like sage just waiting for the right student to appear. Nothing could be further from the truth. Most of my mentorship has come in the form of books, podcasts, webinars, peer groups, and in some rare cases, one-on-one interactions, which I have sought out.

If someone has the experience you want, and they have the capacity and desire to invest into your life, remember that their time and attention is their most valuable nonrenewable resource. Come prepared, take notes, apply the lessons, and report back the results. This is the best way to respect your mentor's time and efforts.

I also highly recommend professional coaches. These are people who have either achieved mastery in their discipline, or who've worked with those who have. A good coach knows how to speak truth into your life, help you see your blind spots, and then build strategies to help you grow through them.

A LUCKY MEETING

"A cord of three strands is not quickly broken."
—ECCLESIASTES 4:12 (NIV)

In 2015, I attended an event in Napa Valley called Mastermind Talks. It is a brilliant gathering created by Jayson Gaignard, who carefully curates a fascinating group of entrepreneurs and thought leaders. These people come together for a three-day event to create meaningful connections and to learn and grow from each other's experiences.

The level of detail that Jayson puts into placing participants with common interests in the vicinity of each other is nothing short of world-class. As a result of his meticulous planning, I sat next to a young, bright, and scrappy entrepreneur named Matt Bertulli. I soon discovered that we were both business owners from Toronto and that we both shared a common passion for mountain biking. A special relationship was born.

Matt and I became good friends, spending time together riding bikes, talking about business, and eventually joining an EO forum together. After one of our EO forum meetings, we found ourselves sitting in an airport lounge in Boston waiting on a delayed flight. Matt started sharing with me some of the challenges he was experiencing with a new company that he had invested into.

Interestingly, Matt had met the founder (Jeremy Lang) at the same event where we were introduced to each other. Jeremy had invented the world's first compostable phone case. He had perfected the science that underscored the product, but he wasn't an expert when it came to telling the story to the market. That was until Matt came along and not only felt compelled by the potential of the environmental impact but also recognized the value he could add. Matt subsequently decided to invest into the company. Matt was the perfect investor for the company as he had built a very successful business that focused on developing direct-to-consumer e-commerce brands. He was a brilliant marketer and had grown his company into becoming one of the largest digital marketing agencies in Canada. With Jeremy making the product and Matt focusing on the marketing, the company was suddenly growing at an incredible rate however the infrastructure was not able to keep up.

While we sat in the airport lounge, Matt explained that the demand for the product was outstripping their ability to supply. I was intrigued, as all the problems that Matt described, I had extensive experience in solving from my previous experiences in the world of toys. At first glance, it seemed that there could be a potential fit and that my talent and connections could complement what Matt and Jeremy had already started.

While the idea was compelling, I didn't want to repeat the mistakes from my past. This time I would take the time to ensure that we could be good business partners.

To determine this, we agreed to meet in person to discuss our dreams, philosophies and hopes for the future. We compared our personality profiles (we used DISC) to see if there was a match and to identify potential conflicts. It was a great starting point and in the process we discovered that our working styles were compatible. More importantly, we learned that we had similar worldviews, values and hopes for the future.

After taking the time to learn about the possible fit, we started to plot out and imagine the future for the company. We drafted the business's vision, mission and core values and set out a five-year plan. As we all began to envision this brave new world we intended to create, we could sense excitement, optimism, and a strong bond beginning to form. We realized that the three of us coming together was not going to be simply additive, but rather exponential in leveraging our experiences and strengths.

How lucky I was to attend that Mastermind Talks event, how lucky that our flight from Boston was delayed...how lucky that I had been fired from Basic Fun!

THE GOOD LORD'S GARDENER

"Lucky breaks are nothing more than unexpected rewards from intelligent choices we've chosen to make. Success doesn't just happen because someone's stars line up. Success, both in business and personally, is something that's consciously created."

—ROBIN SHARMA

Once, there was a masterful gardener who invited a friend to have tea in his beautiful garden. The friend walked through the beautiful botany, admiring the flora, and then stated, "This garden is a miracle that you and the good Lord have created."

The gardener looked around at the natural work of art he'd brought to life, and then said, "You're correct. The good Lord brought the elements, such as the rain, the soil, and the sunshine. His miracle of life made the plants bloom. But," he added, "you should've seen this place when God had it all to himself."

The story is a clever one, and it illustrates the part humans are to play in working along with our Creator to co-create a future. We can control nothing of rain, wind, and sunshine, and likewise we have no hand in where we are born or what's in our DNA. However, we have a choice on what to do with what we have been given and how we use those gifts. It's as if the Divine started the good work of creation, placed us into it, and gave us freedom, just to see what we'd come up with.

The Genesis account of creation indicates that there's something special about the human species. As the story goes, during the first six days, God was very busy focusing on two things: taking the chaos and turning it to order and then subsequently filling the newly ordered planet with creation. At the end of every day's work, God reflected on what He had created and said "it is good." Then, on the sixth day, humans were created.

According to Genesis, we were created in God's image, after which He describes the resulting humankind as "*very* good."[42] I don't think that being created in "God's image" necessarily means that we physically *look* like God; but rather, that we are endowed with the God-like gifts of being able to imagine and then to create, just like him.

In fact God gave humans this mandate, "be fruitful and increase in number; fill the earth and subdue it. Rule over the fish in the sea and the birds in the sky and over every living creature that moves on the ground." With these words, He commissioned us to become His stewards of the garden, to be His caretakers and to continue the work He started.

Part of our tasks are to *subdue*; in other words, do what God had been doing in the creation account in taking what is chaotic and creating order from it. He also encouraged us to "fill the Earth." That word "fill" is interesting, as it is different from multiply (propagate). When you think about it, the Earth was already pretty full as God had been pretty busy in creating all kinds of living things. I believe that with the commission to "fill the

---

42   Emphasis mine.

Earth," He was inviting us to continue His work and to become co-creators with Him. As God labored in creation, He subsequently appointed us to do the same, by filling the world with additional creation that would create value to support all life on the planet.

Fruit trees grow, but they thrive under the right soil, spacing, moisture, and occasional pruning. The sun produces solar energy, but we must invent the panels that capture it. Plants can produce healing medicines to save lives, but we must first discover processes that transform them into supplements. Precious metals and materials, such as gold, silver, copper, and lithium all offer incredible value, but they must first be mined, refined, and turned into something of utility.

As Erwin McManus says, "You were created to create; you are both a work of art, and an artist at work." Everything is created twice: first in our minds and then if acted on, are manifested in reality. As such we all possess the unique ability to both imagine, and then create it. In doing so we continue what God started by filling the Earth with ongoing creation that builds value for both people and the planet.

Lastly and most importantly, we must understand we are the Earth's stewards. As part of our original job description, I think it is important that we understand the meaning of when God asked us to *rule* over creation. If we look back over history it becomes quickly apparent that we have achieved a failing grade in practicing benevolent rulership. We've been *takers* instead of *caretakers* ignoring the consequences of our selfish actions.

When we were tasked with ruling over this precious planet, it meant not exploiting the resources but rather to be regenerative gardeners who care for it. We are the only species that has the ability to make decisions that in turn dramatically impact and alter our ecosystem. With this great power comes great responsibility.

What ultimately influenced my decision to join Matt and Jeremy was the realization that by successfully scaling the business, it would create an opportunity to act as a force for good. The opportunity perfectly checked the boxes of the requirements for my next venture. Furthermore I was determined that as part of my next endeavor, I wanted to invest my life resources into opportunities that mattered and would ultimately make a positive impact on both people and the planet.

WHAT LUCKY WAVES WILL YOU SURF?

As founders we find ourselves to be like surfers; riders of the waves of luck that will build and then break over the course of our lives. We cannot create the waves and we cannot determine when they will come nor predict the size, speed, or direction. Yet, the only opportunity we can have to surf them is if we are in the water, watching the horizon, paddling and anticipating their arrival.

For a successful surf session, it is all about timing. You need to be in the right spot and when you see the swell beginning to build, turn your back to the horizon, paddle for all your worth, and then at just the right moment stand up and ride. Likely, you will miss many times before you get it right; either watching the wave go past you or getting thrown from your board and spun in the whitewash.

If you are willing to learn from your mistakes, seek out mentorship and embrace the necessary grit to keep at it; then one day, you'll stand up and suddenly feel that surge of acceleration as you propel down the face of the wave. In that moment, you will experience an extraordinary feeling of joy, an ecstatic rush of excitement and a deep desire to never want the wave to end. It is addictive and once you have felt the rush, you will be in the never ending pursuit to catch the next swell.

We all have access to the waves that are abundant in the ocean of life. The question is will we be victims, who retreat from the beach blaming the sun, the sand, and waves for inflicting damage on us? Will we be the bystanders who watch from the comfort and safety of the shore line? Or will we choose to tread into the intimidating waters to seek out opportunity and to discover the full potential of what is possible for us to surf? The ocean is immense and powerful and the waves can seem overbearing; they are both tempting and taunting as they inquire of us if we really have what it takes to ride.

My hope is that you will grab your board, dive in and paddle, as it is the only way for you to surf the lucky waves of your life.

"Being out there in the ocean, God's creation, it's like a gift He has given us to enjoy. And if you talk to any surfer, they'll tell you it's a privilege to share the waves with God's creatures. But to be successful, you have to be lucky and a little bit crazy."
—DUKE KAHANAMOKU

CHAPTER 10

LEAVE A LEGO LEGACY

*"Life is no straight and easy corridor along which
we travel free and unhampered, but a maze of
passages, through which we must seek our way,
lost and confused, now and again check in a blind
alley. But always if we have faith, a door will open
for us, not perhaps one that we ourselves would ever
have thought of, but one that would ultimately
prove good for us."*

—A.J. CRONIN

When we think of most toys, we think of what you do with them once they are a finished product—you hug a teddy bear, you throw a ball, you fly a kite, you play Monopoly. Someone else has already done all the "putting together" of the toy that you have the opportunity to play with. However, when we think of LEGOs, most of us think of all the *pieces* of the set.[43] The toy has potential that has not yet been revealed and the fun part comes when we are building a tower, a city, or the Roman Colosseum.

The Danish carpenter Ole Kirk Christiansen founded the LEGO company in Billund, Denmark, in 1932, the same year that his wife passed away. A fire and the Great Depression had hurt his carpentry business, and he needed a way to financially provide for his four sons.

He decided to use his woodworking skills and apply it to toy making and soon discovered he had a knack for making high quality wooden toys. He was known for being committed to excellence and was unwilling to accept anything less. According to LEGO's official company history, Christiansen made his son Godtfred unbox an entire completed inventory of toys in order to apply an additional coat of lacquer. Apparently, Godtfred had attempted to save the company some money by reducing the number of coats.

Through the early days, LEGO had a rough go of it. Christiansen was raising his sons as a widower, the economy was a mess (they were in the middle of a global financial crisis), and they survived yet another fire. Things went from bad to worse when one of their largest orders was suddenly canceled, resulting in excess inventory and a strain on their businesses cash flow. Despite the several start-up challenges they somehow always found a way through and managed to survive.

Eventually, Christiansen made a large bet on an injection molding machine, marking the beginning of the company's move towards making toys out of plastic and not just wood. Soon after, they designed the original

---

43   Especially if you have young children and you've stepped on one!

LEGO brick. It was very different from what you see today as the bottom of the brick was hollow. From this humble beginning, the LEGO block would soon become a sought after play thing.

In 1958, two major events happened: Christiansen passed away, and the modern LEGO brick was born. Until then, LEGO sets were selling, but with the hollow design the structures that could be built were entirely unstable. Before his passing, Christiansen solved this problem, by coming up with the tubular base that allowed the bricks to "snap" together to create a snug fit.

In 1961, the new design was patented under the name "the stud and tube principle," and with its introduction the sales of the toys really started to soar. The business scaled at an unprecedented rate with the resulting demand, forcing the local community to invest into an airport to help manage the inflow of business travelers looking to source LEGO.

In 1968, LEGO opened its first theme park—which was interestingly constructed several years *before* Walt Disney World. All told, *eight* LEGO-themed parks would be opened around the world.

The family-owned company was passed down from generation to generation and for the most part experienced steady growth. Their defining moment came in the early 2000s, when the company faced a series of setbacks. In an attempt to diversify and respond to the onslaught of digital playthings entering the retail market, LEGO invested into gaming, action figures, and content creation. These bets failed and by 2004, the company had experienced $225 million in losses and was $800 million in debt.

To address the problems, the company brought in new management, resulting in a wind-down of the new initiatives and a refocus on the core construction business. They decided to pursue a strategy of licensing and famously launched new LEGO sets featuring prominent brands such as Star Wars and Harry Potter. The move proved to be genius, turning the tide of their prior misfortunes and resulting in fast growth and much needed profitability.

All the little pieces—setbacks from fires, financial crises, pivots, and iterations—have all paid off and have resulted in the company becoming a top 10 global brand. The US National Toy Hall of Fame, established in 1998, subsequently named LEGO as their first inductee. Furthermore both Fortune magazine and The British Toy Retailers Association named LEGO the toy of the *century!*

Today, the Danish company is still a private family-owned business that in 2015 bypassed Mattel to become the world's largest toy maker. Even though he would never live long enough to see all its success, Christiansen had a vision and started something that would ultimately grow to become an iconic global brand. LEGO did not always get it right and even found itself on the brink of disaster a few times, but over several decades, they have created something truly extraordinary, simply building brick by brick.

Every start-up founder who wants to build something enduring and durable should draw inspiration from this incredible example. As we will soon learn, these invaluable lessons from LEGO can be applied in our own journey as entrepreneurs.

FROM SLAVERY TO GRACE

"The future is not a result of choices among alternative paths offered by the present, but a place that is created—created first in the mind and will, created next in activity. The future is not some place we are going to, but one we are creating. The paths are not to be found, but made, and the activity of making them changes both the maker and the destination."

—JOHN SCHAAR

Captain John Newton worked in the slave trade during the mid-18th century, where he made a living by trading people as commodities. This fact is quite surprising given that he was once a rescued slave himself.

In 1748, John was on a ship off the coast of Ireland when a terrible storm threatened him and his crew's lives. At that dire moment, John bargained with God, praying that, if he were to be spared, he would turn his life around and commit to serving Him.

John did survive the storm and subsequently began the necessary steps to living a more virtuous life. He continued to work in the slave trade, but a transformation had begun. Somewhere between that storm and 1788, John's perspective on slavery reversed and he joined the abolitionist movement, writing about the inhumanity and horrors he had witnessed.

In his essay titled "Thoughts Upon the African Slave Trade," he wrote "a confession," which he claimed "comes too late," but was necessary nonetheless: "I hope it will always be a subject of humiliating reflection to me, that I was, once, an active instrument, in a business at which my heart now shudders."[44]

He joined forces with William Wilberforce and through their combined efforts, the Slave Trade Act was approved by the British Parliament in 1807, officially putting an end to the African slave trade within the British Empire.

John Newton lived eighty-two years, and for the majority of his life, he participated in one of the world's greatest atrocities. Only in his final twenty years did he discover his life's true purpose, which would profoundly impact humanity in a lasting way.

You may not have been aware that he was a key player in birthing the movement that would eventually ban slavery, but you will never forget his timeless and immortal words found within the hymn "Amazing Grace."

---

44 John Newton, *Thoughts Upon the African Slave Trade* (London: 1788), reprinted in The Internet Archive, 2010, https://cowperandnewtonmuseum.org.uk/wp-content/uploads/2020/07/thoughts-upon-african-slave-trade-john-newton.pdf.

The next time you hear the powerful chorus of "Amazing Grace—how sweet the sound, that saved a wretch like me…" take a moment to reflect on the depth of meaning behind those words. They were penned by a man whose life had been irrevocably changed. John Newton knew firsthand the horrors of the slave trade, having made his living trading people as property. He recognized the gravity of his actions and the immense harm they had caused, describing them as nothing short of "wretched."

Despite the weight of his past, Newton found hope and redemption through forgiveness. Though he once felt lost and despondent, in the twilight of his life, he was able to start anew with a renewed sense of purpose. The transformation he underwent was profound and serves as a testament to the true power of redemption.

The passing of the Slave Trade Act in 1807 was a significant moment in John Newton's life, one that marked the end of an era and gave him a sense of closure. It was also the moment that brought the pieces of his life together and completed the picture of his true purpose. John lived to see the day that the British African slave trade was officially abolished, and though he passed away just a few months later, his legacy lives on as a reminder of the transformative power of forgiveness and the power of living with intention and purpose.

"The two greatest days of your life are the day
you were born and the day you find out why.
Purpose in life is far more important than property
or possessions. Having more to live with is no
substitute for having more to live for."

—MARK TWAIN

MY NEWTON MOMENT

Nothing in my own life compares to the dramatic story of Newton's, but I did experience my own moment of transformation, when I decided to join Matt and Jeremy.

I had a lucky meeting with Matt that led to being introduced to Jeremy and ultimately resulted in becoming a co-founder of the company. What was key in the decision to become part of Pela and to help create Lomi, was the opportunity to make recompense over my previous involvement in proliferating an unsustainable consumer economy.

For more than twenty years, I had developed products that filled shelves around the world with playthings. I loved that I was responsible for helping bring happiness and smiles to children's faces, however, something never sat quite right with my conscience.

The toy industry is very large, with global sales of $100 billion per year. Once a toy is sold, there's a high likelihood that it will end up as trash within twelve months or less. Throughout my career, I've literally shipped billions of pieces of plastic in the form of playthings. While they were designed to promote happiness, by now the majority have ended up in landfills, contributing to the destruction of our environment.

I have always been unsettled about the lack of sustainable practices in the making and selling of consumer products. The entire retail industry thrives on creating an insatiable desire to buy more. Both retailers and suppliers are complicit in propagating this "need for more" economy that drives economic growth, but then lacks accountability for the end of life of the products.

Believing that there are no costs to creating consumer waste is a simple form of ignorance. Newton's law proves otherwise, stating that for every action, there is an equal and opposite reaction. Intuitively, we understand that increased consumption leads to more waste, both directly and indirectly.

When we buy new products we are both disposing of the old replacement and the packaging from the new, creating additional waste. The problem is we do not see the accumulation as we adopt an "out of sight, out of mind" approach. We put our trash and recycling into bins and expect them to be taken away every week, with the assumption that they will be disposed of responsibly. This, however, is far from the truth. Waste management is a big business ($2 Trillion per year globally) with massive profits and a complete lack of transparency in terms of where waste goes and how it is processed.

Within waste management recycling has become a big part of the revenue stream and is arguably the greatest greenwashing scam of the past century. In North America, the methods of collecting and sorting recyclable materials are, at best, inconsistent and varied. The system has historically relied on cheap labor to do the sorting, but those options vanished as most Asian countries ceased this practice. As a result less than 10% of what we put into recycling bins actually gets recycled, which is unacceptable for an industry that has had over 30 years to improve. This means that the probability of materials being recycled more than once is unlikely, causing the majority of recyclables to end up in landfills, which are quickly reaching capacity.

Waste management companies do not want the public to know this dirty secret, so they attempt to distract people with their disingenuous efforts to be environmentally friendly, by rebranding themselves as "environmental solutions" and painting their trucks green and converting them to cleaner fuel sources.

I have always had a deep conviction of trying to do what was right for the environment. At home, I was the manic recycler—clawing through the garbage can to pull out anything that should be recycled. I want to believe in the concept and since inception have felt a deep sense of responsibility in doing my part to support it. However unless we have a major innovation to make sorting and processing better, we will not make it viable as the current infrastructure simply does not work. Recycling is like the idea of world peace; I love it and want to believe it is possible, but the reality is that in all recorded history we have never known a world without some level of conflict and chaos. We should continue to strive to achieve a world with more peace and a recycling system that works, however I believe the better solution to deal with the growing waste stream is to adopt more compostables.

Upon exiting the toy business, I was given the time for introspection. During this period I read, reflected, and journaled to help ponder what I wanted to do with my future. Through this process I landed on three guiding principles that needed to be true in my next venture, in order for it to be fulfilling and align with my values:

* My life plan needs to come before my business plan.
* Only work with awesome people.
* Commit my resources towards projects that create meaningful impact.

These became the filter by which I examined every opportunity, with the last one forcing me to carefully consider what (and to whom) I would dedicate my most precious resource, my time and attention. Several months later, I had the fateful delay at Logan airport in Boston, where Matt and I engaged in a discussion about the challenges he was having with trying to scale Pela.

When Kelly and I pray together, we frequently ask God to guide our steps. We ask that He open the doors that He wants us to step through and close those He wants us to avoid. In retrospect, it would seem that the "lucky" two-hour delay in Boston was an answer to that prayer. An ordained gentle nudge from the Divine to explore the possibilities by stepping through the open door of Pela.

The opportunity checked out in being able to live within the three principles I had established. It wasn't just our unique gifts and personalities that enticed me…it was the potential of leaning into the 3rd principle of impact by helping create a waste-free future. Pela's first product using this compostable plastic was to create a phone case; which on its own happened to be a very big opportunity. However, beyond building a meaningful mobile accessories business, the hope was to inspire other companies to adopt compostable materials and in so doing, ensure more products would achieve a graceful end of life. Pela's mission has always been to demonstrate to the world that all products can be made from materials that take into account designing the end of life at the beginning.

We believe garbage is optional and that waste has inherent value. In nature, all waste from one organism becomes valuable fuel to help another grow; the entire planet works within a circular economy. Human's created *trash*. We've created all sorts of incredible materials, from which we've built amazing and wonderful tools and inventions. However along the way, we didn't think through the full lifecycle in order to build in the proper graceful end-of-life solutions. We have created this problem with our human ingenuity, and we'll now need to use our resourcefulness to solve it.

I have come to believe that business can be the greatest force for good, to improve the lives of people and the overall quality of life on our planet. When I met Jeremy and Matt, I discovered we were aligned on our beliefs and I saw the same spark in them to want to meaningfully impact this problem. With this business vehicle I could see a path to actually *creating a compostable clean economy* that would then usher in the waste-free future we have envisioned.

A phone case made of traditional plastic will last hundreds if not thousands of years, while a phone made of Pela's compostable materials degrades into soil in a matter of weeks. This unique value proposition and our ability to communicate the benefits has helped sell millions of phone cases globally. However with the proliferation of the phone cases, we faced a major challenge. Most of our customers did not have access to home composting facilities and the industrial composters in their area would not accept products made of bio-plastics. As a result many people would send back their phone cases to us to provide the end of life solution or discard them through the traditional waste management system. This is a better outcome when compared to the lack of biodegradability of a traditional plastic phone case, but by going to a landfill, it does not capture the inherent value of the organic waste.

We decided we needed to solve this infrastructure problem and so we embarked on a journey that would ultimately result in the creation of Lomi.

Lomi is the world's first smart waste appliance that magically turns your organic waste into a regenerative soil supplement, while you sleep. Lomi uses a combination of heat, humidity, maceration, and microbes to accelerate the natural process of organic degradation. Most importantly, Lomi is able to process waste from both food and compostable materials— and it does it in hours, not months.

About a 3rd of all household waste is made up of food waste and there's a general misconception that food waste in landfills is OK. *It is not.* Most organic waste is put into plastic garbage bags that in turn ends up in landfill where it is buried with clay and dirt. This means the organics will be forced to break down anaerobically (lacking access to oxygen) and in the process generate both a harmful leachate and methane gas. It is believed that methane gas is up to 80 times more harmful than CO_2 in affecting climate change as a greenhouse gas.

Lomi transforms "garbage into gold" by taking something that was considered waste and turning it into a nutrient dense superfood for your plants. In addition, it reduces the volume of organic waste by up to 90 percent, dramatically decreasing the strain on landfills. Best of all, the output acts as a natural carbon synch, pulling it from the atmosphere.

I firmly believe that if Lomi was to be adopted en masse, it could be one of the most democratized solutions in helping reverse climate change while also providing a solution for soil degradation. Lomi empowers the users with a tangible way to participate in helping build a more sustainable future.

It would appear that we are not alone in these beliefs. We launched Lomi as a crowdfunding campaign in the spring of 2021, and quickly sold twenty thousand units in less than ninety days! Lomi went on to become the largest crowdfunding campaign of the year and the largest cleantech crowdfunding campaign of all time.

It's hard to connect the dots looking forward. It's only possible by stopping, reflecting and looking *backward* that we can see logical progression. That is not to be confused with adopting a narrative fallacy (the belief that you had a predetermined plan) but rather the importance of having a clear North Star right from the start.

Our vision of creating a waste-free future has always remained the same; however, our approach at how we realize it has evolved over time. It started with creating a compostable phone case. It then evolved into developing other sustainable products in complementary categories. Now we are building out the infrastructure necessary to support the emergent compostable economy. We know we cannot create this vision on our own. It is our hope to inspire other companies to join our cause and benefit from our experience with materials and the Lomi infrastructure.

The greatest threat to our planet is not climate change; it is not nuclear war nor the plastic pollution problem. The greatest threat we face is the false belief that someone else is going to solve our problems. We have to self-select that we must be part of the solution and it starts by imagining a better future, fueled by the curiosity of how we can create it, and then having the courage to act and bring what we have imagined into reality.

While I may have begun my journey creating products from materials that cause environmental destruction, grace found me amidst the storms of my life and helped transform me into an ambassador dedicated to saving the planet. Pela and Lomi are part of the initiatives that are contributing to this change. However, the world needs more innovation and we intend to use these examples to imagine and inspire additional opportunities that will help create a better and more abundant future.

John Newton holds a special place in my heart, and his story of finding grace followed by then taking action to make restitution, resonates with me deeply. My life as a toymaker led me to an awareness of the unsustainable practices driven by consumerism and the realization of the profound environmental issues we face. Without that experience, I would not have understood the urgency of finding solutions to these problems, nor would I have had the knowledge and abilities to help found companies like Pela case and Lomi.

> *"We make a living by what we get,*
> *but we make a life by what we give."*
> —WINSTON CHURCHILL

What "Pela" Means in Spanish

At Pela, we're trying to achieve a waste-free future. We've adopted a contrarian point of view that waste is optional, and in fact it has value.

The very name *Pela* is a perfect metaphor. In Spanish, it means "peel," describing the protective coating that covers fruits such as apples (just like how our first product, the Pela Case, covers an Apple iPhone). Most importantly, a peel is something you throw away, but when you do, it breaks down and returns to the plan-et gracefully and becomes the source of nutrients for other living things to grow.

LEGO LESSONS

The lessons we could learn from LEGO are endless, just as when you play with them and in the process realize that there are endless possibilities for what you can create. (Visit Legoland for awe-inspiring displays!)

There are so many life lessons learned from these tiny bricks, but there are four critical ones I don't want you to miss. These are so important and aren't just for business, but affect our entire life.

Use Every Block

First, when you begin building a LEGO set, it doesn't look like much. In fact, when you dump all the pieces on the ground, you have little more than a pile—they're all mixed and the colors clash. In the midst of erect-ing a small town or Han Solo's Millennium Falcon, it can be difficult to envision how the final product will have any meaning (the messy mid-dle). However as you work, bringing order to the chaos, beauty begins to emerge. With each connection made, what started out as thousands of random small pieces suddenly is transformed into purposeful art.

Block by block, as you snap the pieces together, you'll eventually end up with a remarkable design. Whether a vehicle, a small town, a robot, or your own creation, what started out as a mess eventually turns into some-thing you can stand back and admire.

And that, I think, is a lesson worth learning.

Each brick on its own is relatively valueless; a simple chunk of plastic. While each block has incredible potential, it's dependent on being *connected* to another block, in order to start forming something of architectural value.

If you build with only a single color or shape, that limits the potential, resulting in a monochrome structure—freestanding, perhaps, but rather lackluster. Without the diversity and quantity of bricks, we limit the shape and detail to build something truly extraordinary. You can only build a beautiful tapestry out of LEGOs by using bricks of various colors and shapes, as each block becomes a small but important piece of the final design.

Likewise, we each have a variety of gifts we've been given: skills, relationships, experiences, education, etc. We could use only one of these, and we may be able to build something of some value. When we put them *all* together, we're able to create beautiful *art*.

You're a unique individual, with a variety of building blocks in your life that make up your full God given faculty of skills and experience. Your real value comes when you learn to use these gifts to realize your true potential.

Follow the Process

Through a disciplined and deliberate approach, you take your dependencies (the connective supports) and assemble them in a way to form an independent structure, something unique and liberated and full of meaning. However, you can't just randomly connect blocks together. Particularly for the most challenging LEGO sets, you must have the discipline to plan your work and then to work your plan; why would our lives (which are infinitely more complex than LEGOs) be any different?

Anyone who's ever built a complex LEGO set and has attempted to design it freeform (not follow the instructions), has come to a moment of impasse. Without the right sequencing, you're often left with extra parts, or you discover that the way you had chosen to build it will not allow you to complete the design. Then comes the unhappy process of taking the structure apart so that you can rebuild it again, this time in the right order to achieve the intended design.

In our lives, we must always take the time to get clear on our beliefs and values. Only from there can we set out meaningful goals and intentions. With this clarity, you are then able to effectively plan out your priorities, knowing that the only way you're going to achieve your goals is by ensuring you're being intentional and methodical.

PAUSE AND REFLECT

When we create a life of meaning it looks like a tapestry of beautiful woven colors, or in the case of LEGO, an assembled structure of unlikely block combinations. Often, the pieces of our lives feel like a meandering, wandering conglomeration, and the daily struggle sometimes camouflages the deeper purpose of our journey.

Just as we buy a package of LEGOs, stare at the picture on the box, and think, "I'm going to create that," so often, we start our life with a vision of what we intend to create. However, somewhere in between steps one and four hundred, we stumble and fall, and nothing seems to make sense.

In those moments, that's a great time to stop, zoom out, step back, and look at the overall arc of your life. Look how far you've come—at the outset, you had a bunch of blocks, now, even if all the parts aren't *quite* there yet, and the original vision isn't completed, some things are taking form and being pieced together.

Reflection is valuable for taking stock of where you have come from in order to better plan where you are going. Sometimes when facing difficulties it is easy to get bogged down in the minutia, losing track of where each step is leading. If you ever lose sight of the greater purpose, the first step is to ask "am I confusing activity for accomplishment?" or "am I drowning in the doldrums of the daily grind?" It is important that our activities are aligned with our values and virtues and are making progress towards supporting our goals. Much of what it takes to be successful is a monotonous and boring process and it is easy to lose the plot of what you ultimately are trying to achieve. When you feel uninspired or lost, often the best thing to do is pause, step back, and make space in order to get a better perspective. Getting renewed clarity on the outcomes you want to achieve and acknowledging the progress that you have made will help make sense out of the mound of remaining pieces you are assembling.

PUT SETS TOGETHER

*"Rome wasn't built in a day, but they were laying
bricks every hour."*
—JOHN HEYWOOD

One LEGO structure is amazing. However where LEGOs *really* shine— is when you can assemble a number of vastly different and independent structures together. How awesome it is to develop a cityscape, a group of *Star Wars* characters coming together to form a battle scene, or to re-create the landscape of *Harry Potter's* Hogwarts. That's when LEGO building goes from fun to awe-inspiring artistry.

Stephen Covey's *The 7 Habits of Highly Effective People* has had a profound impact on my life. A key idea he discusses is the progression from dependence to independence to interdependence. Covey explains that each of us are born and raised in a world where we're *dependent* on others to survive.[45] At some point, through a school graduation or some other transition, we (hopefully) become *independent*—able to stand as a solid structure

---

45 Covey, *7 Habits.*

on our own. If we achieve independence then most of us will stop there, just short of the most glorious representation of ourselves, becoming *interdependent*. This is when we join with others, standing on our own two feet, and when combined together, we become a much more meaningful design.

We start our lives like loose LEGO blocks—full of potential, but dependent on the connections to our parents, teachers, and coaches to provide for our physical needs and to shape our beliefs and values. These influences provide the building blocks that help give our lives structure. Block by block, they form the needed supports to create the walls, platforms, and pillars of our potential. If we keep progressing, on our own, we may achieve an independent, fully formed structure. But is that all there is?

Once you've achieved independence, you'll eventually realize that true joy and satisfaction only comes from transcending to interdependence. We're designed to be in relationship with others and to live inter-connected. We create true meaning, joy, and fulfillment in our lives when we strive for the four Cs and in the process we grow and we give. We can only live out our true potential when we use our agency and resources to build and support communities.

Playing with LEGOs can teach us a lot about how we depend on each other to make outcomes exponentially better. Imagine you have built a beautiful clock tower, like Big Ben. On its own, it's an amazing structure that you can be proud of. If you step back, you will see that there's so much more you can create! You can add more buildings like the London Eye and Tower Bridge and suddenly you have built an awesome cityscape that is infinitely more impressive.

We are created to be interdependent on each other to produce extraordinary outcomes. Working together is the key to not just surviving, but ultimately moving to a place of thriving. Take your independence and upgrade it to *inter*dependence, recognizing that in order to go far, we need to go together.

How to Build Interdependence

Interdependence is a big concept. In *The 7 Habits of Highly Effective People,* Covey provides a recommended path to go from dependence to independence and then to interdependence, suggesting that you must pass through each phase (you cannot go from dependence straight to interdependence).

Covey admonishes us to apply the principles of the seven habits in order to achieve interdependence, noting that we aren't all given the same opportunity for such self-discovery. I've summarized the principles in my own words.

1. **Be proactive:** Get engaged and lean in. Life is in session, this is not the practice run. Know what is in your control, and with that, focus on growing your circle of influence while not being overwhelmed by your circle of concern.

2. **Start with the end in mind:** This is our vision for the future and how to create your own personal vision and mission statements. As we know, everything is created twice: first in our minds, then in reality. Imagine a LEGO tower that you're putting together; in order to make sense of the pieces, you need a final mental picture to determine which piece goes next. Write your eulogy and then live according to your words.

3. **First things first:** Ensure alignment between your values and your priorities. Your calendar tells the truth about what you truly value. We are addicted to being busy and spend time doing what's urgent and important or by doing what's urgent

and unimportant (what Covey calls quadrants one and three). To truly make meaningful progress toward our goals, we need to focus on work that is important but not urgent (quadrant two).

4. **Think win-win:** Think about creating win-win from an abundance mentality versus a scarcity mindset. Scarcity assumes the pie is only so big; therefore, the outcome is binary, with the winner getting the bigger piece. Abundance assumes that the pie is ever-growing. As we create more value, we can all share in the value created. In business and in life, every transaction must be a win-win or there should be no deal. Your perception needs repair if you're asking who's winning in relationships (such as marriage or your business partnerships). Relationships will only endure if they are set up as a continuous win-win for both parties.

5. **Seek first to understand before being understood:** You'll be more effective and have more influence if you first take the time to understand the other person's point of view. People don't care how much you know until they know how much you care. Be genuinely interested; most do not listen to understand, rather they listen just enough to prepare a reply. Be humble and remember the words of Ezra Benson: "Pride is concerned with who is right. Humility is concerned about what is right." In other words, we should stop trying to be knowers who know what is right but rather become learners who in turn want to get it right. Remember when communicating with others that to truly be listened to and to be heard is oxygen for the soul.

6. **Synergize:** We should be trying to create opportunities where the whole is greater than the sum of its parts. Where our differences become our strengths. Where the collective combined perspectives of different people create exponential outcomes. None of us are as smart as all of us. Surround yourself with people who will challenge you, while complementing your strengths and supplementing your weaknesses.

7. **Sharpen the saw:** The habit that ties the other six together is an investment into yourself. You must ensure you invest into your health and have the right ratio of education to entertainment. If you choose to invest in you, it will be the best investment you will ever make. In the words of Jim Rohn, "Work harder on yourself than you do on your job." Develop the discipline and practice of growing yourself to become everything that God intended for you.[46]

Sharpening the saw, this is something that you should expect to do for the rest of your life. As John Archibald so eloquently stated: "We live on an island surrounded by a sea of ignorance. As our island of knowledge grows, so does the shore of our ignorance." This means that the more we learn and discover about ourselves and the world around us, that should only open up our awareness of the need for new discoveries. This includes relationships. The relationships we are growing (including the one with ourselves) are not problems to be solved but rather mysteries to be discovered. We are on a never-ending journey of self-discovery by growing our knowledge and understanding and revealing the mysteries of the relationships we are engaged in.

---

46   Covey, *7 Habits.*

PLAY WELL

When the Danish widower Ole Christensen originally founded the LEGO company in 1932, he named it "LEGO," a derivative of the Danish phrase *leg godt*, which means, "play well."

This is an awesome commission for what it means to fully live out the best of our human experience. We are born playful and through play we discover our truest potential and unlock our unique possibilities. We've each been given building blocks in the form of talents; some of us can paint, others can dance and some of us can build businesses. With our gifts we have the opportunity to develop meaningful relationships and in turn we can create memorable experiences.

We are all blessed to be located in this awe-inspiring place in the universe that features towering mountains, forests that sprawl over vast landscapes, immense oceans full of life, and caverns that invite us into the depths of darkness. All of it beckons us to approach, to savor, to behold, to investigate, to explore and to craft, and with what we build, to enrich the lives of those around us and at the same time to preserve and protect our planet.

There is an ancient First Nations quote that goes, "We did not inherit the land from our ancestors, but, rather, we are borrowing it from our children." It is a striking mandate that should force us to pause and be mindful of the generational consequences of our actions.

Our Creator has designed this incredible playground that provides infinite opportunities for us all. Despite our human history filled with tumult and conflict, I believe His true desire is for us to live out our full potential, all while being good stewards by loving each other and His creation. Pela and Lomi have provided me with an amazing opportunity to do this and to build something meaningful that aligns business enterprise with my values.

I believe that our human potential to imagine and create a better future is boundless, and that we have the ability to solve our greatest problems. What if we all made a commitment today to construct a brighter future for the coming generations? Anything that is valuable and enduring starts small and takes time to build. All it takes is to imagine the possibilities, decide to commit to a course of action and then start putting the pieces together... Every LEGO masterpiece was once a pile of potential that was created by simply connecting one block at a time.

> *"Life is no brief candle for me. It is a sort of*
> *splendid torch which I have got hold of for the*
> *moment, and I want to make it burn as brightly as*
> *possible before handing it on to future generations."*
> —GEORGE BERNARD SHAW

Conclusion
Red Wagons Are Not
Meant to Rust

*"Let's run the risk of wearing out rather than
rusting out."*

—TEDDY ROOSEVELT

We began our journey together in the air and now, we'll land on the ground, with lessons learned from the Radio Flyer red wagon. This product was aptly named after the founder's fascination with both the radio and Charles Lindbergh's nonstop flight across the Atlantic.

In 1914, Antonio Pasin, an Italian by birth, packed up all his dreams and set out for a new land, arriving in America. A few years later, the young Pasin (not yet twenty years of age) moved to Chicago and started building quality wood wagons.

According to *Timeless Toys*:

> During the day, Pasin lugged a ragged old suitcase containing an unassembled wagon from store to store and when prospective buyers would allow, he'd assemble the parts to illustrate just how well the wagons were made.[47]

Soon demand for his wagons outpaced his ability to manufacture them. So Pasin looked to the auto industry, borrowing their innovation of stamping steel and making his wagons from metal. The new design was in production only a couple years before the Great Depression set in.

During the financial crisis, he defied conventional wisdom and took a bold step by committing fully to an audacious marketing strategy: building a forty-five foot tall statue of a boy with his red wagon. This statue, known as "Coaster Boy," was proudly displayed at the 1933 Chicago World's Fair. Pasin believed that showcasing this statue would increase awareness and boost sales of his miniature red wagons as souvenirs. His risk paid off, and the sales of Radio Flyer began to soar, eventually making it an iconic brand and a cherished symbol of childhood in America.

---

47 Walsh, *Timeless Toys*.

The company has been passed down three generations, and is now led by Robert Pasin. He has kept up with his Italian grandfather's adventurous spirit, creating a number of new and innovative Radio Flyer products including developing a partnership with Tesla.

In 2017 the company celebrated its one-hundred-year anniversary, proving that they have been able to do something remarkable in the toy business: transcend time and create something enduring. Truly, if there's a limit to where a little red wagon can take you, the Pasin family has yet to find it.

100 KILOMETERS LATER

*"Nothing can resist a human will that will stake its
very existence on its purpose."*
—BENJAMIN DISRAELI

On one of my early visits to Hong Kong, I met a local man named Paul who had previously served in the British forces. Paul and I became friends, and I enjoyed listening to stories about his military experiences and the history of British rule in southeast Asia.

Through our conversations, I learned about the Gurkhas, and how they had a training camp in Hong Kong in the events leading up to World War II. Composed mostly of Nepalese soldiers, these warriors were highly trained and known for their ferocity. They were widely respected and considered an early version of the modern-day Navy SEALs. Their skills were so impressive that when Great Britain relinquished control of its former colony, they chose to retain many of these warriors in their employment, many of who continue to serve in the military to this day.

Hong Kong is a renowned coastal city that is flanked by mountains draped in dense jungle. These mountains are home to several trails that wind through the hilly terrain, which can be extremely challenging to navigate. As part of the final rites of passage, members of the aspiring Gurkhas had to run a one-hundred-kilometer race through these mountain trails, carrying heavy backpacks, with a time limit of just eighteen hours to finish.

During my high school years, I specialized in sprinting and never considered myself a long-distance runner due to my stocky, five-foot-nine build. However, upon hearing about the Gurkhas—who are similarly known for their short, muscular physiques—I became inspired and wondered if I could accomplish a similar feat. My research led me to discover a modern-day equivalent of their rite of passage: the Hong Kong 100 ultramarathon. As the name suggests, this is an incredibly grueling race spanning 100 kilometers, with runners facing a climb of over 17,000 feet in elevation. Although the challenge seemed daunting, I remained curious and wondered if I had the stamina and endurance to complete it.

Kyle, who was our head of product development, had moved to Hong Kong and was also an avid runner. Often, during my visits, we would venture out into the New Territories to go on runs or hikes. During one occasion, we discussed the ultrarace and I mentioned that one day I planned on entering the race.

Years of busyness and other priorities passed us by and finally one day Kyle asked: "Brad, when are you going to attempt the Hong Kong 100?" By now I was well into my forties; I was getting older, and my youthful advantage was beginning to fade. Realizing that I was out of integrity with my commitments, I made the decision to follow through and register for the January 2016 event—giving myself fourteen months to train.

When I began training, my endurance was terrible. I was reasonably fit but my focus had been on strength training. The interesting thing about training for an ultra-distance event is that it's no different than training to do anything that seems daunting. You have to be willing to suck and start small. In my case, I started very, very small.

There is an age-old adage, "How do you eat an elephant?" The answer is "One bite at a time." I ran three kilometers on my first day of training, and I remember feeling terrible. It was only a fraction of what I'd need to be able to endure, however I had taken one step in forcing myself outside my comfort zone and into exploring my possibilities.

My training was grueling and intense; I hated running and every day of training was a physical and mental struggle. I was not sure I was seeing any real progress and on many days, my recorded times and endurance seemed to *regress*.

Many months into my training I saw my endurance start to improve where I could run 10–20 km comfortably. Fourteen days before the race, I managed to complete my first marathon distance. It wasn't a pretty run, and I didn't feel energized nor did I experience the "runner's high" so many people speak of. During the run I realized that so many of the challenges I needed to overcome were mental. I could see that once you've broken through your perception of what you previously thought were your limits, your vision for the possibilities for the future begins to expand.

When I showed up to the starting line of the Hong Kong 100, I was amongst two thousand other runners on a cool and wet day in January 2016. I had hardly slept the night before, as I was anxious about the physical exertion that was about to take place. The lack of rest was not helpful and I wondered if I had unintentionally sabotaged the probability of success, knowing I would soon be stressing my body to never explored levels.

On an unusually chilly day, with ominous weather forecasts looming, I joined a group of 2000 runners and took off into the misty jungle at the sound of a pistol. Little did we know, we were headed straight into a freak ice storm that was about to hit the region. Despite the worsening weather conditions, I pushed myself to the limit and managed to reach the sixty-four-kilometer checkpoint. By that time, my clothes were drenched, and the icy temperatures had caused my gear to freeze over. Seeking to escape the freezing cold, I took shelter inside a tent for a few minutes to warm up. Then, once I felt ready, I got back into my gear and prepared to rejoin the race.

As I stood outside the tent, watching ice pellets fall down from the sky, I couldn't help but shiver uncontrollably. Despite having come this far, I had a gut feeling that something was wrong. The terrain ahead was only going to get tougher, with some of the steepest ascents yet to come. Faced with this difficult decision, I was conflicted, but ultimately decided to call it quits. The risks of continuing under such adverse conditions were simply too great.

Although I initially felt like a failure for being unable to finish the race, I later found some solace in learning that it was eventually canceled due to the extreme weather conditions. Upon further reflection, I began to recognize just how much I had accomplished. Despite being fatigued from lack of sleep and suffering from hypothermia, I had managed to run four times the distance I had covered just a month earlier and in the process I'd climbed over ten thousand feet!

I took a couple days to rest and recover before flying home to Canada. In my mind, I was done. I had put in my best effort and despite the terrible weather, I'd accomplished more than I thought possible. I had nothing left to prove, or at least that is what I had told myself.

In the months that followed, something continued to nag at me. I couldn't help but wonder whether I would have been able to finish the race had the weather been less challenging. The idea of leaving that box unchecked, of not having accomplished what I had set out to do, left me questioning whether I truly wanted to give up.

I decided to go back; only this time it would be different. Instead of grinding and forcing myself under a time-crunched, miserable practice routine, I stretched out my training. I decided to make my training both enjoyable and fun and a great way to catch up on podcasts and audiobooks.

Interestingly, even though I was more relaxed and pushing myself less, I was posting times comparable with my original training. I was proving that I could go nearly as far and as fast only this time I was also enjoying the journey.

In January 2017, I returned to the starting line of the Hong Kong 100. I was in better shape, had more confidence, and felt prepared.

At 8:00 a.m. we once again started out, however, this time the weather was perfect. I was keeping a comfortable pace and feeling good, however during a steep descent near the forty-kilometer mark, I twisted my right knee. My ACL had been compromised from a prior injury and I was aware of the risk of potentially blowing my knee out. In my mind I was done, and I decided that at the next check point I would drop out.

I arrived at the halfway point and started to pack my gear bags to leave. I told myself: "I've done my best. I just wasn't cut out to be an ultra-distance runner." With my mind made up and some dry clothes on, I suddenly received a text on my phone from Kelly. She was back in Canada and had stayed up late tracking my progress. The text read: "Brad, I love you, and I believe in you. I know you can do this."

I froze, but this time not from the temperatures, but rather the impact of the message. I looked at my packed bags and carefully considered my next moves. I don't know how Kelly knew that I was struggling, but her timely inspiration was the difference between quitting or continuing. I put my running gear back on and once again set off.

From that moment on, one fortuitous event after another occurred, each at a key inflection point, that would allow me to continue. A friend of mine who had previously run the Hong Kong 100 race, was operating as my support. He said he'd meet me at the sixty-four-kilometer checkpoint with any special food request I had. I told him a *Big Mac with fries*…(when you run a race like this, you burn a lot of calories and my body was craving fat and salt.) That meal became a significant motivator for me to press on to the next checkpoint; however, when I arrived, I couldn't find my friend. I had run all that distance and was relishing a hot meal, but he was nowhere to be found. Then I suddenly realized, "This is exactly where I bowed out last year." This time, swollen knee and all, I was feeling energized and despite being disappointed at not being able to satisfy my fast food craving, I decided to press on.

Through the darkness, I could make out the lights from the Hong Kong cityscape in the distance, while my feet carefully navigated the path avoiding tripping on roots and rocks. I was on my own, running in the dark, when out from the bushes, I heard a voice shout, "Brad!" Initially I was startled but then I realized that it was my friend who stood there holding a brown bag with yellow arches. Despite trying, he couldn't reach the planned meeting point; however, since he knew the race route, he had navigated through the jungle to intercept me along the path. There on the side of a mountain, I devoured one of the most delicious meals ever to grace my lips. It would prove to be part of the sustenance I would need to continue into the early morning hours.

By the seventy-three-kilometer checkpoint, the pain in my knee had now become problematic. My spirit was high, but my knee appeared to be getting much worse. As I sat down by the fire a local woman who only spoke Cantonese, walked up to me and pointed at my leg. She instinctively seemed to know I was in trouble and despite not speaking any words, she rubbed ointment on my knee. The pain and throbbing started to subside and using nodding and gestures, I thanked her, and started running again.

I reached the eighty-three-kilometer checkpoint and was completely exhausted. I was warming by the fire and started visiting with a couple of German runners. They had opted to drop out of the race and no longer needed their supplies and in the process one offered me a can of Red Bull. It was just the boost I needed to push myself another ten kilometers.

At the ninety-kilometer checkpoint, I once again paused to recalibrate. It was now 3:00 a.m., and I was only ten kilometers from the finish line. Ahead was Tai Mo Shan, the highest peak in Hong Kong and the trail up was very rugged and formidable, especially in the dark. There had been some rain, and the mountain was now covered in a dense fog.

Typically, by this late stage in the race, you'd be lucky to find even one runner, however at that exact moment *four* of us converged at the final checkpoint. We decided to run the last treacherous foggy section together, combining the lighting of our headlamps to stay on the trail and helping mitigate the risk of injury.

Twenty-one-and-a-half hours after starting, I crossed the finish line! I'd become someone different, I had discovered newly found potential within me along the way. I had learned to dig deep within myself to push past my perceived mental, physical and emotional limitations. It was never about running the race or winning, but rather evolving to become the person who could look past their current moment of pain and push to find their true potential.

When you stretch any part of your life—such as your physical capabilities—the other areas grow as well. Nothing enlarges in a silo; you are a complete being, made up of mind, body, and spirit. When you push your body beyond what you think is possible, your muscles are not the only thing you strengthen. Through the physical struggle, you experience every emotion possible: your brain constantly reminds you of the pain and stress you're voluntarily enduring. At that point, you must dig deep to discover the possibilities that lie within.

Many times while I was stumbling along the path through the lonely darkness, my mind was screaming for me to stop. When I hit my low points, I would recall a quote from Tim Grover's book *Relentless*: "Get comfortable being uncomfortable, or find another place to fail."[48] This became

---

48 Tim S. Grover, *Relentless: From Good to Great to Unstoppable* (New York: Scribner, 2013), 64.

my mantra, and I remember yelling it out, to overcome the negative voices in my mind.

The real battle was never in my body, but rather the six inches between my ears. Yes—the race was grueling and the adversity had almost crushed me physically and emotionally. However, this was ultimately a mental battle. As Henry Ford famously said, "Whether you think you can, or you think you can't—you're right." Ultimately, I'd ignored the negative voices, pushed through the pain, and eventually succeeded, revealing more of my potential. The pain was temporary; however, the physical, mental, and emotional growth would last a lifetime.

> *"The purpose of life, as far as I can tell, is to find*
> *a mode of being that's so meaningful that the fact*
> *that life is suffering is no longer relevant."*
> —JORDAN PETERSON

THE LIMITLESS WAGON

Wagons, like all the best childhood toys, are limited only by the imagination of the user. As a toddler, wagons may simply be the transportation device parents use to easily tote their children. The parent, of course, sees four wheels and a flatbed, and thinks about the practical use; however, with this same wagon, a child finds nearly limitless opportunities.

It may start out as a walker, helping kids navigate across the floor. Perhaps it becomes their carrying device to go shopping throughout the house. On other days, it's really their ship, of which they're the captain, navigating the high seas.

As children grow up, they may move onto other toys; however, many children keep that red wagon as their handy ever-changing vehicle of possibility. Many find good use for wagons by turning them into racers and using the handle to steer. With the push of a sibling, you can find yourself careening down a paved path and if your neighbors have similar wagons, you may find yourselves in a race.

In the end, wagons seem to have just the right amount of engineering—four wheels, two axles, and one steering column—to form a foundation for infinite playtime. That simple design is more than enough to offer unending possibilities for those with the right imagination.

The interesting thing about the classic Radio Flyer red wagon is that if they are not cared for, they will eventually rust. You've probably seen this before—an abandoned wagon with rusty parts, that is a mere shadow of its former glory.

The end of life for every red wagon seems to have two possibilities: it can wear out from many years of memorable and abundant use or it is tossed aside and neglected, only to quickly find its rusty demise.

Wouldn't you want your life to be like the first wagon?

You need to know that I am dying…but then again so are you. Most people drift through life and seem oblivious to the fact that the sands of time allotted to their time on this planet are slowly slipping away. Today is the first day of the rest of your life, which is exactly twenty-four hours less than the same time you had at this point yesterday. Each day is a gift and an opportunity to make the most of our God given potential or to watch it slowly rust away.

One day, this will all fade into a backdrop of nothingness and the question we all will be faced with is: "Did I carefully invest the gift of time I was given or did I spend it on things that were trivial?" What is certain is that the end will come, and we all have the option to either realize the opportunities and abilities within us, or merely allow our untapped potential, skills, and experiences to go undeveloped.

I am afraid of death and dying, which is a natural human emotion; however, what haunts me more is answering the question, "am I really living?" It is said that the wealthiest place in the world is the graveyard. Therein, the bodies of people lie dormant, with the majority of their potential still buried within them. Books not written, songs never sung, artwork never painted, awards never realized, businesses never founded, innovations never revealed, and relationships never healed.

Whenever I step outside of my comfort zone to try and do something that I am intimidated by, my initial reaction is one of hesitation. It is uncomfortable and risky exploring uncharted territory. When I feel the resistance (that is usually a figment of my imagination), the question I have learned to ask myself is "Why not me? Why not now?" The alternative is to stay comfortable and let the opportunities of life pass me by, deferring the inevitable and haunting question we all will face "What *could* I have done?"

For those of us who are still among the living, *we* have the power of choice. We get to decide what we will allow to become our fate. Will we let the rust of underuse slowly consume the potential of our gifts, or will we instead utilize our gifts, talents, and experiences to fill our red wagon full of life?

By the end, I want to ensure that I've explored every facet of life and fully embraced its richness. I want to be like a sponge, soaking up all the good things life has to offer and to then squeeze those opportunities dry of every possibility.

What is vital to all this is to stay young at heart. To remain youthful, curious, creative and courageous in exploring your potential in the opportunities that come your way. I am committed to dying young…but to do so as late as possible.

> *"The future has many names. For the weak it is*
> *unattainable. For the fearful it is unknown. For*
> *the bold it is ideal."*
> —VICTOR HUGO

WE WERE BORN CREATIVE

*"The most effective kind of learning is that the
child should play among lovely things."*
—PLATO

In 1992, doctors George Land and Beth Jarman published a book containing the conclusions of a study that was based on a creativity test originally produced for NASA. After delivering his test to NASA Dr. Land tried the same test on children.

He found that 98 percent of four- and five-year-olds tested in the genius zone of creativity. Dr. Land couldn't believe it. He conducted the same test on the same group five years later and found only 30 percent scored at genius level creativity. They took the test again at fifteen years old, and the creative genius had eroded to 12 percent. Astonishing by age twenty five, only 2 percent of the original cohort was found to have creative genius. Down from 98 to 2 percent genius in two decades.[49]

The origin of the word *genius* means to have been touched by the divine. Based on Dr. Land's study, apparently, the majority of us were born with God given genius. Yet, as we venture into the world, we're hit with the cold reality that we can fail, and face rejection. Fear sets in and starts to tighten its grip on our minds and hearts. We default to scarcity thinking and every time we take a hit, we downsize our hopes and dreams, constraining ourselves to the increasingly limited version of who we could be. We respond to pain by trying to avoid it, seeking out comfortability, downgrading our expectations, trying less, and shrinking more.

So the question is: How do we continue to maintain our genius and reveal our innate touch of the Divine?

---

49 George Land and Beth Jarman, *Breakpoint and Beyond: Mastering the Future Today* (New York: HarperBusiness, 1992).

EXPAND THE EDGES OF
YOUR COMFORT ZONE

Our comfort zone is what is keeping our dreams at bay. As we age and face the many challenges of life, our comfort zone shrinks. As our comfort zone decreases in size, so does our capacity for using our creativity and imagination.

During a research experiment, a marine biologist placed a shark into a large holding tank with several small bait fish. Predictably, the shark attacked and ate the fish. The biologist then inserted a strong clear fiberglass divider into the tank, separating the shark from the rest of the tank. The biologist then once again inserted the bait fish only this time the shark slammed into the divider repeatedly and eventually gave up after weeks of trying. The biologist then removed the divider, but the shark no longer attacked the fish. The shark had become conditioned to believe that a barrier existed and, in an attempt to avoid more failure, it decided to remain on its side of the tank. The shark's comfort zone had shrunk, and it was no longer willing to risk further discomfort—even at the cost of starvation.

Consider young children, where by default, everything is outside of their comfort zone, and every day is full of fresh and exciting experiences to learn and grow. In order to develop their potential, they must constantly live on the edge of what they know how to do. They are in a constant state of exploring, playing, and learning. With a limited history of biases, they let their imagination paint a vivid picture of what is possible.

Therein we see the contrast: young children see future possibilities and are constantly pushing to expand their comfort zone as they grow and develop. On the other hand, adults become conditioned by historical biases of discomfort and failings that naturally *contract* their comfort zone when facing new challenges. What is certain is that the outside world *will* create resistance, and this is actually a key part of developing our human potential.

Unfortunately in an effort to avoid discomfort, most adults shy away from this pain or pressure. In doing so, they inadvertently allow their comfort zones to contract and their dreams to gradually fade into mere fantasies.

If we choose to remain "childlike" and use our imagination to focus on possibilities, we will then intentionally push *outward* against challenges, and in the process our comfort zone will expand. We do this by working up the courage to talk to the girl we think is outside of our league, by launching a new business venture, or trying to get into the school that we think is beyond what we deserve.

Living with the intention to seek out ways to expand our comfort zones is what I believe it means to really thrive in our human experience. It just so happens that *Thrive* is one of my favorite words and I use it often when doing personal affirmations. For me it conjures up images of living my best self and maximizing my full potential. To Thrive is to be truly living…to be fully alive!

If you desire to truly thrive in the way you live your life, then I encourage you to check out FullSpectrumLife.com/Resources where as a community, we strive to unlock our full potential.

> *"The universe is full of magical things patiently*
> *waiting for our wits to grow sharper."*
> —EDEN PHILLPOTTS

WE NEED STRUGGLE

To survive there are a few essential things we all need, including: air, food, water, shelter, and companionship. These are the baseline that form the foundation of Maslow's hierarchy of needs. However, the missing piece that is rarely mentioned is that we need to struggle.

We need difficulties in our life to fully develop our human potential. Absent of difficulty and the resistance they bring, we begin to die. We may continue to exist physically, but internally our dreams wither, and our spirits let go. It is my belief that the death of our future hopes is worse than dying physically.

Consider Immanuel Kant's observations of the important factors that result in a bird being able to fly. The bird must feel the resistance of the air against its wings in order to enable its ability to create lift when flapping. You might think that by removing the resistance you would be doing the bird a favor. The reality is that if you were to put that bird into a vacuum, thereby eliminating the resistance, you would be taking away the very thing that enables the bird to experience flight.

The same principle holds true for us. Through our struggles, we find strength, and challenges will reveal our character. Always sunshine, only desert: the storms of life are what bring the rain that allows us to flourish and grow.

While it is natural for us to embrace challenges as children, as adults we often shy away from difficulty and even go so far as to shield our own children from experiencing hardship. While this is natural it is not optimal. Consider for a moment what it takes to build one's physique. To achieve a fit body, then an unavoidable step is to engage in challenging exercise where you break down muscle tissue, thereby stimulating growth and increased strength. Beyond fitness, this is the same principle for how we develop all of our human potential.

Success tends to be a poor teacher. In the end, we don't learn from easy things; the hard reality is that challenges tend to be the best teacher. As we step outside of our comfort zones, we should expect difficulty and to fail. We ought to *plan* for that, and while you shouldn't seek pain, know that if you're living courageously, you will encounter it. You can either let the challenges you face beat the strength out of you or build the strength into you!

In the apostle Paul's letter to the Romans, he wrote, "We rejoice in our sufferings, knowing that suffering produces perseverance, perseverance produces character, and character produces hope." This passage provides the correct formula. When we are experiencing suffering and in that moment learn to suffer well; we are building perseverance, resilience and tenacity. We are changed as a result and in the process we are reshaping our character. Discovering this new potential gives us a fresh perspective and a new hope that we can become and accomplish more than what we previously thought was possible.

WHERE DO WE START?

Bronnie Ware is a nurse who spent several years working in palliative care, looking after patients during the last few weeks of their lives. During her time, she recorded their thoughts on epiphanies that her patients had discovered. Ware later published these epiphanies in a book called *The Top Five Regrets of the Dying*.

You can only imagine the incredible clarity and wisdom people gain as they approach the end of their lives. According to Ware, when individuals were asked about any regrets or actions they would have done differently, recurring themes emerged. Notably, of the top five regrets, only one involved an action taken: they wished they had worked less. Amazingly, four of the top regrets pertained to opportunities *not pursued* and that they wished they would have experienced. This should serve as a warning for us all knowing that in their final weeks alive, the majority of her patients consistently cited their greatest regrets were of *not doing* things they wished they had.

Thought leader and author John Maxwell further expanded on this idea, when he wrote:

I've been an observer of people all my life, and I've noticed that most people are pretty passive about their lives. An indication of this is that when asked to describe significant regrets in their lives, eight out of ten people focus on actions they did not take rather than actions they did. In other words, they focus on things that they failed to do rather than things they failed at doing.[50]

Incredibly, the regrets of the people in the study are of those adventures left unexplored, those relationships left undiscovered, those inventions left unlocked, and those gifts left unused. They say things like, "I wish I'd lived more in the present," "I wish I'd traveled more," "I wish I'd taken more risks," or "I wish I'd followed my passions."

When faced with important life choices, we need to ask ourselves a question:

"Will I say: 'I'm glad I did?' or 'I wish I had?'"

Jeff Bezos bases his famous "regret-minimization" decision filter on this framework. He fast forwards to his eighty-year-old self and asks whether he will be glad or regret a decision he is about to make. Will you get to the end of your life and wish you had chosen differently? If so, start choosing differently today. The best time to plant a tree? Ten years ago. The next best time? Today!

What could you do with the red wagon of your life?

Will we allow ourselves to rust out, and our dreams to die within us, or will we instead find the edge of what the red wagons of our lives can carry, constantly stretching our capacity, and unlocking all that is possible within us?

I invite you to live your life with the latter in mind: I hope that you'll constantly find the edge of possibility for yourself *and then expand it.* I invite you to play outside your comfort zone and to reenter your childhood

---

50 John C. Maxwell, *The Power of Significance: How Purpose Changes Your Life* (New York: Center Street, 2017), Kindle.

genius. Instead of asking yourself, "What's easy?" or "What's comfortable?" ask yourself, "What if?" followed by, "Who do I need to become?"

You've only got one life to live; why would you not plan to leave all your potential behind on the field of life? Dare to dream big, live boldly, and in the process become the best and brightest version of yourself!

> *"Twenty years from now you will be more*
> *disappointed by the things you didn't do than by*
> *the ones you did. So throw off the bowlines, sail*
> *away from the safe harbor."*
> —MARK TWAIN

OIL YOUR RUSTY RELATIONSHIPS

When I was first fired from Basic Fun, I was initially resentful towards my partners, as I had felt betrayed. My first instinct was revenge, and I wanted to hit back hard at my former co-founders; however, after listening to some sage advice, I chose a more civil path that ultimately led to a graceful exit.

After the dust had settled, I decided to "seek first to understand before being understood" as I wanted to consider the situation from Jay's vantage point. Basic Fun was a newly formed company with high potential; however, the two founders had conflicting working styles. This resulted in frequent clashes and was leading to an unhealthy culture.

Matthew 12:25 states, "Every kingdom divided against itself will be ruined, and every city or household divided against itself will not stand." As I reflect, I can now see that the way we were operating and leading the business, would have eventually compromised the integrity of the company.

I came to the realization that when Jay and the board agreed to fire me, it was not out of personal malice but rather in the best interest of protecting the business. They did the best they could with what they knew at the time. While I did not like the tactics, I learned to accept that his actions were meant for de-risking an unhealthy dynamic. The unexpected outcome was that this decision ultimately led to providing for my personal freedom and the ability to design a new life.

As I have pondered these events, I have come to a place of gratitude. When the board sent Justin to that fateful breakfast to *remove me* from my role, he unexpectedly *released me* to new and better possibilities. Jay and I had been frustrated in trying to figure out how to lead the company together, and now I had been set free to choose and imagine a new future somewhere else!

With that realization, I no longer felt bitterness toward Jay and instead had a desire to "bury the hatchet." My belief is that in order to be released from our past, you first need to have the courage to confront it.

On a trip back to Florida the following year, I decided to meet Jay over lunch. To my surprise, he responded quickly and expressed his happiness in hearing from me. However, he inquired about my intentions for the meeting. In response, I explained that I was seeking to reconnect with him, gain a better understanding of what had happened in the past, and ultimately find healing.

When we got together, we first exchanged the usual pleasantries and then we moved into the difficult conversation of unpacking what had happened. Jay explained that he had labored over the decision to let me go. In fact, he was leaning away from doing so, but the other board members thought it was best. He went on to say that he was surprised at the way it happened and suggested that the way it was handled was out of character for him. He explained that he was concerned over how my dismissal may have tarnished his reputation.

I listened carefully as I appreciated him opening up to share these insights with me. I then explained to him that over time I had come to understand why it happened; that I did not like how it happened, but that ultimately it had been a gift. I went on to tell him the story of how I was now directing my energy toward new opportunities and how I felt empowered by the new possibilities and that I was thriving.

We had an amazing meal and I will never forget Jay's final remarks; he thanked me and then made reference to my spiritual beliefs about seeking forgiveness and how he had witnessed them firsthand. As good as he felt about the exchange, I am convinced that I was the greatest benefactor as I felt fully released from many of the insecurities from my past.

I now recognize how easy it would have been to be the victim, holding onto my resentments and living in a spin cycle by replaying over and over the past tragedy. Choosing to live in a world of victimhood, I could have allowed myself to easily be consumed by the four B's. I could have been willfully blind to the part I had played in co-creating the dynamics that led to the firing. I could have blamed my partners for the professional and emotional damages they had caused in forcing me out of a company I had founded. I could have been begrudging them by watching them continue to build and scale the business without my direct involvement. That would ultimately have led to bitterness that I have since learned will insidiously infect all areas of your life.

Instead I chose to follow the way of the champion and embrace the four Cs. I tacked the challenge head on by mustering up the courage to reach out to Jay to seek reconciliation. I was able to explain to him how the adversity had been turned to my advantage and with my newfound opportunities, I could make a meaningful impact on the charitable landscape through the use of my creativity and resources, supporting causes that I believe in. Most importantly I had been given the opportunity to reestablish a meaningful connection and renew a relationship with someone who I value.

A legacy piece of my former business partnership with Jay is that we have a property in South Florida. Despite no longer being a part of Basic Fun, my wife and I have chosen to keep it as during the long winter months in Canada, it offers an amazing reprieve. Beyond that, we have built a meaningful community in the area with people we have come to love and cherish. We consider Jay and his family amongst those people, and when we visit Florida we continue to connect on a regular basis.

I share this story to explain how our efforts to wear out and not rust out should extend to all areas of our life, including the formerly valuable relationships that we have neglected. Socrates admonished that "the unexamined life is not worth living." In response to that, where in your life do you have unfinished business? To whom or what are you holding resentment and grudges that are keeping you from living out becoming the champion in your own hero's journey? I encourage you to get comfortable being uncomfortable and deal with the broken relationships of your past in order to be fully released to embrace the better future that awaits you.

> *"Resentment always hurts you more than it does the person you resent. While your offender has probably forgotten the offense and gone on with life, you continue to stew in your pain, perpetuating the past. Those who have hurt you in the past cannot continue to hurt you now unless you hold on to the pain through resentment. Your past is your past! Nothing will change it. You are only hurting yourself with your bitterness. For your own sake, learn from it, and then let it go."*[51]
>
> —RICK WARREN

---

51 Rick Warren, *The Purpose Driven Life: What on Earth Am I Here For?* (Grand Rapids, MI: Zondervan, 2002), Kindle.

ELISE

My journey of competing in the Hong Kong 100 race would not be complete without telling you the story of Elise. Elise was the vice president of marketing for Tech 4 Kids and had been responsible for helping us launch many of our most successful products.

Prior to working with us, Elise had successfully worked her way through the ranks of several toy companies to become a senior executive. Along the way she had achieved spectacular results in both brand management and performance marketing. She appeared to be successfully climbing the corporate ladder until one day, she suddenly resigned and picked up her family, relocating to Boulder, Colorado. It seemed like a risky career move however, she had decided that she was going to prioritize her life plan and Colorado was the best place for her to do that. Elise and her husband were athletes and avid outdoor enthusiasts, and living in Boulder gave them access to a backdrop that supported their active lifestyle.

When hiring people, my overarching philosophy has been to focus on finding the best talent irrespective of the geography. I firmly believe that great people will build value regardless of where they live. So when we needed to find a leader for our marketing team and we learned that Elise was available we pursued her. She agreed to join our team and we initially started off working under a contract for specific brands. We quickly discovered that beyond being an amazing cultural fit within the company, that she produced excellent work. Seeing the massive value she was building, we decided to move her into a full time position.

Elise was incredibly talented and made a massive positive impact as we started to scale Tech 4 Kids. What I loved most about Elise was that besides being a gifted marketer, she was full of life and vitality. She was very adventurous, constantly looking for ways to grow her abilities through new experiences. On a number of our trips to Hong Kong, I would plan to go into the new territories to train for the upcoming ultramarathon. When she found out what I was doing she would volunteer to come out and join to help me train. The terrain and weather could be challenging but she was always eager to challenge herself. Elise's value of spending time exploring nature would consistently show up in the way she lived every part of her life. She never wanted to miss the moment to reveal new possibilities.

New York City has always had a deep connection to the toy industry. For many years it was the home of the toy building, as well as iconic stores such as FAO Schwarz, and the location for the annual toy fair. It is also a place that I have been very conflicted about. I have incredible memories of going to the theater, taking a run through Central Park, the spectacle of Times Square, and numerous meals in amazing restaurants. However, whenever I visit, I am also reminded of my personal connection to the tragedy of 9/11 and how it is also the place where I suffered the greatest professional loss of my career.

On a blustery winter day in February 2016, our marketing team was busy getting the showroom ready for the much anticipated toy fair. Elise had just finished having breakfast with a few of our other team members and was walking alone for a few short blocks from our hotel to the Jacob Javits Center. With the hood of her jacket up to try and avoid the snow and wind, she attempted to cross Eleventh Avenue and was struck and killed by a large dump truck.

That cold and tragic day our company lost a very special individual and someone who was indeed a very bright light to the whole industry. Even more sickening, Elise left behind a daughter and loving husband who were at home in Boulder, unassuming and expecting that she would return home in a few short days. Instead, within a few hours they would be on a plane to New York City to grieve the loss of their precious mother and wife.

Since that day I have replayed the tapes over in my mind, asking all kinds of "what if" questions in an attempt to see if there could have been a way to avoid this horrific incident. It is both frustrating and haunting. While I am left unsatisfied with the explanation, I have come to appreciate that it is impossible for me to fully understand why our human condition is rife with hardship and calamities such as these.

What I have come to appreciate is that while Elise was alive she embraced the philosophy of wear out not rust out. The right career choice would have been for her to remain in the large city, near the head offices of the toy companies where she was employed. For the ROI of both her career advancement and her ability to earn an income, that certainly would have been the prudent decision. Instead she chose to focus on her ROE (return on experience), where she understood that for her to get the most from her all too short life, she would choose to live in a place where she could live abundantly and in the process make incredible memories with those she loved. In the end, how much money we earn or have in the bank will not matter; the only thing we will truly value and appreciate are the memories we have made in our pursuit of the four Cs.

Her life was tragically cut short, but while she was alive Elise truly lived, and for those of us who had the privilege of knowing her, she has left an indelible mark and many fond memories that I will always cherish.

PUTTING IT ALL TOGETHER

"And the end of all our exploring will be to arrive
where we started and know the place for the first
time."
—T.S. ELIOT

My intention is to live a life that is truly "successful" however, that term has been used so often, it has lost real meaning. If I asked you the question, "What is the true definition of success?" What would you say? Is it money, fame, status? We have already discussed the allure and trap of the four Ps, so that cannot be the right answer.

As I consider the lessons we have shared together in this book and what it means to be a fully thriving human, the two words that come to me are enlightened *alignment*. Enlightened simply means to have a greater knowledge and understanding about a subject or situation. Alignment is achieved when what you believe and value is truly congruent with your attitudes and actions, which in turn drive your results. The important caveat is that the only results that matter must build value for both yourself and for the world around you. And what does it mean to build value for yourself? The single word for me is:

freedom.

With that in mind, I believe the best definition of success that I have been able to come up with (so far) is:

$$S=F3V$$

Success is freedom (doing what I want, when and the way I want, with whom I want to do it) invested into my values, anchored by my virtues and expressed with vitality.

Said another way, it is living a life that is in integrity with what I believe, that in turn develops my character (to become the best and brightest version of what God has intended for me), creating value for others and that ultimately produces freedom.

As we have journeyed together through these chapters, we have discovered the many hidden and often surprising lessons that can be taught by the toys of our youth.

In my life, I've experienced bankruptcy because I forgot the lessons of the G.I. Joe: to mind my flanks. Through my downfall, I learned to constantly monitor the critical components of my business so that I will not get flanked again. I learned that my business's capital, people, and systems must grow commensurate with the company itself.

If the game of Monopoly has taught me anything, it's this: life is only worth living when I am growing and giving, and I do so by striving for the four Cs: challenges, connections, creativity, and charity.

Where you invest your time is what you value. After watching the World Trade Center Twin Towers fall, I decided I needed to focus on the vital values of the four Fs: faith, family, fitness, and finances. I learned that to "win in life," just like in Jenga, there are some blocks that can't be moved.

Just like Peter Parker, I've had my own battles with my inner villain of self doubt. I'm not sure I will ever defeat my inner dark wolf, but I remain vigilant and aware of what feeds him. I am reminded of my coach's sage words of advice, that a good hunter knows how to hunt but a masterful hunter knows how he is hunted. I now better understand how my external character is a manifestation of my belief system, values, and virtues, and how I must constantly work on who I need to become as a part of the be-do-have process.

On its own, an Etch A Sketch seems a tad colorless and dull, but it's the unmistakable joy of starting over that has made this toy a world-renowned bestseller. Throughout my life, I've learned that hope and fear are the two primary motivators of humanity. Both shape our decisions, but we can choose the more powerful force of hope to guide our actions.

My toy box—our team—at my initial startups didn't include the right mix of characters. Andy's toy box needed both diversity in thought and experience in order to complete the most important missions. Most importantly, the toy box needed to be filled with toys that contributed to a cohesive culture that could then be mobilized around an important purpose. I now focus on attracting, empowering, and retaining the most talented and mission-driven teams possible.

I have learned that a Hula-Hoop is easier to keep spinning than starting to spin from scratch. When I get into rhythm in business, I focus on spinning it longer and faster, capitalizing on the momentum and not jumping from idea to idea.

I now understand the importance of trust and candor in building relationships. In conflict, we have two options: we can stay soft and pliable, allowing the trusting conflict to help shape us, or we can dry out and become hard, brittle and broken.

I'm not a Laird Hamilton–level surfer, but I've learned that to enjoy the ride of life, we must have the courage to surf the waves we're given. Not all waves are equal and that luck (timing) plays an important role in our outcomes. In order to catch the lucky waves of life, you cannot be standing on the shoreline observing. You need to be in the water paddling.

I'm beginning to see how the LEGOs of my own life are fitting into place. My journey in the toy business resulted in me being able to build an independent structure. Now I am adding in new blocks with different colors and shapes, to create something new and more aligned with my values. For it to be truly impactful and "universe denting," we must be interdependent by not simply building a single free standing structure but rather creating an entire landscape.

Lastly, I intend to wear out and not rust out as I am compelled by the words of Jim Rohn, which I believe are worth repeating: "In life you might not be able to do all you find out, but make sure you find out all you can do." That is exactly what I intend to do as I have learned that the only shortcuts we will find in life come from our willingness to go the extra mile.

I am striving to realize success by having the courage to develop and utilize the full faculty that God has gifted to me. To be known as a man of integrity who has first and foremost modeled my life in a way that would honor Jesus. To know that I was a loving husband, father, friend, and business leader who has given his best to make a positive impact on the world.

One day while I am lying on my deathbed, I hope to reflect back on my life and have no regrets over the things I wish I had done. I want to be able to say with certainty that I fought the good fight, I finished the race, and through it all, I kept the faith.

I hope this book helps to inspire you to commit to creating your most beautiful life. That you will choose to stay young at heart, that you will play well and live a life filled with joy as you discover and then realize all of the potential and possibilities that are within you!

> *"What lies behind us and what lies before us are*
> *tiny matters compared to what lies within us."*
> —RALPH WALDO EMERSON

Afterword

The authoring of this book has been an unexpected journey that has led me down a path that has been both spiritually rewarding and emotionally painful.

I opened the book with a tribute to my beloved father. A short nine months later, I would find myself writing the end of this book and at the same time my dear mother would be completing the final chapter of her life.

Both of my parents were casualties of the pandemic. My father directly, succumbing to the debilitating effects of the virus on his body and my mother indirectly due to a much-needed heart surgery that was delayed because of the strains on the medical system. Ironically, she was given a date for the lifesaving procedure just a few days prior to her suffering a massive heart attack.

In a strange and yet-to-be-fully understood way, I now find myself bookending the final chapter with a tribute to my mother.

My mother was a truly remarkable woman who lived a very full life. Her love language for others was best expressed with food, and there was never a visit to mom's house that did not involve a spectacular feast.

My mom was a polymath. During her life, she was an artist, a musician, a seamstress, a baker, a wedding-cake maker, a first mate, a fisher, an orthotic maker, a naturopath and a lover of people. My father used to joke that my mother was the only woman he knew that would go into a public restroom and come out with new friends. She delighted in the beauty of flowers and the singing of song birds and she demonstrated daily what it was like to find joy in the journey.

At the celebration of my mothers life, my Uncle Neil noted that my mom had one notable flaw—she was consistently late. Both of my parents were infected with the COVID-19 virus, and both ended up going into the ICU. My mother, already having compromised health, was not expected to recover. Ironically, she was spared and the virus took my father's life. Miraculously, we were given the precious gift of another nine months of memories with her. It was as if she had let God know that her time of passing was going to be on her time—she was going to be late.

C. S. Lewis once said, "God whispers to us in our pleasure and shouts at us through our pain." The pain of losing two precious people in such a short period of time has left a scar on my heart. I have wept to the point of exhaustion but recognize that tears are often the best words our hearts can speak. This season of loss has forced me to reflect deeply on the blessing of being raised by such wonderful parents, the many memories of my youth, and the lessons that both my mom and dad taught me.

While I am wrestling to understand the purpose of this pain, what I do know is that our greatest human potential is often birthed out of our deepest human hurts. Pain and eventually death are the imminent outcome of our broken human condition. While pain is inevitable, misery is optional.

That has led me to reflect on the words of the Serenity Prayer: "God, grant me the serenity to accept the things I cannot change, the courage to change the things I can, and the wisdom to know the difference." I cannot help but think of Covey's circle of control, circle of influence and the circle of concern. Accepting the things I cannot change is knowing that there is an infinite sphere around my life of things that are out of my control.

We are a speck, on a speck, in a remote galaxy floating in what appears to be an infinite and expanding universe. When one reflects on this, it is humbling to realize that the vast majority of what happens is out of our control. This makes up our circle of concern and is the space that needs to be surrendered to God.

The courage needed to change the things I can, represents my ability to choose my response or my circle of control. I can only affect what I think, what I say, what I feel, and then what I do. That's all I can control, and is what ultimately grows my circle of influence. In the context of the universe, my part is relatively small.

The wisdom to know the difference is understanding that I am only responsible for choosing my response. I must surrender that the Divine has far more under His control and this leads to having faith that I am in a small way part of His greater plan.

Many times when I was going through business challenges I would recite the words from Proverbs 3: "Trust in the Lord with all your heart, lean not on your own understanding, in all your ways acknowledge him and he will guide your paths." I once again find myself repeating these words. They both represent and reaffirm the same meaning of what I now understand is the significance of the Serenity Prayer. I need to submit to God's sovereign dominion over all things, with my part being the lesser of having only a few choices within my control.

It is not so much about trying to understand why God allows suffering, but the comfort of knowing that He has walked alongside and never abandoned us in the midst of our suffering. In fact he has felt suffering first hand in that Jesus became fully human, experienced real human suffering, was betrayed and killed in a horrific way and then ultimately defeated death.

I do not understand why there has been so much loss in such a short period of time. Furthermore, I find the timing curious, as these events happened while I was scribing the pages of this book. What I do know is that during this writing project, my soul has been ripped wide open. We impress people with our accomplishments but we connect with people through our challenges. I recognize that a tenderized heart is what is required to meaningfully touch the lives of others.

Mom, thank you for bringing me into this world and providing love and care for me. I love and miss you and look forward to when we are once again together, taking delight in spotting rare songbirds while enjoying a fresh coffee and some of your Black Forest cake.

"The world breaks everyone and afterward many are strong at the broken places."

—ERNEST HEMINGWAY

Acknowledgments

The creation of this book has only been possible because of the influence of so many amazing people. As Issac Newton stated, "If I have seen further, it is by standing on the shoulders of giants."

First of all, I am thankful to my Creator for giving me the gift and opportunity of this life and modeling the ultimate expression of love through Jesus.

To my incredible wife, Kelly, who has been a rock and my faithful life and business partner for almost thirty years. We have created a beautiful life together. Our relationship has been forged by "growing through" many adversities that could have easily broken us apart but rather have galvanized our commitment to one another.

To my amazing children, Bretton and Megan. You are the arrows from my quiver that have been shot into a future that I will never see. I am so proud of you, not for what you do but rather who you are becoming. Your mom and I continue to lift you up in our prayers, asking God to refine your character so that you may shine your light in the world as you pursue excellence.

To those who raised me, including my mom and dad and to my sisters and the many cousins, aunts, and uncles who have made me feel loved. Specifically, I want to call out my grandma Keller, who has been an incredible matriarch to the entire family. Thank you for your never-ending, unconditional love, your relentless prayers of support, and the many stories you love to tell and retell of our heritage. I want to especially thank you for convincing me not to jump off the roof of the shed with the kite strapped to my back. (Although somehow I still believe I would have been able to fly!)

To my co-founders of Pela, Matt and Jeremy. It has been such an incredible journey. I am so proud to watch how you have both grown. Jeremy, thank you for your initial vision; you have such an amazing heart, and when it comes to humility, you are the best amongst us. Matt, you are an extraordinary leader who has done an incredible job of helping guide our company in creating the brave new future we have dreamed of. I am grateful for both of you, to not only be called your business partner, but also your friend.

To my coach, Colin, who next to my wife is the person who has had the greatest impact on helping shape my inner character. We have invested a significant amount of time together, often resulting in either heated words or shedding of tears. It has been hard work challenging many of my stubborn beliefs that have held me back from moving forward, and I am so grateful for your wisdom, servant leadership, and tender heart.

To the many mentors, coaches, and friends who are always a text or phone call away, who have selflessly invested their time. The list is long and not exhaustive but includes notable mentions to: Darren Hardy, Warren Coughlin, Anthony Dimarco, Dan Martell, Vijay Krishnan, and my forum The Dirty Dozen. The way you all live your lives inspires me, and I love how we help ignite each other's imaginations and dream about the possibilities for the future.

To Jayson Gaignard. Thank you for having the courage to create MMT as some of my favorite people in the world (several already listed, including my co-founders) have come as a result of your initial vision.

To my fellow adventurers in the Okanagan, British Columbia. We live in a postcard and I feel so blessed that we get to do life together in this extraordinary playground making magic memories together. I love that I have such a tight community of fellow adventurers and that it is easy to live in a way that we can daily overlay the values of fitness, family, friendship, and fun!

To the extraordinary Pela Case and Lomi teams and the amazing group of leaders that we have put together. I love your passion and commitment to our vision, mission, and values. Helping assemble these extraordinary teams is one of the accomplishments I am most proud of.

To Tucker Max and the Scribe team: thank you for creating the playbook and path to make this book possible. The idea for writing a book seemed incredibly daunting, and your system and approach showed me a step-by-step process that could turn it from just an idea into reality. I specifically want to call out Paul Fair. Thank you for your prayers, your research, and your encouragement that were so helpful through the many hours that we invested together. As we have journeyed, we have developed a friendship and a bond that I know will continue beyond these pages.

Finally, I want to pay a special tribute to the challenges and adversities that I have faced during my life. When people hear my stories, I often get asked the question, "If you could go back and change anything, what would it be?" To their amazement, my simple answer is… "Nothing!" First, let's be clear that my challenges have been tame compared to those of so many others. As my father used to say, "If money can solve your problems, you don't have a problem." I am fortunate that most of my adversities have been in business and few have been with health and family. I had to both *"go through and then grow through"* every challenge I faced in order to become the person that I am today.

As a part of those adversities, I want to offer a special "thank you" to Justin. You fired me and then tried to saddle me with undeserved liabilities but unknowingly you freed me to a better and brighter future. God allowed our paths to cross and you were instrumental in helping us navigate the business during very difficult times. Despite the "good" relationship that we had forged by working through many adversities together, the allure of the four Ps had you choose them over me. I forgive you and I am grateful for all that I learned during our time together.

Inspired by my challenges and keeping to the bull-riding theme from the forward of this book; in the immortal words of Kip Moore: *"Most of all, thanks to the bulls that bucked me off."*

Sources

ON THE HISTORY OF THE G.I. JOE TOY:

Fletcher, Dan. "G. I. Joe." *Time*. August 7, 2009. https://web.archive.
org/web/20090810110440/http://www.time.com/time/nation/
article/0,8599,1915120,00.html.

"Hasbro, Inc. History." Funding Universe. 1997. http://www.fundinguniverse.
com/company-histories/hasbro-inc-history/.

Stamp, Jimmy. "Now You Know the History of G. I. Joe and Knowing Is
Half the Battle." *Smithsonian Magazine*. March 29, 2013. https://www.
smithsonianmag.com/arts-culture/now-you-know-the-history-of-gi-joe-and-
knowing-is-half-the-battle-11506463/.

ON THE HISTORY OF THE JENGA:

Ricketts, Nicolas. "Jenga. Jenga? Jenga!" *Play Stuff Blog*. National Museum of
Play. January 20, 2009. https://web.archive.org/web/20110807140452/
http://www.museumofplay.org/blog/play-stuff/2009/01/jenga-jenga-jenga/.

Suggitt, Connie. "Teen Smashes Jenga Record by Removing 32 Blocks in One
Minute." Guinness World Records. February 10, 2022. https://www.
guinnessworldrecords.com/news/2022/2/teen-smashes-jenga-record-by-
removing-32-blocks-in-one-minute-689116.

ON THE HISTORY OF SUPERHEROES:

Anthony, Ted. "A Universe of Flawed Heroes: Stan Lee Was Ahead of His
Time." *Associated Press*. November 13, 2018. https://apnews.com/article/
d355ac3dbc154c7abee0e01a998b371d.

TheComicBooks.com. "Creating the Superhero." Accessed October 21, 2022. https://www.thecomicbooks.com/old/Hist1.html.

Eidman, Alex. "Comic Book Creator Takes on Publishers Marvel and DC for Right to Use Term 'Superhero.'" *Daily News*. April 25, 2013. https://www.nydailynews.com/news/national/comic-book-creator-fights-term-superhero-article-1.1327860.

Game. "The World's Favourite Superhero Universe? Marvel vs DC." April 13, 2021. https://www.game.co.uk/webapp/wcs/stores/servlet/HubArticleView?hubId=2855754&articleId=2855755&catalogId=10201&langId=44&storeId=10151.

Heilbrunn, Jacob. "The Flawed Superhero of Marvel Comics." *Washington Monthly*. January 10, 2021. https://washingtonmonthly.com/2021/01/10/the-flawed-superhero-of-marvel-comics/.

Humanities Washington. "How American History Created the American Superhero." *Humanities Washington* (blog). March 9, 2016. https://www.humanities.org/blog/how-american-history-created-the-american-superhero/.

Idato, Michael. "Stan Lee's Heroes, and Their Flaws, are Part of the DNA of Our Culture." *Sydney Morning Herald*. November 17, 2018. https://www.smh.com.au/entertainment/books/stan-lee-s-heroes-and-their-flaws-are-part-of-the-dna-of-our-culture-20181116-p50ggu.html.

Khalil, Hafsa. "Spider-Man Remains One of the World's Most Popular Superheroes. Here's What Makes Him a Fan Favorite." *CNN Entertainment*. April 28, 2022. https://www.cnn.com/2022/04/28/entertainment/spider-man-national-superhero-day-marvel-comics-cec/index.html.

Miller, Yvette Alt. "Stan Lee, Creator of Flawed Superheroes Has Died." Aish. November 13, 2018. https://aish.com/stan-lee-creator-of-flawed-superheroes-has-died/.

Murray, Christopher. "Like Many Marvel Characters, Stan Lee Was a Flawed Hero." The Conversation. November 13, 2018. https://theconversation.com/like-many-marvel-characters-stan-lee-was-a-flawed-hero-106867.

Reif, Rita. "Antiques: Collectors Read the Bottom Lines of Vintage Comic
Books." *New York Times*. October 27, 1991. https://www.nytimes.
com/1991/10/27/arts/antiques-collectors-read-the-bottom-lines-of-vintage-
comic-books.html.

Thomas, Roy. "How Stanley Lieber Wrote His First Comics Story and Became
'Stan Lee.'" *Time*. November 13, 2018. https://time.com/5452565/stan-lee-
name-change-history/.

https://www.pbs.org/opb/historydetectives/feature/the-golden-age-of-comics/

ON THE HISTORY OF ETCH A SKETCH:

Coopee, Todd. "Etch A Sketch from Ohio Art Company (1960)." Toy Tales.
September 21, 2015. https://toytales.ca/etch-a-sketch-from-ohio-art-
company-1960/.

Playthings Staff. "Etch A Sketch Creator Dies." Gifts & Decorative Accessories.
January 13, 2013. https://web.archive.org/web/20130202214323/http://
www.giftsanddec.com/article/559614-Etch_A_Sketch_Creator_Dies.php.

Wee, Heesun. "Etch A Sketch's Incredible Toy Legacy—and Burden." *CNBC*.
February 22, 2013. https://www.cnbc.com/id/100471234.

ON THE HISTORY OF THE SURFBOARD:

Couldwell, Andrew. "History of the Surfboard." Club of the Waves. April 11,
2006. https://clubofthewaves.com/feature/history-of-the-surfboard/.

McCarthy, Erin. "A Brief History of the Surfboard." Popular Mechanics. June 12,
2012. https://www.popularmechanics.com/adventure/sports/a7666/a-brief-
history-of-the-surfboard-8347626/.

Olympics. "The Legend of Duke Kahanamoku, the Father of Modern Surfing
and Double Olympic Champion in Antwerp." Olympics.com. Updated July
11, 2022. https://olympics.com/en/news/the-legend-of-duke-kahanamoku-
the-father-of-modern-surfing-and-double-olympic-ch.

Rhodes, Margaret. "The Fascinating Evolution of the Surfboard." *Wired*. February 25, 2016. https://www.wired.com/2016/02/fascinating-evolution-surfboard/.

Sheppard, Brodey. "Surf & Surfboard History: 1778 to 2018 an Indepth Time-Machine." *Surf Nation* (blog). June 28, 2018. https://www.surfnation.com.au/blogs/news/surf-surfboard-history-1778-to-2018-an-indepth-time-machine.

ON THE HISTORY OF LEGOS:

Battered Fish Brick Productions. "How the LEGO Company Almost Went Bankrupt: A History." *FireStar Toys* (blog). November 9, 2020. https://blog.firestartoys.com/how-the-lego-company-almost-went-bankrupt-a-history/.

Ekstract, Steven. "From Almost Bankrupt to Most Profitable Toy Company; Lessons from LEGO." License Global. March 19, 2021. https://www.licenseglobal.com/trends-insights/almost-bankrupt-most-profitable-toy-company-lessons-lego.

Encyclopaedia Britannica Online, s.v. "LEGO." By Adam Augustyn. Last updated September 23, 2022. https://www.britannica.com/topic/LEGO.

Goodenberger, Sara. "The Patent Behind the LEGO 'Toy Building Brick.'" Suiter-Swantz Intellectual Property. October 24, 2019. https://suiter.com/patent-of-the-week-toy-building-brick-lego/.

LEGO. "LEGO History." Accessed October 21, 2022. https://www.lego.com/en-us/history/.

LEGO. "LEGO History: The Stud and Tube Principle." Accessed October 21, 2022. https://www.lego.com/en-us/history/articles/d-the-stud-and-tube-principle.

Nolan, Claire. "LEGO's Comeback: From Nearly Bankrupt to a $6 Billion Empire." *CNBC*. January 26, 2021. Video. 11:26. https://www.cnbc.com/video/2021/01/26/legos-comeback-from-nearly-bankrupt-to-a-6-billion-empire.html.

Rosenberg, Jennifer. "The History of Lego." ThoughtCo. Updated
January 17, 2021. https://www.thoughtco.com/lego-toy-bricks-first-
introduced-1779349.

Toy Retailers Association. "Toy of the Century." Accessed October 21, 2022.
https://www.toyretailersassociation.co.uk/toy-century/.

ON THE HISTORY OF RADIO
FLYER RED WAGONS:

Clayman, Andrew. "Radio Flyer, est. 1917." Made in Chicago Museum. Accessed
October 21, 2022. https://www.madeinchicagomuseum.com/single-post/
radio-flyer/.

Harris, Karen. "History of the Radio Flyer: The Little Red Wagon that Defined
Childhood." History Daily. August 5, 2021. https://historydaily.org/radio-
flyer-facts-stories-trivia/2.

Radio Flyer. "Radio Flyer History." Accessed October 21, 2022. YouTube video.
4:07. https://www.youtube.com/watch?v=Y5Y7jwDa8Gc.

Radio Flyer. "Tesla: Model S for Kids." Accessed October 21, 2022. https://www.
radioflyer.com/tesla.

Stumpf, Mindy. "Celebrating 101 Years: 10 Fun Facts About Radio Flyer." *Word
on the Sidewalk* (blog). Radio Flyer. July 17, 2018. https://blog.radioflyer.
com/content/share/blog/celebrating-101-years-10-fun-facts-about-radio-
flyer.

TIMELESS TOYS

Walsh, Tim. *Timeless Toys: Classic Toys and the Playmakers Who Created Them*
(Kansas City, MO: Andrews McMeel Publishing, 2005).

Made in the USA
Monee, IL
06 September 2024

99c9673b-74c4-491a-8b54-4dbdd6c38401R01